D1432322

structure
language
and style

a rhetoric-handbook

structure
language
and style

a rhetoric-handbook

W. Ross Winterowd

University of Southern California

WM. C. BROWN COMPANY PUBLISHERS
Dubuque, Iowa

For Jeff and Tony

Preface

During my years of work on *Structure, Language, and Style,* I have kept certain goals foremost in my mind.

First, I wanted to write a book that would be flexible and eclectic, that would not tie the instructor to a rigid development of a body of subject matter, but that would leave each teacher free to pick and choose and to arrange and rearrange. To a large extent, I think that I have accomplished that goal. The chapters (though they present what seems to me a logical progression of subject matter) are self-contained and can pretty much stand alone; hence, the teacher can adapt the book to the course rather than being forced to follow the alternate route of adapting the course to the book.

Next, I had become, during my years as a teacher of writing, thoroughly tired of the sententious pedantry of many handbooks, of their dogmatic dullness, of their plodding lack of inspiration. What I wanted to do, then, was to produce a lively discussion of the lively art of writing. A certain conventional reticence prevents me from judging the success of my effort. Those who use the book must be the final judges of my success.

I wanted, also, to be up-to-date and scholarly. Much is happening right now in the study of grammar, rhetoric and creativity, and I have attempted to ascertain that *Structure, Language, and Style* was not fossilized even before it reached print. Within these pages you will find, among other things, the latest theories of grammar (in their pure state and as they apply to writing); a modern rhetoric that calls upon such diverse authorities as Wayne Booth, Kenneth Burke, and Francis Christensen; an approach to the creative act of writing that reflects twentieth-century thinking.

Which brings me to the next point: I wanted this book to reflect the best modern theory, but to be practical in its utility as a textbook in a course in composition. Once again, the reader must judge my success in this respect.

Finally, I wanted *Structure, Language, and Style* to be challenging— not unduly difficult, but containing enough intellectual substance to engage both teacher and student. Books that are "written down" and that do not present a challenge to both kinds of users (teachers and students) finally must fall short of complete success as texts, for such books do not really need to be taught and discussed. I have worked carefully to achieve a nice balance between challenge and understandability. The chapter on grammar may well present the most difficulties, for the concepts therein will be foreign to many readers, but, on the other hand, that chapter may well be the one that most engages the students, for it will take them into unfamiliar territory. In general, it seems to me that this book is substantial enough to engage the student, but clear and elementary enough not to intimidate him. Parenthetically, in this regard, some responses within the profession to new materials are baffling and discouraging. A minority—but a depressing minority—of teachers resist the new as if it were contagious and fatal. In the sciences, the intellectual community is eager to explore the new and to judge it valid or invalid, valuable or valueless. In the humanities, there is always, among some few, a protectiveness and defensiveness which amounts to outright hostility against such developments as the new grammar and the new rhetoric, as if to understand those areas is to be irrevocably contaminated. *Structure, Language, and Style* is indeed heavily *weighted with* the new, but not necessarily *slanted in* that direction. To overlook what is going on in the scholarly fields allied to composition is vandalism, but to opt for this or that new development (over traditional materials) would violate the spirit of eclecticism that I hope characterizes this book.

I said that one goal I had in mind was to produce a handbook that would engage the user. In this regard, I have the feeling that most exercises—grouped at the ends of chapters, used by some teachers as handy make-work assignments—disengage students. But I recognize the pedagogical function of exercises: theory without practice totals very little. My solution was to make the exercises an integral part of the text. They occur throughout the chapters frequently, to reinforce or illustrate points, and often to lead the student to discover essential concepts. I would urge both teacher and student to pay attention to these exercises, for they are not tacked on, but are an integral part of the text.

Getting this book into print has been tedious and exciting, frustrating and elating, arduous and easy. Undertaking the kind of project that I set out for myself was tedious, but the prospect of getting together the kind of text I wanted was exciting. My many failures, backtrackings, and rewritings were frustrating, but the moments of success in getting a point across were elating. The job of writing the book, taken as a whole, was arduous, but thanks to the help of some good people, much of what could have been drudgery became easy.

Among the people who helped make the task as easy as possible must be listed: Professor Barnet Kottler of Purdue University who labored through two versions of my manuscript, each time with the result that I heeded almost all of his advice and revised to make for a better book; the editorial and production staff of WCB for their cooperation and guidance while my manuscript was maturing into an extraordinarily accurate set of proofs; and especially my editor, Richard C. Crews, whose encouragement and suggestions, about minor details and major concepts, made my job as an author less difficult and improved the quality of the book.

To my wife, Norma—three thousand thanks and a promise that subsequent projects will be less hectic.

For the virtues of *Structure, Language, and Style* I happily share the glory with those who helped me so generously. For the defects— well, heavens, at this point let's hope that they're not significant.

Contents

IV. THE SENTENCE

V. PUNCTUATION

VI. THE WORD 181

VII. THINKING STRAIGHT 207

I ✍ Writing an Essay: An Overview

WHAT IS THE ESSAY?

Venerable and long established, the essay is a part of our literary heritage, in exactly the same way that poems, novels, and plays are. Montaigne, Lamb, Bacon, De Quincey, Addison and Steele, E. B. White, Walter Lippmann, Loren Eiseley, and countless other names make up the anthology of essayists from yesterday and today who have spoken to us on a whole universe of subjects—from the discovery of roast pig to the last national political convention—for the essay is that literary form which analyzes, explains, and interprets, which allows the individual writer to put his personal viewpoint before the public. The essay is not a work of imaginative literature like a poem or novel (which is not to say that essays should be unimaginative); the essay is a vehicle of *expository prose*, and expository prose is prose that explains anything, from one's most intimate thoughts about love and life to the machinations of a politician taking every opportunity to gain votes. An essay is *not* a story. A story is narrative, i.e., its main principle of organization is chronology: first this happened, and then that happened, and so on. The story is also imaginative, but the prime ingredient of

1

the essay is not fictional. Some essays are written in verse, for instance, Alexander Pope's *Essay on Man. An essay is a (relatively) brief piece of writing, usually in prose, the purpose of which is to analyze, interpret, and explain events, facts, opinions, states of mind, processes and so on.*

It is useful to distinguish between *formal* and *informal* essays. The formal essay is more tightly structured than the informal; it is not so chatty and is more reserved. The informal essay is frequently very personal, even whimsical; though it may be completely serious, it is never portentous.

> *Exercise.* The best way, of course, to get an idea of what essays are all about is to read two or three or four of them. From the following list, read at least one informal essay and one formal essay; then be prepared to discuss the nature of each and the differences between the two.
>
> > *Informal essays.* Charles Lamb, "A Dissertation on Roast Pig"; James Thurber, "The Psychosemanticist Will See You Now, Mr. Thurber"; Leigh Hunt, "Getting Up on Cold Mornings"; almost any of the short pieces in "The Phoenix Nest" section of the *Saturday Review;* Thomas De Quincey, "Levana and Our Ladies of Sorrow"; E. B. White, "Once More to the Lake."
> > *Formal essays.* Francis Bacon, "Of Studies"; Ralph Waldo Emerson, "Self-Reliance"; Bertrand Russell, "A Free Man's Worship"; George Orwell, "Politics and the English Language"; Henry David Thoreau, "Civil Disobedience."

All of these essays are widely reprinted; you can find them in the collected works of their authors.

The father of the essay was the French philosopher Montaigne (1533-1592). After he had retired from active life, Montaigne set about compiling a *commonplace book,* that is, a collection of pithy sayings, maxims, words of wisdom from the classics, and other short bits of prose and poetry which he felt contained wit or wisdom or both. (The commonplace book was a very *common* book in the Renaissance. It was a treasury of wit and wisdom on which one could draw for ideas in writing or speech. Whatever appealed to the compiler was put in and thus stored away for future use.) A collection of these bits and pieces on a single topic was known as a *leçon morale,* but to the traditional, fragmented "moral lesson," Montaigne added something new: his own attitudes and thoughts, for he came to the conclusion that he was a representative man and hence had much to say to other men. The result was a literary form that combined the "wisdom of the ages" with the personal viewpoint of the author, and in 1580 Montaigne published a collection of these pieces under the title *Essais,* which meant originally "attempts" or "trials" and which, thus, constitutes an apt term for a form of writing intended for the trying out of ideas.

For the essay is indeed an "essay." It represents an attempt to work ideas out to the satisfaction of the author and his reader, and hence one can say that the essay is usually tentative, never dogmatic. The method of the essay is *dialectic,* and, according to *Webster's Collegiate Dictionary,* dialectic is

> That branch of logic which teaches the art of disputation and of discriminating truth from error; esp[ecially] the art of reasoning about matters of opinion.

The art of reasoning about matters of opinion. We should underscore that phrase in our minds. The essay consists of reasonable and reasoned personal opinion on topics of general interest.

WHY THE ESSAY?

One of the first and most important tasks of the college student is learning to write mature, responsible, accurate essays. Virtually every college and university in the United States offers a course in freshman composition. Most institutions of higher learning require students to complete a course in composition. Furthermore, no course is more maligned by students than freshman English, and some of the complaints are just. Too often, the course is not rigorous; it does not require that students put their best thought and their complete effort into the arduous task of learning to write. But more often, complaints against freshman English rest on shaky foundations. Let's examine some of these complaints:

1. "Why should I learn to write essays? I'm here to learn accounting." The student who enters a university just to learn a given skill is shortchanging himself and the society in which he must live. A person is a human being—and citizen and member of society—first, an accountant second. The university is and ought to be a universe of knowledge, not a training school to impart isolated skills. Which leads us to the second complaint.

2. "I write good enough. People get my meaning. Why should I spend my time learning to write like Lord Bacon?" The answer here is twofold. No one communicates well enough. The gap between man and man—the achievement of understanding—is bridged by language; the more effective the language, the greater the understanding. The

student who claims that he can "get his meaning across" may simply never have tried to convey much subtle meaning. Next, graceful, lucid, accurate language has esthetic and social values that less accomplished use of language does not. It is one's right to prefer the ugly to the beautiful, the awkward to the graceful, the imprecise to the precise, but such a preference hardly seems reasonable. As a matter of fact, also, certain kinds of language constitute the *dialect* that educated people accept. The person who cannot handle that dialect proficiently has a difficult time in getting the educated to take him seriously.

3. "There is no need for me to take freshman English. I just can't learn to write well." The student who makes such a statement is probably rationalizing. Obviously he thinks that he has native ability and some intelligence, or he would not be in college. And anyone with a bit of gray matter can learn to write.

The essay is the form of writing in which educated men explain themselves and their concerns to other men. If ideas are unimportant—well, then, indeed the essay is unnecessary. If ideas are unimportant, certainly learning to use language skillfully is a waste of time.

Writing essays, however, can be an intensely rewarding activity. Everyone ought to give it an eager try. When the results of the effort are successful, the writer feels a kind of exhilaration that is difficult to equal.

THE CREATIVE PROCESS OF WRITING

We know precious little about the creative process—what it is, how it works, or why at times it refuses to work. Every writer can attest that at times the words come tumbling out in a miraculous fashion, seeming to express just what the writer wanted to say in just the way he wanted to express it; no revision is necessary; the piece takes form as if by magic. At other times, even the most experienced writer suffers agonies untold. He starts and is dissatisfied. He crumples the sheet and starts again. Again, his beginning seems unsatisfactory . . . and so, often into the wee hours of the morning—at which time, the sturdy retire to their rest and the more vulnerable either pace the floor or resort to nail biting. But one thing is certain: the more one writes, the easier the process becomes. No one who has ever taken a course in composition or who has written extensively or who has become a recognized master in the field will ever say that writing is easy. No other activity so involves the whole human being—his intellect, his personality, his emotional constitution, his whole outlook on life.

Writing that is worthwhile demands a total effort, but when the effort is successful, there comes a sort of deep satisfaction that is hard to equal.

What we must do now is investigate the situation in which essays come into being, and do so with a view toward helping the learner overcome his mental "writer's cramps."

RHETORICAL STANCE

Think for a moment of the following spectrum:

1. a lyric poem on the beauty of the sunset
2. a philosophical treatise about the nature of reality
3. a war novel with a pacifist message
4. a sermon inculcating honesty
5. a campaign speech by a presidential candidate
6. a commercial for a detergent
7. a letter proposing marriage

One can detect two sorts of movements in this list: the items become progressively more persuasive, and the audiences at which the pieces are aimed become increasingly more specialized. The lyric poem, we might speculate, is written by the poet for himself; he is aiming at no given audience. He has no persuasive purpose, but is trying to record a visual and emotional experience. Above all, he is certainly not arguing for sunsets. The other examples are more or less persuasive and, we feel, must be aimed at definite sorts of audiences. When a writer aims his discourse at an audience he is employing *rhetorical stance*. Rhetorical stance is the attitude that the writer takes toward his presumed readers.

Exercise. Answer the following:

1. Do you speak the same way to little children, your friends, your parents, and your professors? In what ways do you adjust the way you talk?

2. Think of a currently popular ad on TV. What audience does it obviously aim at? How do you know?

3. Do printed advertisements for Fords and Chevrolets and Cadillacs and Continentals apparently aim at the same general audience? Explain.

Any discourse—spoken or written—which persuades must, by definition, use rhetoric, for *rhetoric is the art of finding the available means of persuasion in regard to any subject whatever*. It is perfectly obvious that one of the available means of persuasion that a writer must employ is rhetorical stance. As a first step in successful expository writing, the writer must define some kind of audience and then write for that audience. One of the great flaws in the writing of beginners is that it is too frequently aimed at no one in particular, and as a result, it loses the life that focusing toward a given audience would lend it.

There is, of course, much expository writing that seems aimed at no one in particular and that is monotonic in nature. The language of the newspaper certainly is aimed at a given audience, but we feel that the "personality" of the writer—the element that gives writing life—is submerged in the journalistic formula. But memorable expository writing always seems, somehow, to reveal the personality of the writer. That apparent revelation of the writer's personality has much to do with what we call rhetorical stance.

We should now ask, "How does the writer go about adopting the proper rhetorical stance for his audience?"

Write for a definite audience. Don't sit down merely to write; always write for someone or some group, the class, the student body at large, the group of citizens who might be opposed to such and such a national policy. The more clearly you can visualize an audience, the more surely you will be able to adjust your writing to that audience. After all, when you speak, such adjustment is automatic and almost always relatively successful. Of course, the student in freshman English is at a tremendous disadvantage simply because his main audience and perhaps his only audience is an instructor who will grade the result of the effort. Regardless of how one tries to define an audience other than the instructor, the instructor is always a psychological presence that will exert influence toward shaping the essay in the direction that the student thinks the instructor wants it to go. But it is well to remember that any respectable member of the academic community keeps an open mind and is happy to receive diverse points of view. Many teachers of writing, in fact, encourage students to take diverse stances toward *them*: "Address your argument to me as if I were an extreme conservative"; "Pretend in your paper that I am a member of the Catholic church and that you are writing against birth control." Your instructor will not insist that you please him in your viewpoints. He will insist that those viewpoints be well developed and that they be aimed at someone or some group, imaginary or real.

> *Exercise.* The following are the opening sentences of some diverse pieces of writing. What is the nature of the audiences to which the pieces are addressed? How do you know? (Sources of the quotes are in the footnote at the bottom of the page, but do not check the sources until you have completed the exercise.)

1. Once upon a time there were Three Bears, who lived together in a house of their own, in a wood. One of them was a
Little, Small, Wee Bear; and one was a Middle-sized Bear, and
the other was a Great, Huge Bear.

2. I, Nephi, having been born of goodly parents, therefore
I was taught somewhat in all the learning of my father; and having
seen many afflictions in the course of my days, nevertheless, having
been highly favored of the Lord in all my days; yea, having had
a great knowledge of the goodness and the mysteries of God,
therefore I make a record of my proceedings in my days.

3. There was a time when American women considered it
their responsibility to grace the land with gentility and beauty.
The soft word. The flower in the vase. The bountiful table. The
gentle smile. And all that went with it.

4. Responsibility implies a sense of obligation. A man's obligation can, however, only be understood in terms of "meaning"—the
specific meaning of human life. The question of such a meaning is
of supreme interest and comes up very frequently, whenever a
doctor has to deal with a psychically ill patient who is racked by
spiritual conflicts.

5. I love junk stores, I ooze over second-hand stores, I get
little shivers of pleasure just reading the words "Goodwill" or
"Salvation Army" or "Veteran's Thrift."[1]

In fact, the ability to adopt the correct rhetorical stance for the
situation comes with practice. There are no definite formulae for success—except, perhaps, try and try again until you begin to succeed.
Nonetheless, it is helpful to understand a few of the elements that go
to make up rhetorical stance. One of these, obviously, is *subject*. Not
every audience will be interested in every subject; some audiences
will be more interested in a given subject than will other audiences.
Another aspect of rhetorical stance is *style;* one must adapt his style
to audience and purpose. And, finally, rhetorical stance is a matter
of *tone*, the attitude that the writer adopts and that is reflected in the
writing (condescending tone, hostile tone, arrogant tone, humorous tone,
friendly tone, serious tone. . . .)

In subsequent parts of this book, we fully discuss style and tone.
But first, what about choosing a subject?

---

[1] The examples are from (1) Robert Southey's "Story of the Three Bears";
(2) *The Book of Mormon;* (3) Peter Hastings, in *McCalls;* (4) *The Doctor and the
Soul,* by Victor Frankl; (5) "Flea Market at Universal City," by Liza Williams, Los
Angeles *Free Press.*

CHOOSING A SUBJECT

The student writing to fulfill an assignment is admittedly working under an artificial constraint, for most writing springs from more natural causes than the need to pass a course. In fact, the reasons for writing are manifold and run the gamut from a mere urge for self-expression to the necessity for making a living by writing a daily newspaper column. But, in any case, the student has every right to feel put upon by the weekly or bi-weekly theme assignment: whether or not you have anything to say, whether or not you are "inspired," write a five hundred to one thousand word theme on. . . . It is safe to say that by and large, no undergraduate task is dreaded by so many students as those inevitable theme assignments. But there is, after all, another side to the story: themes give the undergraduate one of his few opportunities to tell it like he thinks it is, to experiment with untrammeled self-expression, to theorize and argue for the "right."

In any case, it is certain that most students magnify the work and multiply the worries of theme writing, which actually can be a pleasant and exciting kind of task. What follows constitutes practical suggestions for making the theme assignment easier and more rewarding, if not joyous.

The first rule of thumb (one that some students never seem to learn) is this: cover a relatively narrow topic thoroughly; do not cover a broad topic superficially. Here is a theme which violates this simple principle:

Fishing

Both ocean fishing and stream fishing have their advocates, and both have their advantages. Any kind of fishing takes skill and patience. Whether on the stream bank or the seashore, the fisherman gains fresh air and a sense of being away from it all.

But even though ocean fishing has a number of advantages, it is simply not as much fun as stream fishing. Most people who can take their choice between the two will choose stream fishing every time. Of course, some people love the salt air and the sound of the surf.

A great many famous people have found their escape from the problems of life by getting out on a mountain stream and pitting their skills against the wily trout. Indeed, trout fishing demands real knowhow and finesse—much more so than ocean fishing. Just in the matter of choosing the right equipment, stream fishing takes a real expert, whereas any duffer can catch salt-water fish.

All in all, the man who really likes to fish chooses stream fishing every time.

Exercise. Before the discussion undertakes a critique of the above example of student writing, ask yourself some questions about it.

1. How many ideas are left undeveloped? (How many questions do you have about this, that, or another aspect of the theme?) For instance, would you like to know more about the "knowhow and finesse" that trout fishing demands? Would you like to see a discussion of equipment?

2. Does the essay have a clear purpose? What exactly does it seem that the author has set out to do? Has he accomplished his purpose? (Might a better title than "Fishing" be "The Superiority of Trout Fishing"?)

"Fishing" is an example of an ill-defined topic that is underdeveloped. It is a safe guess that the author is an enthusiast for trout fishing and knows a great deal about it. Therefore, the reader feels cheated; if he is interested at all in the topic, he wants the details, the nitty gritty. But the essay handles its subject in such a general way that the reader learns virtually nothing, and, to put it bluntly, the essay says virtually nothing: it is just words words words. Second-guessing the author, we can speculate about what has taken place in the composition of this feeble theme. The author has fumbled about to find a subject, perhaps vaguely aware that it is a good idea to write about something that one understands and in which one is interested. And so a subject is chosen: fishing. The theme then gets under way, but the author probably has little idea of where it is going, though he seems, in the first paragraph, to want to make a comparison between ocean fishing and stream fishing. However, by the time he gets into the anemic second paragraph, he is beginning to veer toward trout fishing, and in the third paragraph, he has almost forgotten about ocean fishing, except for the after-thought at the end. In other words, the theme lacks direction as well as development. (And unfortunately, "Fishing" is all too typical of the sorts of things that inexperienced writers produce.)

Now then, in summary we can say that the author of that theme needed to *focus his topic more clearly and develop it more fully.* In focusing, he might have made a point-by-point comparison of ocean fishing and stream fishing:

skills involved in	sorts of fish one catches in
ocean fishing	ocean fishing
stream fishing	stream fishing
equipment necessary for	advice for beginners at
ocean fishing	ocean fishing
stream fishing	stream fishing
	and so on

Or the author might have decided to write only on stream fishing or ocean fishing. And, of course, there are countless other possibilities. The point is this: the more sharply defined the purpose in the author's mind, the more meaningful the resultant theme.

But above all, this advice: *write about something that you know.* You are an expert on a great number of subjects. You may not be an economist, but you understand the effects of inflation on your family's budget; you probably are not a member of the Republican or Democratic National Committee, but you have a considered opinion about candidates; you undoubtedly have no connection with NASA, but surely you have your own views about the space race.

Once upon a time, a student came to a university from Cut Bank, Montana. (There is such a place, and there was such a student.) For the first month or so of the fall term, the student seemed overwhelmed by freshman English. What was he to write about? He had spent his whole life on a huge cattle ranch, he had never been to a big city, and he had never been interested in "literary" matters. Surely, he thought, the professor and the sophisticated students in the class would be uninterested in such dull affairs as the operation of a ranch, being caught for two days on the plains in a raging blizzard, the economic vicissitudes of cattle ranching, antelope hunting, breaking mustangs, the local political fight to bring electricity to isolated homesteads. . . . These were some of the subjects that were near and dear to the student's heart, topics that he knew best and genuinely wanted to talk about. But for some time, he was under the impression that he should pontificate about such generalities as goodness and truth and such earth-shaking topics as the cure for cancer and halting inflation (both of which he understood only in the vaguest way).

And another student—this one from the black ghetto in Watts. And yet another student, a shy, attractive girl who had spent her life cloistered in a Beverly Hills mansion. And a Laotian exchange student who had been in the United States for only six months. And a student from Topeka, Kansas. Another from Brooklyn.

Diverse backgrounds, diverse personalities. A group of individuals with unique experiences of life, various attitudes toward their fellow men, and personalities running the whole spectrum. It turned out, strangely enough, that each of them had intensely interesting things to say about a wide range of subjects. But in each case, the young writer had to discover that he must use his own experience, his own background, his own "voice." The boy from Montana could not—and should not want to —write like Walter Lippmann, nor could the girl from Beverly Hills even approximate the tone or subject matter of

Malcolm X. Each had first and foremost to learn to speak for himself about himself. Once each student had learned that simple (and yet, apparently, not so simple) lesson, exciting things began to happen in their writing; they had interesting things to say and could say these things with force and clarity.

The most common sort of theme assignment consists of a list of general topics, one of which the student chooses for his own. It is then up to the student to narrow that topic and focus it. That is, the student must reduce the general topic to a specific topic that he can handle. Suppose that the general topic assigned is "The race war in America." Obviously, the individual writer needs to zero in on some one aspect of that very general subject:

> The problem of integrating Washington High School
> The white power structure in the Watts ghetto
> The attitudes of Montana ranchers toward the race problem
> An outsider looks in—the experiences of a Laotian with American racism
> Two worlds—Beverly Hills and Watts

and so on.

All of which is not to say that one must draw exclusively upon his own immediate experience for his materials. After all, each intelligent person has attitudes toward and ideas about the problems of society. These attitudes (based on reading, watching TV, arguing with parents), if fully and coherently developed, constitute valid subject matter for themes.

> *Exercise* Look at the following list of general topics. For each, name two *specific* related topics on which you would be qualified to write: inflation, the Vietnam War, education, literature, religion, politics.

Notice the process of narrowing and focusing that the following series illustrates:

> education
> higher education
> University of Southern California
> undergraduate courses at University of Southern California
> grading in undergraduate courses at University of Southern California
> the pass-fail system of grading in undergraduate courses at University of Southern California

> Carry out the same kind of narrowing process for two more of the general topics listed above in this exercise.

"The pass-fail system of grading in undergraduate courses at University of Southern California" is certainly a topic that would be manageable for an undergraduate at USC; it is sufficiently narrow that it could be handled in detail within, say, 750 to 1,000 words, or perhaps even less. But notice what can happen to that specific topic:

> Because the pressure for grades puts a false emphasis on learning, the pass-fail system should be adopted in undergraduate courses at University of Southern California.

Now a genuine idea has taken shape; the topic has a sure direction, and the writer knows exactly where he must go. In fact, he has two major ideas that he must establish by evidence and arguments: (a) that the pressure for grades puts a false emphasis on learning and (b) that the pass-fail system would remedy the situation. A *topic sentence* or *thesis statement,* like the one above, often takes the subject for a theme out of limbo and puts it firmly in the realm of the possible.

> *Exercise.* In the last exercise, you systematically narrowed two topics. Now write topic sentences for each of these.
>
> Of the six topics listed in the last exercise, you now have topic sentences for three. Formulate topic sentences for the remaining three.

It is possible to put too much stress on the importance of the the topic sentence. Often the process of writing is a process of discovery. Strangely enough, it is quite possible to write an essay in order to discover what one thinks about a given subject! The essay might well be an exploratory adventure for the writer, in which case, he will not be able to formulate a topic sentence before he begins. But the point is this: after the essay is written and revised, a topic sentence representing the thesis of the essay should be easy to formulate; otherwise, the piece is quite likely to be chaotic and unfocused.

DEVELOPING STYLE

If for its success an essay depended only on a clear subject thoroughly handled, the whole business of writing would be immeasurably simplified. But into the process of aiming at an audience, of adjusting rhetorical stance, there enters another, subtle matter: style. It is largely through *style* that we come into contact with the personality behind the essay. The British critic Bonamy Dobrée has said,

> It is not, we see, by a man's thoughts alone that we become acquainted with him in his books any more than we do in actual life;

and it is not for a writer's thoughts alone that we read a book, though some books we plunge into mainly for the sake of the thought. . . . How then, it will be asked, do we come into contact with the man? The answer seems to be 'By the sound of his voice.' For whenever we read a book, although we do not read it aloud, or even consciously form the words in our minds, we are aware of a voice. It is as though someone had been speaking to us, telling us something, or working upon our feelings. It is this voice that we roughly call style, and however much a writer may ignore his personality . . . he cannot disguise his voice, his style . . .[2]

Some writing, of course, does not reveal any personality and in that sense is style-less: one can think of sets of directions, some government reports, the impersonality of most newspaper writing. But the essay certainly needs the personality that a lively, lucid, graceful style can give it.

What are the components of style?

First, it is obvious that the mere *structure of sentences* has a good deal to do with style, regardless of the words used.

> Being an ardent fan, Hector attended the game even though it was raining.
> Hector attended the game even though it was raining, being an ardent fan.

> It is well known that cigarettes cause lung cancer.
> That cigarettes cause lung cancer is well known.

> I know a man. He is a lawyer. His office is on Hill Street.
> I know a man who is a lawyer with an office on Hill Street.

> The old lady baked me an apple pie. She is my grandmother.
> The old lady, my grandmother, baked me an apple pie.

The *words* that go into structures also help to determine style:

> We made many excursions to the lake after that, and had many a narrow escape and thrilling adventure which will never be recorded in any account.
> We made many trips to the lake after that, and had many a hair-breadth escape and blood-curdling adventure which will never be recorded in any history.
> —Mark Twain

> Thrilled with the idea of my trip to London, I arose.
> Elated with the thoughts of my journey to London, I got up.
> —James Boswell

---

[2]Bonamy Dobrée, *Modern Prose Style* (2nd ed.; Oxford: 1964), pp. 2-3.

If, then, *these* are the instrumentalities by which Levana works, how deeply must she respect the causes of sorrow.

If, then, *these* are the ministries by which Levana works, how profoundly must she reverence the agencies of grief!

—Thomas DeQuincey

Figures of speech are an important part of style:

Literal: What if man is not the most important thing in the universe?
Metaphorical: What if we are not playing on the center stage?

—Loren Eiseley

Literal: The movie was terrible.
Ironic: Oh yes. The movie was *really* an immortal masterpiece.
Literal: The building is thirty stories high.
Hyperbolical: The building rears itself to heaven.

These are examples of three of the elements of style. Each is handled in detail in subsequent parts of this book. Our purpose now is to gain awareness, not to investigate deeply. Most beginning writers have a good deal more sense of style than they might think. And, furthermore, style is a much less mysterious subject than it might appear. After all, style must come from the arrangement of words into the limited number of structural possibilities that the language affords; to paraphrase Jonathan Swift, style comes about from proper words in proper places. And the native speaker of a language has a good deal of intuition about those proper words and proper places. This principle is easily demonstrated:

Exercise. Rewrite the following—a garbling of a passage from Mark Twain's *Roughing It*—so that it is stylistically more satisfactory.

We fished a good deal. We did not average one fish a week. We could, winging about in the emptiness under us, see trout by the thousand. Or maybe they were, in the shoals on the bottom, sleeping. They would not bite. The line could be seen perhaps too plainly by them. We frequently selected the trout we wanted. Then we rested the bait patiently and persistently on the end of his nose. The bait was at a depth of eighty feet. He would only shake it off with an annoyed manner. Then he would shift his position.

CAUTION: DO NOT READ WHAT FOLLOWS UNTIL YOU HAVE COMPLETED THE EXERCISE.

If Mark Twain had written in the style of the practice passage, he would have rapidly sunk into well deserved obscurity. But, as a matter of fact, he wrote like this:

We fished a good deal, but we did not average one fish a week. We could see trout by the thousand winging about in the emptiness under us, or sleeping in shoals on the bottom, but they would not bite—they could see the line too plainly perhaps. We frequently selected the trout we wanted, and rested the bait patiently and persistently on the end of his nose at a depth of eighty feet, but he would only shake it off with an annoyed manner, and shift his position.

And the point to understand here is this: one's intuitive sense of style and the language allows one to avoid the worst mistakes that flaw the sample passage in the exercise. As we shall see later, we all have a highly sophisticated sense of language, of what sounds "good" and what does not. So for a start in the struggle for a mature style, this advice holds: use your innate sense of language to unscramble your writing. Go over it—after the first draft is completed—and do the polishing that your feeling for language enables you to do. The initial writing is important, but the revision is equally so.

Again, all of these matters will be handled in detail in later sections of this book.

TONE

Tone in writing is a subtle, almost ineffable matter. It develops from countless factors, among others: diction, structure, subject. It is almost synonymous with rhetorical stance, for it is the sense that your audience has of your attitude toward itself. Thus, tone may be informal, condescending, formal, friendly, hostile, humorous, serious, grave, light-hearted, elevated, vulgar, and so on. Tone, always vital to style, is more easily illustrated than defined:

From a learned journal:
The place of Sebastian Brant in the intellectual currents of his time is far from settled. Many scholars view him as an essentially medieval mind, longingly and resignedly looking towards the past, and only accidentally helping to usher in the new age.[3]

Mark Twain to Livy, his wife:
A happy Christmas to my darling, & to all that are dear to her! You are at home, now, Livy, & all your labors and vexations are over for a while. Poor child, I am afraid you are pretty well worn out. But you must be quiet, for a few days & recruit your strength, & then I shall find you restored & well when I see you a week hence.

From Time *magazine*:
For years, old movies have been television's backbone—one reason why TV often appears to be totally spineless. All that is about to change. The networks are running out of films, features are giving way to talk shows and, in historic reversal, TV is starting to invade the movies.

---

[3]Ulrich Gaier, "Sebastian Brant's *Narrenschiff* and the Humanists," PMLA, LXXXIII (May, 1968), 266.

A college freshman to his parents:
Dear folks:

You guessed it. Your check last month didn't stretch quite far enough. Honestly, I'm really strapped, and I haven't been living it up much either. I bought a new jacket that maybe I shouldn't have, and I took Joanne out to dinner last Sunday. (You don't expect me to be like a monk, do you?) Anyway, how about sending $25 to keep me from starving? I'll really take it easy with my bread from now on.

Most neophyte writers have no problem in adjusting the tone of what they have to say, whether in writing or speaking, until they come to the frustrating situation of a paper that they must write for a class, and then their personalities become wooden. They write for no one— or, perhaps more accurately, for some kind of insensate computer that will not respond to humor or pathos or cheer.

Once again, this advice holds: write for a well defined audience (as everyone does when he writes a letter to his parents or to a friend). If, when you are writing, you can see a face or a group of faces, chances are that you will begin to adjust your tone to your audience.

Exercise. Describe the tone of the four examples above. Try to be as specific as possible. What evidence can you find in the pieces to support your description?

BEGINNING

A good essay gets to the point. It does not wander about in a morass of generalities. It begins crisply, and it ends decisively. The beginning actually begins something, and, furthermore, it grasps the reader's interest. Here are the beginnings of two essays. Which is better? Why?

It was in Burma, a sodden morning of the rains. A sickly light, like yellow tinfoil, was slanting over the high walls into the jail yard. We were waiting outside the condemned cells, a row of sheds fronted with double bars, like small animal cages. Each cell measured ten feet by ten and was quite bare within except for a plank bed and a pot of drinking water. In some of them brown silent men were squatting at the inner bars, with their blankets draped around them. These were the condemned men, due to be hanged within the next week or two.
—George Orwell, "A Hanging"

Since ancient times criminal law and penology have been based upon what is called in psychology the pain-pleasure principle. There are many reasons for inflicting pain—to urge an animal to greater efforts, to retaliate for pain received, to frighten, or to indulge in idle amusement. Human beings, like animals, tend to move away from pain and toward pleasure. Hence the way to control behavior is to reward what is "good" and punish what is "bad." This formula pervades our programs of child-rearing, education, and the social control of behavior.

—Karl Menninger, "Verdict Guilty—
What Now?"

One might argue that both beginnings are good. Each gets its subject under way; neither is long-winded or beside the point. But for drama, for gripping the reader immediately, the Orwell beginning without a doubt is superior to that by Menninger. Since an essay is relatively brief, it must gain attention immediately, and it must get to its point quickly. Because of these requirements, there are no definite formulas for beginnings. The good beginning is the one that fits its subject. But there are some valid tips about choosing devices for beginning—ways of starting that will grasp the reader's interest and that will begin the development of the subject. Here are some useful ways to begin essays.

*Outlining a situation and then asking
the reason for that situation*
The world is aflame with man-made public disasters, artificial rains of brimstone and fire, planned earthquakes, cleverly staged famines and floods. The Lord of Creation is destroying himself. He is throwing down the cities he has built, the works of his own hand, the wealth of many thousand years in his frenzy of destruction, as a child knocks down its own handiwork, the whole day's achievement in a tantrum of tears and rage.

What has displeased the royal child? What has incurred his world-shattering tantrum?

—Susanne K. Langer, "The Lord
of Creation"

Straightforward announcement of the subject
The survival of democracy depends on the ability of large numbers of people to make realistic choices in the light of adequate information. A dictatorship, on the other hand, maintains itself by censoring or distorting the facts, and by appealing, not to reason, not to enlightened self-interest, but to passion and prejudice, to the powerful "hidden forces," as Hitler called them, present in the unconscious depths of every human mind.

—Aldous Huxley, "The Arts of
Selling"

*A brief, but original, generality, which will
be supported in detail by the rest of the essay*
America appears to be the only country in the world where love is a national problem.

—Raoul de Roussy de Sales,
"Love in America"

The paradoxical and ironic twist

The discovery of America has never been a more popular pastime than it is today. Scarcely a week goes by without someone's publishing a new book of travels in the bright continent. The anthropologists, native and foreign, have discovered that the natives of Middletown and Plainville, U.S.A., are as amazing and as interesting as the natives of such better known communities as the Trobriand Islands and Samoa. Magazines here and abroad provide a steady flow of articles by journalists, historians, sociologists, and philosophers who want to explain America to itself, or to themselves, or to others.

—John A. Kouwenhoven, "What's American about America?"

A series of questions to be answered in the essay—
a device to be used sparingly and with caution

What, then, is the rightful limit to the sovereignty of the individual over himself? Where does the authority of society begin? How much of human life should be assigned to individuality, and how much to society?

—John Stuart Mill, "On Liberty"

An anecdote that will relate to the subject
of the essay

Not long ago I was at work in my study writing, when, as was her custom, the lady across the way burst into song. There was something about that lady's voice which prevented the use of human intelligence, and I called upon the janitor to give her my compliments and then silence her. She replied with a good deal of conviction that this was a free country and she would sing when the spirit moved her; if I did not like it, I could retire to the great open spaces.

—Walter Lippmann, "The Nature of the Battle over Censorship"

A definition

This was the American dream: a sanctuary on the earth for individual man: a condition in which he could be free not only of the old established closed-corporation hierarchies of arbitrary power which had oppressed him as a mass, but free of that mass into which the hierarchies of church and state had compressed and held him individually thralled and individually impotent.

—William Faulkner, "On Privacy: The American Dream, What Happened to It"

There are, of course, many other effective ways to begin essays. It cannot be stressed enough that an essay is organic, a unity; nothing must seem tacked on. But not every essay should begin with a general announcement of the subject; not every essay should get under way with a tendentious statement. No essay should begin with a long and only partly relevant generality. Start. Get into the subject. Don't beat around the bush.

ORGANIZING

The table of contents of any book is an outline of that book, a map of its organization. Does the author prepare the table of contents before or after he has written the book? Perhaps the most typical process is this: when he starts to write, the author has an extremely general table of contents in mind (or on paper). As he writes, he adjusts and alters. After he has written and revised, he prepares a detailed table of contents. The relation of an outline to a theme is exactly that of a table of contents to a book; the outline is a map of what the theme turns out to be. It is also safe to say that most—the great majority—of good writers do not work on the basis of a detailed outline. Their subject grows and forms itself as they write.

> *Exercise.* Explain what Henry James means in the following statement about his composition of *Portrait of a Lady*:
>
>> Trying to recover here, for recognition, the germ of my idea, I see that it must have consisted not at all . . . in a plot . . . in any flash, upon the fancy, of a set of relations, or in any one of those situations that, by a logic of their own, immediately fall, for the fabulist, into movement, into a march or a rush, a patter of quick steps; but altogether in the sense of a single character, the character and aspect of a particular engaging young woman, to which all the usual elements of a "subject," certainly of a setting, were to need to be super-added.

My own method of organizing runs something like this: I start with a general idea and then work it out in a series of subtopics that I scribble on any piece of paper at hand. As I progress with my writing, I scribble more notes, rearrange topics, and make various reminders to myself. Writing from a formal outline can result in letting oneself be straightjacketed, can restrain the creative process of writing, where one idea suggests another and that suggests yet another and so on.

All of which is not to say that any writing should be chaotic. All writing should be tightly organized, but that organization will probably come from the logic of the subject as it is developed. A good way to check organization and logic is to make a formal outline of the piece. Another function of the formal outline is to give the reader a bird's-eye view of the piece.

Let it be said clearly that each writer develops his own methods, and certainly many writers work best on the basis of a preliminary formal outline. If such is the case, then by all means: Use the outline. However, the outline should always be an aid, never a straightjacket. The whole human thought process seems to be a wonderful chaos from which order can emerge. We do not know the exact methods whereby that order comes about. Use the outline as a tool, not as an inviolable law.

There are two kinds of formal outlines: *sentence* and *topic*. The two should never be mixed.

Sentence outlines have their heads in complete sentences:

Fly Fishing

I. Choosing the proper equipment is the most important step in successful fly fishing.
  A. The most important item of equipment is the rod.
    1. The most expensive and probably the best rods are made of tonkin cane.
    2. Fiberglass rods of good quality are completely satisfactory.
      a. Dual purpose fiberglass rods are popular, but not really satisfactory.
      b. The hollow fiberglass single-purpose rod is the best choice for a fisherman with limited means.
  B. Next in importance to the fly fisherman is his line.
    1. The line should be matched to the pole.
    2. Special lines for dry fly fishing and wet fly fishing are necessary.

The same outline in topic form looks like this:

Fly Fishing

I. Choosing the proper equipment
  A. The rod
    1. Tonkin cane rods
    2. Fiberglass rods
      a. Dual-purpose fiberglass rods
      b. The hollow fiberglass single-purpose rod
  B. The line
    1. Matching the line with the pole
    2. Lines for dry fly and wet fly fishing

On the principle that nothing can be divided into one part, if there is a subhead I, there must be at least a subhead II; if there is a subhead A, there must be at least a subhead B; if there is a subhead 1, there must be at least a subhead 2; if there is a subhead a, there must be at least a subhead b.

If the outline is topic, all the heads must be phrases, not telegraphic sentences, thus:

I. *Choosing proper equipment first step in fly fishing*
    A. The rod
        1. *Most expensive rods made of tonkin cane*
        2. Fiberglass rods
            a. *Dual-purpose fiberglass rods popular but not really satisfactory*

Headings must be equal and must not overlap:

II. Kinds of water for fly fishing
    A. Sloughs
    B. Small mountain creeks
    C. Geyser Slough
    D. Millcreek
    E. Large, slow rivers
    F. The Clark Fork

Obviously, these headings should be rearranged:

II. Kinds of water for fly fishing
    A. Sloughs
        1. Geyser Slough
        2. Johnson Slough
    B. Small mountain creeks
        1. Millcreek
        2. Ten Mile Creek
        3. Kramer Creek
    C. Large, slow rivers
        1. The Clark Fork
        2. The Bitterroot

SUMMARY

So much for general remarks and upbeat propaganda. It is now time to get into the real subject matter of the book. But a few points have been made in the foregoing pages.

The essay is a literary form in which ideas are interpreted, analyzed, and explained; therefore, the essay is a vehicle for expository prose, which is prose that explains. The essay may be intimate and informal or fairly impersonal and formal—depending, of course, on the purpose and the audience. It is a good idea to think of the essay as an attempt, a trial, the working out of ideas *dialectically.*

Perhaps the basic accomplishment in a liberal education is learning to express oneself fluently, gracefully, and forcefully. Conversely, the person who cannot express himself is not educated.

We know precious little about the creative process—about how ideas get formed into sentences, sentences into paragraphs, and paragraphs into essays. But we do know that through practice and with instruction students can overcome their mental "writer's cramps" and develop the ability to express themselves. But in order to achieve "fluency" in writing, one must apply himself totally, for "No other activity so involves the whole human being—his intellect, his personality, his emotional constitution, his whole outlook on life."

One of the most common failings of the beginner is to write with no audience in mind. When writing is directed at no one in particular, it is usually vapid, lifeless, dull. It is important, therefore, that every writer envisage an audience to whom he can address his discourse. When one does address a given audience, he has assumed a rhetorical stance.

The beginner often complains that he has nothing to say, nothing to write about. Such an attitude, of course, is completely fallacious. The mere fact that one is an individual, a unique human creature, gives him a whole universe of topics for writing. The trick is to write about subjects that one knows thoroughly—and, furthermore, that interest one at the deepest level. Another problem is the tendency for the beginning writer to be too ambitious, to want to cover a field that is beyond the scope of a relatively brief essay. Therefore, it is necessary to reduce topics to a manageable size, to narrow and focus. A well developed essay on education in America is impossible, but a thorough discussion of some aspect of education in some given school is not only possible, but intriguing.

Every literate person has a sense of style, for everyone reacts against this "clumsy" construction or that "hazy" sentence. The trick is to put our senses of style to use in our own writing, and the way to do that is to rely on the intuitive sense of what is good and what is bad. If one reads his own essays with the same critical "ear" that he uses when he reads someone else's writing, he will be on the way toward the kind of revisions that make for good style. And style, of course, must be adapted to audience and purpose.

Tone is a subtle matter of which the writer must be aware. A humorous tone in a funeral sermon would be out of place. A flippant tone in a state-of-the-union address would alienate the electorate. The writer must learn to adjust the tone of his writing to his audience and his purpose.

Getting under way with an essay is often one of the writer's greatest problems. The beginning must accomplish two purposes: grasp the reader and get the subject under way. There are countless ways to begin, but one of them is *not* beating around the bush.

An essay should be coherent and organized—but to assume that organization must come about before the writing is an error. Some people work well on the basis of a formal outline before the fact, but some don't. The main point is this: after the essay is completed, it should be a coherent whole that one can outline with little difficulty. The outline itself is a tool that the writer should use to his advantage. The outline should never be a straightjacket.

II ✑ The Paragraph

An essay is a series of carefully related paragraphs. But what is a paragraph? Is it, according to the common definition, an essay in miniature? Does a *topic sentence* control all well-built paragraphs? What are methods of paragraph development? We will be examining these and other questions in some detail. At the moment, however, it will be instructive and interesting to see if we can determine something about the anatomy of the paragraph.

The sentence is a convention. That is, native speakers of the language intuitively know what constitutes a sentence, and given a fairly long stretch of discourse with all sentence indicators removed, a group of subjects will agree with surprising unanimity on where the sentences conclude and begin. To put this idea another way: the subjects will agree on the punctuation marks needed to separate independent clauses. We can very easily test the soundness of this contention.

> *Exercise.* Wherever needed, insert either a semicolon (;), a period (.), an exclamation point (!), or a question mark (?) into the following passage. (All four of these marks of punctuation set off

25

independent clauses, i.e., clauses that are capable of standing alone as sentences.)

I have said that all branches of knowledge are connected together because the subject-matter of knowledge is intimately united in itself as being the acts and the work of the Creator hence it is that the Sciences into which our knowledge may be said to be cast have multiplied bearings on one another and an internal sympathy and admit or rather demand comparison and adjustment they complete correct balance each other this consideration if well-founded must be taken into account not only as regards the attainment of truth which is their common end but as regards the influence which they exercise upon those whose education consists in the study of them I have said already that to give undue prominence to one is to be unjust to another to neglect or supersede these is to divert those from their proper object it is to unsettle the boundary lines between science and science to disturb their action to destroy the harmony which binds them together such a proceeding will have a corresponding effect when introduced into a place of education there is no science but tells a different tale when viewed as a portion of a whole from what it is likely to suggest when taken by itself without the safeguard as I may call it of others

—John Henry Cardinal Newman, *The Idea of a University*

The important point about the above exercise is not where *you* inserted punctuation, but how nearly a whole group, in this case the class, agreed on inserting marks of punctuation that set off independent clauses. If the class achieved anything near agreement, then we can conclude that for that particular group of subjects, the sentence must be a convention. This is not to say that every member or any member of the class can define "sentence," but somehow, intuitively, the whole group has what is sometimes called "sentence sense." Unless your class is a completely atypical group of college students, the results of the experiment were satisfactory: there was indeed wide agreement about where independent clauses should be set off.

This question then arises: Is it possible that the paragraph is a convention in somewhat the same way as the sentence? In a stretch of writing with all paragraph indentations removed, would the class generally agree on the stretches of sentences (or single sentences) that should be set off as paragraphs?

Exercise. The following is an essay by a student in a composition class. As you can see, paragraph indentations have been removed. Insert the paragraph mark in front of those sentences that you think should begin new paragraphs:

The Young American:
Affluent and Unfulfilled

(1) An unkempt, bearded hippie in the Haight-Ashbury district takes a psychedelic trip, and, as Dr. Timothy Leary says, turns the microscope in upon his soul. (2) A young activist on the Berkeley campus marches and demonstrates for a cause, seeking justice certainly, but seeking also direction and identity in the movement. (3) And a young Roman Catholic in New Jersey attends mass in his home that he may participate more fully and thus involve himself personally in the celebration. (4) Though vastly dissimilar in most particulars, these three individuals reflect, in varying degrees, a common characteristic of modern man—the lack of a definite sense of self, of what might be termed identity. (5) Each of the three feels this lack (perhaps not consciously) and pursues identity in his own way, attempting to clarify and intensify those qualities and convictions which mark him as both a definite and unique individual: the hippie, by substituting a powerful, drug-induced inner experience for the hard inner core of belief which he did not inherit; the activist, by commiting himself to a cause, which at once clarifies his identity (he is, if nothing else, one who espouses that particular cause) and allows him to assert that identity in a direct and purposeful fashion; the young Catholic, by participating directly in an intimate religious ritual, thus expressing his faith through self-involvement (rather than through observation) and becoming more aware of his identity as a Catholic. (6) I do not wish to suggest, of course, that the pursuit of identity is the sole motivating factor in any of these cases; obviously there are other motives that occur to one, such as the desire for "kicks" on the part of the hippie, or the desire for a sense of community on the part of the Catholic. (7) But I do wish to suggest that these incidents are typical of the presently maturing generation in America and result, in large part at least, from the need for identity, a need not consciously felt perhaps, but nonetheless real and compelling. (8) The lack of identity is peculiarly modern, for our ancestors were fortunate enough, individually and collectively, to inherit a definite and consistent system of values, and their sense of identity was clarified and buttressed by the cultural, technological, and geographical stability of the pre-industrial period. (9) Our pre-industrial ancestor knew what he believed and where he was going—knew who he was—with a clarity and certitude that seem, to most moderns, incredible, and his ties to the land, familiar landmarks, and to kin past, present, and future so re-enforced his sense of identity as to make it unshakably firm; he had what is popularly called "character." (10) William H. Whyte, in his book *The Organization Man,* describes this character, this identity, as a gyroscope which gave our forbear a sense of equilibrium even in the most precarious situation: in other words it provided a means by which he could evaluate any given situation and his relation to it. (11) As Loren Eiseley puts it, "Custom directed the vagaries of the will. (12) Among the fixed institutional bonds of society man found the security of the animal. (13) He lived in a patient renewed orbit with the seasons. (14) His life was directed. . . ." (15) But as the Industrial Revolution

made its inexorable advance into the nineteenth and twentieth centuries, disturbing forever the ancient patterns of life and settlement, the "inner-directed" man gradually gave way to the "outer-directed"; the gyroscope of inner conviction, of identity, gave way to the radar screen which looked outward to others for direction. (16) If the screen showed no consistent pattern, and in our rapidly changing social environment it often did not, then the man was directionless, and in confusion followed the path of least resistance, or that which was most appealing to the senses, or perhaps that which was most immediately pragmatic. (17) And if there was a consistent pattern on the screen and the other-directed man followed that pattern, he could be said to have no real identity. (18) For he was only a chameleon: he assumed whatever color he was placed against; he had little or none of his own. (19) But if, as the twentieth century American (and Western man generally) evolved, he ceased to have a clear and consistent identity, he seemed hardly aware of it. (20) He certainly did not suffer the trauma of disorientation felt by certain African tribesmen when colonists systematically and ruthlessly fragmented their tribes and forbade tribal customs. (21) He was not especially aware of any deficiency in himself because, unlike the African tribesmen (and, I suppose, the American Indian), he lost his identity gradually and because the loss was replaced, in a way, by the exciting challenge and promise of the Industrial Revolution. (22) He was so taken up with the notions of economic and social progress—his own and society's—so committed to the work of controlling nature and making for himself a materially comfortable world, so preoccupied, as it were, with things exterior to himself that he did not realize the terrific inner loss which he had suffered. (23) He only began to feel that loss (to feel unfulfilled, at least) when he had accomplished much of what he had set out to do and had set into operation the machinery which would eventually complete the task. (24) It probably is true that "Man does not live by bread alone," but only the man with bread feels the need for something more. (25) It was only the post World War II generation, the generation coming to maturity in the late nineteen-fifties and sixties, that began to manifest clearly, and sometimes consciously, the need for more direction and stability from within. (26) Essays began to appear in psychological journals and other periodicals on the American's loss of and lack of identity, and in time Diana Trilling could write in *The Partisan Review* that modern novels were generally weak in that their characters lacked identity with the assurance that her readers would recognize the quality to which she referred. (27) The term "identity-crisis" became a popular one—almost a cliché—among college students, and, seeking direction and identity, thousands of them participated in marches and demonstrations, often without discrimination, expending as much energy in the interest of four-letter words as in civil rights for Negroes. (28) The rootlessness of youth and their desire for identity was mirrored in a popular song of the sixties: "I'll be a dandy, and I'll be a rover; you'll know who I am by the song that I sing. . . ." (29) Ultimately, the lack of a clearly perceived inner self led to experimentation with drugs in the hope that they could provide self-knowledge and direction, and if not, at least the drugs could intensify the present moment, and that much one could be sure of. (30) It remains yet to be seen what permanent contribution, if any, drugs will make toward filling modern man's need for identity, but it is almost certain that commitment to ephemeral causes will fail to fill that need. (31) It is equally certain that the identity of our pre-industrial ancestor cannot be imposed on modern man, for that identity served man in a simpler, smaller, and in many ways more stable world, though some traditional values and beliefs are undoubtedly yet viable. (32) While modern man should not adopt carte' blanche the values of the past (as some political reactionaries in America have done in desperation, I suspect, to fill the void), his identity must resemble his ancestor's to the extent that there is general collective agreement on some principle or principles. (33) If there is none, if each individual goes his own way, then the result is anarchy, the absence of political and social order (the present juvenile crime rate, but perhaps more significantly the general lack of respect for vested authority among juveniles, is pertinent here). (34) There can be no societal evaluation (except for the most grossly pragmatic) of human creations or acts if there are no accepted premises. (35) If, for instance, there is no common agreement that human life—any human life—is sacred, then the killing of unproductive old men, or of deformed infants, can be justified pragmatically, much as in Huxley's *Brave New World*. (36) Or on another level, if there are no accepted criteria for evaluating art, then the Beatles can be said to be superior to Beethoven, or Grace Metalious to Shakespeare, and there can be no arguing the matter, for argument assumes the acceptance of principles one can appeal to. (37) Ortega y Gasset, in his book, *The Revolt of the Masses*, characterizes the modern age as barbaric because there are few, if any, commonly held principles, and Loren Eiseley supports this conclusion when he observes that now "Ideas, heresies, run like wildfire and death over the crackling static of the air." (38) The fact that ideas "run like wildfire" is indicative not only of the lack of a common American identity; it is indicative also of the individual's felt need for identity, of the need for a firm inner core of belief that at once gives substance and direction (39) The conformity of the other-directed generation does not satisfy the present one, and with a new self-awareness they pursue identity; commitment and involvement become their watchwords. (40) And perhaps, after all, the "wildfire" of innumerable commitments is not without some pattern. (41) The hippies speak of love and live communally. (42) The Ecumenical Movement has as its avowed purpose the bringing together of all Christian churches, of the creation of a Christian community. (43) Campus activities embrace causes that are altruistic: they commit themselves to helping Negroes, or Mexican-Americans, or slum children, or even the Viet Cong. (44) The terms love and community are not new, of course, but they are being given new scope and dimension: they are no longer being interpreted narrowly within familial, or territorial, or racial limits. (45) That one should love one's neighbor and that the world is one's community are, hopefully, those principles which will form the very heart of that identity the present generation seeks. (46) They are not new principles—Christ offered them nearly two thousand years ago—but perhaps man and his world will grow sufficiently to live them.

Now compare your results on this experiment with those of the other members of your class. If there is a significant area of agreement, then we must conclude that somehow the class senses the paragraph as a convention. Perhaps no one is able to give an airtight definition of "paragraph," but somehow most students are able to recognize paragraphs. (This experiment has been performed many times, and the conclusion is that the paragraph is indeed a convention, although perhaps not as clearcut as the sentence.)

The implications of all of this should be obvious. If the paragraph is a convention, then we should be able to advance tentative descriptions of it and to analyze it. This is not to say that we are dealing with a mathematically precise entity that will be subject to equational explanation; nonetheless, the paragraph is not nearly so mysterious an affair as most of us believe.

THE STRUCTURE OF PARAGRAPHS

Much work is currently under way on the nature of the paragraph, and several theories vie for attention. The various theories and hypotheses have great interest in and of themselves, for they bear upon the way that the human mind perceives and organizes ideas; furthermore, the unravelling of the skein of paragraph structure will have great value in the teaching of writing. But in the order of things, theory normally precedes practice, and it will be illuminating to take a disinterested look at the abstract concepts that lie behind analysis of the paragraph.

An examination of any large group of paragraphs reveals that, in the main, they tend to have a discernible movement: from the general to the specific. A general statement is supported by a series of examples; a fairly broad topic is narrowed more and more by qualifications. This kind of movement is natural and to be expected. Think, for a moment, about how ideas develop in a random conversation. Usually the speaker comes out with a general proposition, and then, in supporting that proposition, he is pinned down more and more narrowly to specifics. This tendency to move from the general to the specific is illustrated by the following:

> *Goldman*: Does adaptation mean adapting an already written book or story [for TV]?
> *Burkey*: Adapting material previously produced by another medium, yes.
> *Tunick*: There is also another kind—adapting materials of a newsworthy or of an historical nature.
> *Burkey*: We would call that an original, because it is essentially an original dramatization of material, rather than adapting something previously published or produced.

Tunick: The best example is the Armstrong Theatre, where they do what they call "actuals." Recently we did a show on the Dead Sea Scrolls. The producer came to me and said, "There is a lot of excitement and interest in the Dead Sea Scrolls. Do a dramatic story on the Dead Sea Scrolls."

Well, that is the total assignment. From then on, it is the writer's problem to do this very broad and diverse assignment, on a subject with all kinds of interpretations and angles, and adapt it to the dramatic form; in other words, not to make it a documentary, but to make it a dramatic show.

—The Relation of the Writer to Television

The majority of paragraphs have exactly this same kind of movement. We can take a close look at the anatomy of a typical paragraph.

(1) Most people who bother with the matter at all would admit that the English language is in a bad way, but it is generally assumed that we cannot by conscious action do anything about it.
(2) Our civilization is decadent and our language—so the argument runs—must inevitably share in the general collapse.
(3) It follows that any struggle against the abuse of language is a sentimental archaism, like preferring candles to electric lights or hansom cabs to aeroplanes.
(4) Underneath this lies the half-conscious belief that language is a natural growth and not an instrument which we shape for our own purposes.

—George Orwell, "Politics and the English Language"

Notice how this paragraph runs from a general proposition in the first sentence to a conclusion in the fourth. The second sentence qualifies and explains the first. The third sentence "sums up" the import of the first two. It is interesting to note that the sentences can be rearranged in this way: 2 1 3 4. This order preserves coherence and sense, but no other possible arrangement does. (Read the sentences in the 2 - 1 - 3 - 4 order to prove to yourself that rearrangement is possible.) Not all paragraphs are rearrangeable, however. Try reordering the sentences in the following paragraph:

(1) *I answer that,* Law is a rule and measure of acts, whereby man is induced to act or is restrained from acting; for *lex* [*law*] is derived from *ligare* [*to bind*], because it binds one to act.
(2) Now the rule and measure of human acts is reason, which is the first principle of human acts, as is evident from what has been stated above.
(3) For it belongs to the reason to direct to the end, which is the first principle in all matters of action, according to the Philosopher.
(4) Now that which is the principle in any genus is the rule and measure of that genus: for instance, unity in

the genus of numbers, and the first movement in the genus of movements.

(5) Consequently, it follows that law is something pertaining to reason.

—Thomas Aquinas

Even at the most superficial glance, paragraphs seem to have an inevitable and analyzable order, a structure that gives them what is generally called *unity*. One more brief example. Notice that this one can appear as 1 - 2 - 3 - 4 or 1 - 2 - 4 - 3:

(1) A pilot must have a memory; but there are two higher qualities which he must also have.

(2) He must have good and quick judgment and decision, and a cool, calm courage that no peril can shake.

(3) Give a man the merest trifle of pluck to start with, and by the time he has become a pilot he cannot be unmanned by any danger a steamboat can get into; but one cannot quite say the same for judgment.

(4) Judgment is a matter of brains, and a man must *start* with a good stock of that article or he will never succeed as a pilot.

—Mark Twain, *Life on the Mississippi*

We can sum up by saying that the normal movement of paragraphs is from general statements to more and more specific working out of those statements.

The reverse of the general-to-specific pattern is, however, not uncommon.

I once declared that in England the born lover of ideas could not but feel that the sky over his head is of brass and iron. And so I say that, in America, he who craves for the *interesting* in civilization, he who requires from what surrounds him satisfaction for his sense of beauty, his sense of elevation, will feel the sky over his head to be of brass and iron.

The human problem, then, is as yet solved in the United States most imperfectly; a great void exists in the civilization over there; a want of what is elevated and beautiful, of what is interesting.

—Matthew Arnold, *Civilization in the United States*

A very rough guess might be that no more than ten per cent of all paragraphs have this kind of development.

Another way of looking at paragraph development is to say that sentences are either *coordinate* with or *subordinate* to one another. Professor Francis Christensen of the University of Southern California points out that one of the main reasons for paragraph unity is the coordinate and subordinate relationships among ideas; as long as these relationships are perceivable (other things being equal), the paragraph will be coherent. In the examples that have been cited so far, you will notice that indentation has shown the system of subordination and coordination.

Exercise. Rearrange the following groups of sentences so that they make coherent paragraphs. Be prepared to explain the ranks of coordination and subordination.

1. Men generally, under such a government as this, think that they ought to wait until they have persuaded the majority to alter them.

2. Why does it always crucify Christ, and excommunicate Copernicus and Luther, and pronounce Washington and Franklin rebels?

3. Unjust laws exist: shall we be content to obey them, or shall we endeavor to amend them, and obey them until we have succeeded, or shall we transgress them at once?

4. Why does it not encourage its citizens to be on the alert to point out its faults, and *do* better than it would have them?

5. They think, that, if they should resist, the remedy would be worse than the evil.

6. Why does it cry and resist before it is hurt?

7. Why is it not more apt to anticipate and provide for reform?

8. *It* makes it worse.

9. But it is the fault of the government itself that the remedy *is* worse than the evil.

10. Why does it not cherish its wise minority?

—Thoreau's "Civil Disobedience"

1. And as there takes place an evolution of knowledge, that is, as the truer and necessary knowledge crowds out and takes the place of faulty and unnecessary knowledge, so also does the evolution of feelings take place by means of art, crowding out the lower, less good feelings, which are less necessary for the good of men, to make place for better feelings, which are more necessary for this good.

2. Speech makes it possible for the men of the last living generation to know what the preceding generations and the best leading contemporary men have found out by means of experience and by reasoning; art makes it possible for the men of past living generations to experience all those sensations which men experienced before them and which the best and leading men are still experiencing.

3. In this does the mission of art consist; and so art is according to its contents better, the more it fulfils this mission, and worse, the less it fulfils it.

4. Art is, together with speech, one of the instruments of intercourse, and so also of progress, that is, of humanity's forward movement toward perfection.

—Leo Tolstoy, "What Is Art?"

1. They are symbols taken from our daily experience, and not information about what God did once upon a time or will do sometime in the future.

2. If faith call God "almighty," it uses the human experience of power in order to symbolize the content of its infinite concern, but it does not describe a highest being who can do as he pleases.

3. God is the basic symbol of faith, but not the only one.

4. Faith is not the belief in such stories, but it is the acceptance of symbols that express our ultimate concern in terms of divine actions.

5. So it is with all the other qualities and with all the actions, past, present, and future, which men attribute to God.

6. All the qualities we attribute to him, power, love, justice, are taken from finite experiences and applied symbolically to that which is beyond finitude and infinity.

—Paul Tillich, *Dynamics of Faith*

The art of writing successful paragraphs is the art of making movement and connections clear, of establishing firmly the relationships between ideas, and of showing how one idea leads to the next. We have not, by any means, explored all of the reasons for paragraph unity; our discussion will take us into much deeper water hereafter. For now, it will be useful to explore the configurations (the shapes) that paragraphs take.

The following is typical of a relatively common sort of pattern in paragraphs:

But why kill? I am ready to believe the statistics tending to show that the prospect of his own death does not stop the murderer. For one thing he is often a blind egoist, who cannot conceive the possibility of his own death. For another, detection would have to be infallible to deter the more imaginative who, although afraid, think they can escape discovery. Lastly, as Shaw long ago pointed out, hanging the wrong man will deter as effectively as hanging the right one. So, once again, why kill? If I agree that moral progress means an increasing respect for human life, how can I oppose abolition [of the death penalty]?

—Jacques Barzun, "In Favor of Capital Punishment"

The design of this paragraph can be described as *question* and *answer*— actually a question, an answer, and two more questions. Here is a slight variation on the question-answer pattern:

I am asked what is the end of University Education, and of the Liberal or Philosophical Knowledge which I conceive it to impart: I answer, that what I have already said has been sufficient to show that it has a very tangible, real, and sufficient end, though the end cannot be divided from that knowledge itself. Knowledge is capable of being its own end. Such is the constitution of the human mind, that any kind of knowledge, if it be really such, is its own reward. And if this is true of all knowledge, it is true also of that special Philosophy, which I have made to consist in a comprehensive view of truth in all its branches, of the relations of science to science, of their mutual bearings, and their respective values.

—John Henry Newman, *The Idea of a University*

The paragraph based on the question-answer pattern is fairly rare—one reason being that paragraph after paragraph of this type would bore the reader. When the occasion arises, the question-answer sequence serves a good purpose, but it is not the means for designing all paragraphs.

Some paragraphs present concrete *examples* of ideas being developed in essays. In an essay discussing the effects of television, television advertising, and advertising in general, John Steinbeck inserts this paragraph:

> We were having dinner in a lovely little restaurant in California. At the table next to us were six beautiful, young, well-dressed American girls of the age and appearance of magazine advertisements. There was only one difficulty with their perfection. You couldn't tell them apart. [Elia] Kazan, who is a primitive of a species once known as men, regarded the little beauties with distaste, and finally in more sorrow than anger cried, "It's years since I've seen or smelled a dame! It's all products, Golden Glint, l'Eau de l'eau, Butisan, Elyn's puff-adder cream—I remember I used to like how women smelled. Nowadays it's all products!"
>
> —John Steinbeck, "How to Tell Good Guys from Bad Guys"

Perhaps the most common sort of paragraph, however, represents the general pattern *topic-restriction-illustration*. A topic is announced; it is then delimited and qualified; finally it is illustrated concretely—as in the following paragraph:

Topic	The seediest moving-picture theater in town, I soon discovered, showed every Saturday the same kind of Western picture at which I had yelled and squirmed as a kid, clutching my box of jujubes;
Restriction	but in this context it was different. The children still eagerly attended, to be sure—but also the cowhands.
Illustration	In their run-over-at-the-heels boots and dirty jeans, they were apparently willing to invest a good part of their day off watching Gene and Roy, in carefully tailored togs, get the rustlers, save the ranch, and secure the Right; meanwhile making their own jobs, their everyday work into a symbol of the Natural Gentleman at home.

—Leslie Fiedler, "Montana: Or the End of Jean-Jacques Rousseau."

Now look at the movement in the next example. The paragraph begins with a topic, restricts that topic and illustrates it, and then summarizes, thus: *topic-restriction-illustration-summary*:

Topic	If the scheme of things is purposeless and meaningless, then the life of man is purposeless and meaningless, too.
Restriction	Everything is futile, all effort is in the end worthless.
Illustration	A man may, of course, still pursue disconnected ends, money, fame, art, science, and may gain pleasure from them. But his life is hollow at the center.
Summary or restatement	Hence the dissatisfied, disillusioned, restless spirit of modern man.

—W. T. Stace, "Man against Darkness"

We have seen so far that the normal movement of ideas in a paragraph is from the general to the specific and that this general movement can at times be reversed. The reader must be able to perceive the relationships among ideas, which idea is coordinate with which and which is subordinate to which. We have seen also that paragraphs tend to fall into a limited number of generally describable patterns such as *question-answer, example, topic-restriction-illustration.* There are other patterns undoubtedly, *problem-solution,* for example. (A fairly careful search through 640 pages of essays failed to turn up one clearcut example of the problem-solution paragraph.)

Generally speaking, if we were to draw diagrams of the movement of paragraphs, those diagrams would look like this:

or like this:

but not like this:

_____

_____

_____

_____

_____

_____

For instance:

1. In the language of screen comedians four of the main grades of laugh
    are the titter, the yowl, the belly-laugh, and the boffo.
    2. The yowl is a runaway titter.
    3. Anyone who has ever had the pleasure knows all about a belly-
        laugh.
    4. The boffo is the laugh that kills.
        5. An ideally good gag, perfectly constructed and played, would
            bring the victim up this ladder of laughs by cruelly controlled
            degrees to the top rung, and would then proceed to wobble,
            shake, wave and brandish the ladder until he groaned for
            mercy.
            6. Then, after the shortest possible time out for recuperation,
                he would feel the first tickling of the comedian's whip once
                more and start up a new ladder.

                            —James Agee, "Comedy's Greatest Era"

but not:

    4. The boffo is the laugh that kills.
        6. Then, after the shortest possible time out for recuperation,
            he would feel the first tickling of the comedian's whip once
            more and start up a new ladder.
1. In the language of screen comedians four of the main grades of laugh
    are the titter, the yowl, the belly-laugh, and the boffo.
        5. An ideally good gag, perfectly constructed and played, would
            bring the victim up this ladder of laughs by cruelly controlled
            degrees to the top rung, and would then proceed to wobble,
            shake, wave, and brandish the ladder until he groaned for
            mercy.
    2. The yowl is a runaway titter.
    3. Anyone who has ever had the pleasure knows all about a belly-
        laugh.

Again:

            1. My wife's grandmother, the wife of a distinguished
                lawyer, once declined to dine with the Cartiers of
                jewelry fame because they were, as she put it, "in
                trade."

2. Life for grandmother was relatively simple where social
distinctions were concerned, but while there are still
a few people who think and act much as she did, the
passage of time has eliminated a great deal of that
particular kind of snobbishness from American society.
3. We are replacing it with another kind.
4. The old structure of the upper class, the middle class, and
lower class is on the wane.
5. It isn't wealth or family that makes prestige these days.
6. It's high thinking.

—Russell Lynes, "Highbrow, Lowbrow, Middlebrow"

But notice how the paragraph can be restructured:

5. It isn't wealth or family that makes prestige these days.
6. It's high thinking.
4. The old structure of the upper class, the middle class, and
lower class is on the wane.
3. We are replacing it with another kind.
2. Life for grandmother was relatively simple where
social distinctions were concerned, but while there
are still a few people who think and act much as
she did, the passage of time has eliminated a great
deal of that particular kind of snobbishness from
American society.
1. My wife's grandmother, the wife of a distinguished
lawyer, once declined to dine with the Cartiers
of jewelry fame because they were, as she put it,
"in trade."

Exercise. Analyze and be prepared to discuss the movements of
ideas and the structural patterns (topic, restriction, illustration; example; question and answer) in the following paragraphs:

(1) From the fourth century B.C., rhetoric has been one of the important
intellectual currents of Western man. Throughout the Middle Ages and
Renaissance, higher education consisted of two curricula, the *trivium* and
the *quadrivium*. The trivium included three liberal arts, grammar, rhetoric, and logic; the quadrivium included four liberal arts, arithmetic,
music, geometry, and astronomy. The intellectual world that we have
inherited was shaped, then, by the seven liberal arts, of which rhetoric
was a prominent member. When we think of the intellectual accomplishments of Bacon or the artistic accomplishments of Shakespeare, we must
inevitably take into account the milieu of ideas that produced them.
For this reason, the history of rhetoric is an important cultural subject.

—Winterowd, "Rhetoric: Main Trends"

(2) What shall be said of the Princeton social system and the upperclass
clubs, of which so many bitter and uninteresting things have been said
already? The clubs have been called undemocratic, as if a goosestep
method should be applied to choosing one's friends. They have been

assailed as snobbish, when many a poor but honest student has found that neither poverty nor honesty could keep visitations of upperclassmen and election committees from his door. It has been said that they accustom the undergraduate to a too luxurious manner of living. Even this is, I am afraid, a fiction, for, if the architecture is at times pretentious, the food is unfortunately simple and wholesome—and it is to be remembered that the clubs are, first and last, eating clubs.

—John Peale Bishop, "Princeton"

(3) For the first few days I was lost. My eyes were not accustomed to the skyscrapers and they did not surprise me; they did not seem like man-made, man-inhabited constructions, but rather like rocks and hills, dead parts of the urban landscape one finds in cities built on a turbulent soil and which you pass without even noticing. At the same time, I was continually and vainly looking for something to catch my attention for a moment—a detail, a square, perhaps, or a public building. I did not yet know that these houses and streets should be seen in the mass.

—Jean-Paul Sartre, "American Cities"

(4) The proposition is peace. Not peace through the medium of war; not peace to be hunted through the labyrinth of intricate and endless negotiations; not peace to arise out of universal discord fomented from principle in all parts of the empire; not peace to depend upon the juridical determination of perplexing questions, or the precise marking the shadowy boundaries of a complex government. It is simple peace, sought in its natural course and its ordinary haunts. It is peace sought in the spirit of peace, and laid in principles purely pacific. I propose, by removing the ground of the difference, and by restoring *the former unsuspecting confidence of the colonies in the mother country,* to give permanent satisfaction to your people; and (far from a scheme of ruling by discord) to reconcile them to each other in the same act and by the bond of the very same interest which reconciles them to British government.

—Edmund Burke, "Speech on Conciliation with America"

FUNCTIONS OF PARAGRAPHS

According to their functions, paragraphs can be divided into three categories: (1) those that are full stages in the development of the subject of the composition; (2) those that signal a shift in focus or topic; (3) those that emphasize the importance of a single, relatively brief point. The paragraphs that we have examined so far obviously represent the first type; we need not discuss that kind further now.

The second type, the transitional paragraph, is normally just one sentence and sometimes not even a complete sentence. This kind of short paragraph says to the reader, "Be alert now; we're moving on to a new aspect of our subject."

But to turn to the second aspect of the topic.
Even though the time of the insect hatch is terrifically important in fly fishing, matching the dry flies with the insects is the way to produce catches. *And so on.*

. . . by Sunday, exurban fathers are less thrilled at the notion of consorting with their young than they were before the novelty wore off some time Saturday. It is for this reason that Sunday in some exurban homes sees parents who have grown indignant with popular media of child entertainment, and who have responded strongly and affirmatively to Dr. Frederic Wertham's *Seduction of the Innocent,* urging their small fry to find some diversion of their own. "Daddy is not a toy," Duke says patiently, "Go find something else to play with. Why don't you read one of those comic books where they kill people on every page. That's very exciting."
But exurban kids are less likely to be fascinated by such fare than most.

—A. C. Spectorsky, "A Weekend in Suburbia"

The third type of paragraph merely isolates an idea for emphasis. It is much like underlining or italics:

It is the function of the popular arts to divert, but not to deceive. When they become the only arts of great numbers of people, they can be held to account for what they do.

—Gilbert Seldes, "The People and the Arts"

Nothing has changed since the time of the covered wagons; every year towns are founded in the United States, and they are founded according to the same methods.

—Jean-Paul Sartre, "American Cities"

Our spirit is watered by three streams of thought, originally distinct but here mingled:
The eighteenth-century Enlightenment view of progress toward social reason, or what we Americans know as the Jeffersonian ideal;
The Romanticist view of man's diversity, inventiveness and love of risk by which society is forever kept in flux, forever changing;
And the native tradition of Deafness to Doctrine which permits our Federal system to subsist at the same time as it provides free room for carrying out the behests of our other two beliefs.

—Jacques Barzun, "Innocents at Home"

The brief transitional and emphasis paragraphs are useful, but their utility decreases in direct proportion to their frequency. In other words, the two subsidiary kinds of paragraphs should be used sparingly. A great deal of emphasis de-emphasizes; if a great many short emphasis paragraphs appear in an essay, none of them will emphasize significantly.

TOPIC SENTENCE

It has been common for many years to speak of the "topic sentence" of a paragraph. This sentence, it is said, announces the subject of the paragraph and hence controls the development. Since unified paragraphs invariably order themselves according to hierarchies of idea—that is, on the principles of coordination and subordination—one might say that the sentence to which all others in the paragraph are subordinate is the topic sentence. A simple example:

> It is not possible to form a just judgment of a public figure who had attained the enormous dimensions of Adolf Hitler until his life work as a whole is before us.
>
> Although no subsequent political action can condone wrong deeds, history is replete with examples of men who have risen to power by employing stern, grim, and even frightful methods, but who, nevertheless, when their life is revealed as a whole, have been regarded as great figures whose lives have enriched the story of mankind.
>
> So it may be with Hitler.
>
> —Winston Churchill, "Hitler and His Choice," (1935)

What, however, is the topic sentence in the following passage?

> I was born in Harlem thirty-one years ago. I began plotting novels at about the time I learned to read. The story of my childhood is the usual bleak fantasy, and we can dismiss it with the restrained observation that I certainly would not consider living it again. In those days my mother was given to the exasperating and mysterious habit of having babies. As they were born, I took them over with one hand and held a book with the other. The children probably suffered, though they have since been kind enough to deny it, and in this way I read *Uncle Tom's Cabin* and *A Tale of Two Cities* over and over and over again; in this way, in fact, I read just about everything I could get my hands on —except the Bible, probably because it was the only book I was encouraged to read.
>
> —James Baldwin, *Notes of a Native Son*

The Baldwin passage is, of course, different from that by Churchill. Baldwin is writing mostly narrative—that is, telling a story. But the passage does have a definite topic, even though it does not have a discoverable topic sentence. The topic is, roughly, the development of the author's literary powers.

In fact, it is common for unified paragraphs to function perfectly well with no topic sentence. Most paragraphs probably do have topic sentences; some don't. But coherence and unity do not depend necessarily on the topic sentence. It is far better and more productive to concentrate on the coherent movement of ideas than to try to formulate (or discover) topic sentences.

DEVELOPING PARAGRAPHS

In the first chapter of this book, we discussed the necessity for developing the ideas in an essay fully. The essay should not be an outline; it should, rather, cover its subject with such completeness that the reader never feels that he is being put upon and asked to do the work the author should have done. Now we can turn to the specific methods whereby an essay is developed fully, for development takes place at the paragraph level.

Readers demand that full information be given. The audience—which we discussed in the first chapter—expects that all questions will be answered, that all contingencies will be explained, that all ideas reach a conclusion. Part of the problem in creating a finished, unified essay is, of course, one of organization. But since the paragraphs in an essay are the major "message units," it is the development of paragraphs upon which depends the total development of the essay.

As a start toward understanding the development of paragraphs, we can take a look at the following theme, a not awfully successful effort by a student at University of Montana:

My Greatest Love

1. Recently I returned from Puerto Rico, where I had been on a two-year tour of duty with the Air Force. During these two years, I acquired my greatest love. This love is not only my greatest love, but the love of many of the people of the island: the sport of skin diving.

2. I would venture to say that this is one of the most beautiful and adventurous sports known to man. Most of the diving that I did was at depths from 30 to 40 feet. At this depth, the waters of the Caribbean are of a dark blue, like the sky on a clear day at sunset.

3. Standing on the shore and looking out across the vast body of water makes a person feel smaller than a grain of sand on the beach, but once you plunge into the water, you enter a whole new world where you no longer feel like a grain of sand, but instead like the master of the sea. As you approach the floor of the sea, you enter the world of silence and beauty. All you can see is the movement of the undertow and the beauty of a miniature forest made up of underwater vegetation of the brightest colors in the spectrum.

4. Swimming along at these depths, you will be joined by schools of parrot fish and many other species that will swim next to you for a while and then dart off. These exquisitely colored schools of fish against the beautiful background of the dark blue sea and underwater vegetation are a picture no artist could ever paint.

5. Along with all this beauty, adventure is always present, for there are many ships, caves, underwater streams, and large rock formations to be explored. Always present are the feared sea animals, such as the shark, sting ray, and moray eel that can destroy a diver in a matter of seconds. Many times a diver gets so engrossed with other thoughts that he does not notice these sea animals. For instance, you may have just seen a lobster dart behind one of the rock formations, and with all of your attention on spearing this lobster, you fail to notice the dark figure of a shark swimming not more than twenty feet away. At a time like this, all you can do is hope that he is not hungry, for there is no defense against a shark once he attacks.

6. Even though there are many ways in which a diver may lose his life, the beauty and the adventure seem to compensate for this fact.

Anyone reading this essay must feel that it needs "filling out." In many ways the attempt is imaginative and intelligent, but the interested reader simply does not get the information that he desires; he has the impulse to corner the author and question him about the details that are lacking in the essay. In order to understand what the author might have done, let's examine the essay paragraph by paragraph.

Paragraph 1. The author could have supplied many pertinent details, but the one thing that he desperately needs to do is to document the popularity of skin diving. The paragraph raises a great many unanswered questions. What is the climate like in Puerto Rico? How cold is the Caribbean? How many skin divers are estimated? How often did the author skin dive? The first paragraph is not vivid and full enough to grasp the reader.

Paragraph 2. The main idea in this paragraph is the technical information about the depth of diving. Isn't this the place to introduce information about equipment, techniques, and costs? Instead, the paragraph, such as it is, vacillates between the beauty and adventure of skin diving and the depths of the dive. The writer needs to choose one of those ideas and then go into great detail.

Paragraph 3. The main idea here is the beauty of the underwater world—but the writer does not show us any of that beauty in detail. Compare the vividness of the following:

> So singularly clear was the water, that where it was only twenty or thirty feet deep the bottom was so perfectly distinct that the boat seemed floating in the air! Yes, where it was even *eighty* feet deep. Every little pebble was distinct, every speckled trout, every hand's-breadth of sand. Often, as we lay on our faces, a granite boulder, as large as a village church, would start out of the bottom apparently, and seem climbing up rapidly to the surface, till presently it threatened to touch our faces, and we could not resist the impulse to seize an oar

and avert the danger. But the boat would float on, and the boulder descend again, and then we could see that when we had been exactly above it, it must still have been twenty or thirty feet below the surface. Down through the transparency of these great depths, the water was not *merely* transparent, but dazzlingly, brilliantly so. All objects seen through it had a bright, strong vividness, not only of outline, but of every minute detail, which they would not have had when seen simply through the same depth of atmosphere. So empty and airy did all spaces seem below us, and so strong was the sense of floating high aloft in mid-nothingness, that we called these boat-excursions "balloon-voyages."

—Mark Twain, *Roughing It*

Paragraph 4. Again: lack of detail. Compare:

The shore is composed of a belt of smooth rounded white stones like paving-stones, excepting one or two short sand beaches, and is so steep that in many places a single leap will carry you into water over your head; and were it not for its remarkable transparency, that would be the last to be seen of its bottom till it rose on the opposite side. Some think it is bottomless. It is nowhere muddy, and a casual observer would say that there were no weeds at all in it; and of noticeable plants, except in the little meadows recently overflowed, which do not properly belong to it, a closer scrutiny does not detect a flag nor a bulrush, nor even a lily, yellow or white, but only a few small heart-leaves and potamogetons, and perhaps a water-target or two; all which however a bather might not perceive; and these plants are clean and bright like the element they grow in. The stones extend a rod or two into the water, and then the bottom is pure sand, except in the deepest parts, where there is usually a little sediment, probably from the decay of the leaves which have been wafted on to it so many successive falls, and a bright green weed is brought up on anchors even in midwinter.

—Thoreau, *Walden*

Paragraph 5. This is obviously the most satisfactory part of the essay. The writer has gotten warmed up to his subject and has become involved; hence, he supplies enough details to make the paragraph begin to come to life. Much more could be done, but at least, for the first time, the reader senses a kind of fulfillment of the writer's promise to talk about a subject.

Paragraph 6. The ending is lame. It needs expansion and illustration. It promises more than the essay delivered; the ending tells us that there are many ways in which a diver can lose his life, but the essay has discussed only one.

The essay has other obvious faults, but the important point is this: "My Greatest Love," in its lack of development, is relatively typical of the essays that beginners produce in college. To write fully developed, meaningful essays takes practice. A knowledge of the techniques for developing paragraphs can take the neophyte writer a long way toward maturity, so we will now turn to a discussion of specific methods of development.

A paragraph is not an essay in miniature, but it is—in the sense that a sentence is not—a development of a complete idea. That is, the traditional definition of "sentence" applies more nearly to the paragraph than it does to sentences. Just how to explain paragraph development is a problem, for there are obviously as many different ways of building satisfactory paragraphs as there are subjects that paragraphs discuss. A list of methods of paragraph development doesn't really accomplish the purpose of teaching writers how to develop paragraphs. Writers learn by doing—by reading and then imitating. We should, then, read some paragraphs analytically and see how they are developed—always remembering that a list, no matter how long, won't represent all the possibilities.

Examples. Examples serve two purposes: they illustrate, and they "prove." The use of examples corresponds roughly to what logicians call *inductive reasoning:* A, B, C, and D are all members of genre X, which exhibits characteristic Omega, so E, also a member of genre X, will exhibit characteristic Omega. That, in theory, is how inductive reasoning works. In the essay, examples A, B, C, D can serve to substantiate a general statement about a genre of idea or ideas. For instance,

> *Students at University of Southern California tend to be conservative.*
> Student A is a member of the Young Americans for Freedom.
> Student B voted for George Wallace.
> Student C thinks that all people who wear beards are revolutionaries.
> Student D advocates removing *Das Kapital* from general circulation in the library.
> Student E attends University of Southern California; therefore, he is probably also a conservative.

The above sequence illustrates—in a simple fashion—the way in which one argues on the basis of examples, but it also demonstrates the hazard of that kind of argument: one or two or more examples often cannot establish a general principle, as any scientist knows, but a well-chosen example can make the subject clear and vivid.

> In its special approach to a biblical story, Hollywood often overlooks the real dramatic material that is at hand. The most striking recent example of this instinctive preference for the mediocre is *The Prodigal.* (In defense of this film, to which I seem continually to be returning, I must say that, so far as I know, no one responsible for it issued any pretentiously pious statements of the sort that have accompanied the release of DeMille's epics and of *The Robe* and its sequel.) Jesus' parable of the prodigal son emphasizes the resentment and pacifi-

cation of the good son who stays home; that is the main issue and not the prodigal's addiction to "riotous living." No one would guess it from the movie, although the attitude of the prodigal's brother raises the most interesting character problem in the parable.

—Henry Popkin, "Hollywood Discovers the Bible"

Notice that in this case, the example is called to the reader's attention: "The most striking recent example . . ." Such introductory statements are not at all necessary, as the following paragraph illustrates:

But there is also a different way of violating the Western form. This is to yield entirely to its static quality as legend and to the "cinematic" temptations of its landscape, the horses, the quiet men. John Ford's famous *Stagecoach* (1938) had much of this unhappy preoccupation with style, and the same director's *My Darling Clementine* (1946), a soft and beautiful movie about Wyatt Earp, goes further along the same path, offering indeed a superficial accuracy of historical reconstruction, but so loving in execution as to destroy the outlines of the Western legend, assimilating it to the more sentimental legend of rural America and making the hero a more dangerous Mr. Deeds. (*Powder River*, a recent "routine" Western shamelessly copied from *My Darling Clementine*, is in most ways a better film; lacking the benefit of a serious director, it is necessarily more concerned with drama than with style.)

—Robert Warshow, "The Westerner"

As we said earlier, it is quite possible to set a fairly extended example off as a paragraph in its own right, but the usual movement is *topic*, sometimes then a *restriction*, and finally one or more *illustrations* (examples); the paragraph by Robert Warshow follows that pattern.

Logic. Now, watch how the following paragraph works. It is based on a chain of reasoning—if this is the case, such and such must follow.

Now pragmatism, devoted though she be to facts, has no such materialistic bias as ordinary empiricism labors under. Moreover, she has no objection whatever to the realizing of abstractions, so long as you get about among particulars with their aid and they actually carry you somewhere. Interested in no conclusions but those which our minds and our experiences work out together, she has no *a priori* prejudices against theology. *If theological ideas prove to have a value for concrete life, they will be true, for pragmatism, in the sense of being good for so much. For how much more they are true, will depend entirely on their relations to the other truths that also have to be acknowledged.*

—William James, "What Pragmatism Means"

What we are saying here, perhaps, is that the paragraph built upon ideas must be sequentially coherent and not self-contradictory. Very few paragraphs, if any, will be tightly logical in the sense that they can be reduced to the formulae of the syllogism, a matter that we will be discussing in a later chapter. The paragraph built on logic will be a "thinking through" of an idea, as in the example. In the paragraph based on logical thinking, one idea leads to another in a kind of natural succession.

Data. Another good method of paragraph development is to pile up specific data:

> But one does not have to be interred to take up permanent residence at Forest Lawn. A number of other arrangements can be made, including being inurned after cremation in the columbarium for as little as $145 or entombed in the mausoleum crypt—which can cost as much as $800,000, as in the case of the Irving Thalberg mausoleum. One can also be placed in a large wall out in the open air. Families may be interred, inurned, or entombed as a unit to maintain "togetherness." Should one feel the need for fresh air while spending the "happy Eternal Life" in a crypt, it is possible, at added cost, naturally, to have a ventilating system installed. In the mausoleum, tape-recorded music is played as well.
>
> —Paul Jacobs, "The Most Cheerful Graveyard in the World"

The myth that statistics are dry ignores the vividness that facts and figures can bring to writing, as in the following paragraph on the size of the world's oceans:

> In brief, the sea contains 330 million cubic miles of water. The volume of all land above sea level is only one eighteenth as great. Land's tallest peak, 28,028-foot high Mount Everest, could be sunk without a trace in the ocean's greatest abyss, the 35,800-foot-deep Mariana Trench in the western Pacific. If all the irregularities on the earth's surface were to be smoothed out, both above and below the water, so that there were no dents or holes anywhere, no land would show at all. The ocean would cover the entire globe to a depth of 12,000 feet.
>
> —Leonard Engel, *The Sea* ("Life Nature Library")

Or note this, from that old stand-by, *The World Almanac*:

> *Fees*—The passport fee is $9 plus an execution fee of $1 at Passport Agencies and at Federal Courts and $2 at State Courts. A person on official business for the U.S. Government should submit a sponsoring letter from the Agency instead of the $9 fee. All applicants must pay the execution fee unless exempt by a special Act of Congress. Emergency clearance costs $2 at all Agencies except New York and Philadelphia, where it is $1. Emergency service fee after working hours $10, in addition to passport fee. The only other fees are for postage and emergency service charges.

Anyone applying for a passport will recognize the success of this paragraph.

Enumeration. Many subjects have component parts that need listing; hence, it is possible to build paragraphs on the basis of "enumeration."

> We hold these truths to be self-evident, that all men are created equal; that they are endowed by their Creator with certain inalienable rights, that among these are life, liberty, and the pursuit of happiness. That to secure these rights, governments are instituted among men, deriving their just powers from the consent of the governed; that, whenever any Form of Government becomes destructive of these ends, it is the right of the people to alter or abolish it, and to institute new government, laying its foundation on such principles, and organizing its power in such form, as to them shall seem most likely to effect their safety and happiness.

But in the same paragraph, notice what follows:

Qualification Prudence, indeed, will dictate that governments long established should not be changed for light and transient causes; and, accordingly, all experience hath shown that mankind are more disposed to suffer, while evils are sufferable, than to right themselves by abolishing the forms to which they are accustomed. But, when a long train of abuses and usurpations, pursuing invariably the same object evinces a design to reduce them under absolute despotism, it is their right, it is their duty, to throw off such government, and to provide new guards to their future security.

Conclusion Such has been the patient sufferance of these colonies; and such is now the necessity which constrains them to alter their former Systems of Government. The history of the present King of Great Britain is a history of repeated injuries and usurpations, all having, in direct object, the establishment of an absolute tyranny over these States. To prove this, let facts be submitted to a candid world.

The paragraph began with enumeration, but then that enumeration was *qualified*, and finally the general significance of the whole paragraph was summarized in a conclusion. In other words, the component parts of the argument were listed; certain restrictions were stated; a conclusion was drawn. Such a movement in paragraphs is not at all uncommon.

Analogy. Analogy is drawing a comparison between two things, ideas, emotions, etc., to make one of them clear. The more familiar is used to clarify the less familiar. Drawing on the theories of physics,

Dwight Bolinger points out that language has "particles" (its words and smaller units), the affinities that particles show when they are used in the language, and the "field" relationships among the particles—all obscure enough until the author clarifies with the following analogy:

> Language is not unique in this respect. Other forms of activity have the same three-way organization. A good analogy is that of the roles of players in a baseball game. Each role is a "particle"—pitcher, catcher, outfielder, third baseman. The ways in which the roles interact in a game are its "strings": the catcher at a given moment interacts with the pitcher, and he regularly interacts more with the pitcher than with any other player. The abstract relationships among the players are the "field": a treatise on baseball might compare the function of shortstop with that of catcher on the one hand and second baseman on the other, explaining how the three roles are alike and how they differ.
>
> —Dwight Bolinger, *Aspects of Language*

Another example of analogy:

> In narratives where historical veracity has no place, I cannot discover why there should not be exhibited the most perfect idea of virtue; of virtue not angelical, nor above probability; for what we cannot credit we shall never imitate; but of the highest and purest kind that humanity can reach, which, when exercised in such trials as the various revolutions of things shall bring upon it, may, by conquering some calamities, and enduring others, teach us what we may hope, and what we can perform. Vice, for vice is necessary to be shewn, should always disgust; nor should the graces of gaiety, or the dignity of courage, be so united with it, as to reconcile it to the mind. Wherever it appears, it should raise hatred by the malignity of its practices; and contempt, by the meanness of its stratagems; for while it is supported by either parts or spirit, it will seldom be abhorred. *The Roman tyrant was content to be hated, if he was but feared; and there are thousands of the readers of romances willing to be thought wicked, if they may be allowed to be wits.* It is therefore to be always inculcated, that virtue is the highest proof of a superior understanding, and the only solid basis of greatness; and that vice is the natural consequence of narrow thoughts; that it begins in mistake, and ends in ignominy. (Italics mine.)
>
> —Samuel Johnson, *The Rambler*, No. 18

In this example, the analogy is introduced indirectly, and it is worth noting that this, like most paragraphs, is built not on one device, but on several. The "pure" paragraph, relying on only one means of support, is fairly rare.

Anecdote. The anecdote is a little story used to illustrate a point. It has the advantages of vividness and humor.

> To build city districts that are custom-made for easy crime is idiotic. Yet that is what we do. Today barbarism has taken over many city streets —or people fear it has, which comes to much the same thing in the end.

"I live in a lovely quiet residential area," says a friend of mine who is hunting for another place to live. "The only disturbing sound at night is the occasional scream of someone being mugged."

—Jane Jacobs, "Violence in the City Streets"

When Gentleman Dick Humphries ascended the stage at Odiham, Hampshire, on January 9, 1788, for his widely heralded first match with Daniel Mendoza, his fighting dress consisted of a pair of fine flannel drawers, white silk stockings with gold-colored clocks, pumps, and black shoe ribbons. After twenty minutes of fighting, during which he had been severely punished, Humphries counter-attacked, and Mendoza, "milling in retreat," slipped on the rain-soaked stage, wrenched his ankle, and was forced to give in. Immediately after the fight, Humphries sent word of his triumph to his patron: "Sir, I have done the Jew, and am in good health." Thus, with stylish pageantry and laconic report, did modern boxing begin.

—Steven Marcus, "Annals of the Prize Ring"

The anecdote, of course, must not be mere ornament; it must fit the purpose of the paragraph and the essay. Generally the writer does not need to search for the proper anecdote; it will occur to him, and when it does, it will probably have the ring of naturalness that a "manufactured" anecdote would not.

Cause and Effect. David Hume said, "But the most usual Species of Connexion among the different Events, which enter into any narrative Composition, is that of Cause and Effect. . . ." Naturally, the cause-effect relationship is an extremely important means of developing paragraphs.

Cause	The record shows that the people of the democracies, having become sovereign in this century, have made it increasingly difficult for their governments to prepare properly for war or to make peace.
Effect	Their responsible officials have been like the ministers of an opinionated and willful despot. Between the critical junctures, when public opinion has been inattentive or not vehemently aroused, responsible officials have often been able to circumvent extremist popular opinions and to wheedle their way towards moderation and good sense. In the crises, however, democratic officials —over and above their own human propensity to err— have been compelled to make the big mistakes that public opinion has insisted upon. Even the greatest men have not been able to turn back the massive tides of opinion and sentiment.

—Walter Lippmann, "The Malady of Democratic States"

Comparison and contrast. These devices are self-explanatory, and they appear almost spontaneously in any kind of discourse. (The proverbial father habitually says to his son, "You modern kids take the school bus, but when I was a boy, I had to struggle five miles through snow-drifts to learn my readin', writin', and 'rithmetic.") Comparative studies in all intellectual fields are valuable: the comparison of the family habits of chimpanzees with those of men, the comparison of Shakespeare with Jonson, the comparison of ancient Rome with modern America, and so on.

Contrast　　Flint's or Sandy Pond, in Lincoln, our greatest lake and inland sea, lies about a mile east of Walden. It is much larger, being said to contain one hundred and ninety-seven acres, and is more fertile in fish; but it is comparatively shallow, and not remarkably pure.

—Thoreau, *Walden*

Comparison　　Fashions in academe may be a bit more durable than those of Paris couturiers, but, like hemlines, the popularity of disciplines rises and falls. Much in vogue at the moment, right up there with particle physics and computer technology, is the study of linguistics. Its new popularity, contends Princeton linguist William Moulton, stems from a growing recognition that it is "the most scientific of the humanities and the most humanistic of the sciences."

—*Time*, Feb. 16, 1968

Contrast　　See the exquisite contrast of the types of mind. The pragmatist clings to facts and concreteness, observes truth at its work in particular cases, generalizes. Truth, for him, becomes a class-name for all sorts of definite working-values in experience. For the rationalist it remains a pure abstraction, to the bare name of which he must defer. When the pragmatist undertakes to show in detail just *why* we must defer, the rationalist is unable to recognize the concretes from which his own abstraction is taken. He accuses us of *denying* truth; whereas we have only sought to trace exactly why people follow it and always ought to follow it. Your typical ultra-abstractionist fairly shudders at concreteness: other things equal, he positively prefers the pale and spectral. If the two universes were offered, he would always choose the skinny outline rather than the rich thicket of reality. It is so much purer, clearer, nobler.

—William James, "What Pragmatism Means"

Definition. Often the writer feels that he must define his terms. He may be using a common word in a special way, and hence he will need to formulate a *stipulative* definition:

For the purposes of this discussion, we will take the word "science" to mean any systematic, controlled intellectual inquiry, not merely inquiry under laboratory conditions, as the word has been interpreted in the past. Thus, for instance, the study of language can be as exact a science as chemistry.

Starting with a definition that is not in doubt or in dispute, however, is just a way of beating around the bush. The definition should serve some other purpose than taking up space.

> Originally *dilettante* meant a lover of the fine arts (it comes from the Latin word for delight) and it was used to distinguish the consumer from the producer. Its application spread beyond the arts in English, and in the eighteenth century the Society of the Dilettanti was a club of influential men interested not only in the arts but in the sciences and in archaeology. It meant the man of intellectual curiosity who devoted part of his time to the intelligent cultivation of the arts and sciences, to the resources of leisure and the satisfactions of the mind.
>
> —Russell Lynes, "Time on Our Hands"

Description. The descriptive paragraph in the expository essay serves to bring a subject to life. Suppose the effect and idea of an essay depend upon the reader's "visualizing" a place or thing. Then it will not do to speak in generalities: "Paris is beautiful" or "The clipper ship is graceful." The beauty of Paris and the grace of the clipper ship must be brought concretely and vividly before the mind's eye of the reader.

> The prompt Paris morning struck its cheerful notes—in a soft breeze and a sprinkled smell, in the light flit, over the garden-floor, of bare-headed girls with the buckled strap of oblong boxes, in the type of ancient thrifty persons basking betimes where terrace-walls were warm, in the blue-frocked brass-labelled officialism of humble rakers and scrapers, in the deep references of a straight-pacing priest or the sharp ones of a white-gaitered, red-legged soldier.
>
> —Henry James, *The Ambassadors*

Here is a somewhat less successful descriptive passage from a student theme. Compare it with the paragraph by James.

> Tracking down elk deep in the confines of the dark evergreen forests gives me my greatest thrills. During these days of the dying summer, the elk comes to life with a desire for procreation. He rubs his massive antlers against trees until they take on a hard glassy surface in preparation for the battles that the bulls will soon wage for their mates. Their coats become long and heavy in preparation for the long winter months ahead. In the early morning and late evening, their sharp bugling calls can be heard from canyon to canyon. In this season of the year, elk are constantly watchful for any enemy that may challenge their domain. The mighty animal is truly at his height of splendor. Jack Frost has begun to make his marks on the remains of an Indian summer. The once green grass is now dingy brown-colored with a coating of white dew upon it. The windows now serve as a canvas for the designs of Jack Frost. The

light blue sky is now cold and crisp, and there are no sounds to be heard. The leaves on the trees have turned many different colors while the ground has taken on a new complexion of whiteness, and intermingled with the new covering are many fallen leaves. The outside world has become a living picture without the chirping and singing of the birds, who have left for a new summer place. This picture is painted for me early in the morning during the preparation for the start of the elk hunt in early fall.

This paragraph is not all bad, and certainly the student was headed in the right direction: the description is packed with concrete details. However, the paragraph lacks control. A description must maintain a consistent *viewpoint;* that is, the describer cannot change positions in relation to the thing described at will. If the descriptive passage is from the panoramic viewpoint, then it must remain so until there is a good reason for change; if the descriptive passage is from the inside looking out, then there must not be a sudden, unexplained shift to the outside looking in. In the example paragraph, at first we have the impression that we are in "the confines of the dark evergreen forest," but then we find that "The windows now serve as a canvas for the designs of Jack Frost." What windows? Where are they? (And, parenthetically, what about the whole concept of Jack Frost. Isn't it, after all, so hackneyed as to be useless?)

The effective description will maintain a consistent viewpoint, as if the onlooker either remained in one place or else flew over a larger area.

Successful description is based on close observation and accurate, detailed reporting.

Details. All writing should be detailed. Skimpiness leads to failure. In all of the example paragraphs cited so far, details have been used for development. One more example of how concrete details build meaningful, interesting discourse:

> It was a delicious supper—hot bread, fried bacon, and black coffee. It was a delicious solitude we were in, too. Three miles away was a sawmill and some workmen, but there were not fifteen other human beings throughout the wide circumference of the lake. As the darkness closed down and the stars came out and spangled the great mirror with jewels, we smoked meditatively in the solemn hush and forgot our troubles and our pains. In due time we spread our blankets in the warm sand between two large boulders and soon fell asleep, careless of the procession of ants that passed in through rents in our clothing and explored our persons. Nothing could disturb the sleep that fettered us, for it had been fairly earned, and if our consciences had any sins on them they had to adjourn court for the night, any way. The wind rose just as we were losing consciousness, and we were lulled to sleep by the beating of the surf upon the shore.
>
> —Mark Twain, *Roughing It*

The paragraph says nothing but, "We had a good supper, we enjoyed the solitude, and we slept well." And yet, paradoxically, how much more it says! From paragraphs such as this one, the student can learn worlds about developing his own writing.

Metaphor. For an extended discussion of metaphor, see Chapter V. Briefly, the metaphor is a figure of speech that is based on implied comparison. The simile expresses the comparison through the use of "like" or "as." *He was a lion in battle* is a metaphor; *He was like a lion in battle* is a simile. The metaphor is at the very basis of language. It illuminates strikingly, and it brings a measure of esthetic discovery to prose.

> This bird's-eye view of the general steering function of the college-bred amid the driftings of democracy ought to help us to a wider vision of what our colleges themselves should aim at. If we are to be the yeast-cake for democracy's dough, if we are to make it rise with culture's preference's, we must see to it that culture spreads broad sails. We must shake the old double reefs out of the canvas into the wind and sunshine, and let in every modern subject, sure that any subject will prove humanistic, if its setting be kept only wide enough.
>
> —William James, *Memoirs and Studies*

Virtually the whole freight of idea in this paragraph is carried by metaphor. One can validly question, indeed, whether or not James has used too much metaphor, whether the metaphor of the yeast and the metaphor of the ship do not clash and hence cancel one another out.

Restatement. A paragraph can consist of a series of sentences which restate the subject from different angles, in different lights, as the author moves toward his complete meaning. This kind of development, extremely common, is not mere repetitiveness; it is the accrual of meaning. We have already seen that paragraph movement is usually from the general to the specific, each sentence pinning the meaning down more closely. The movement of a paragraph from "Nature" by Emerson looks like this:

> Space, time, society, labor, climate, food, locomotion, the animals, the mechanical forces, give us sincerest lessons, day by day, whose meaning is unlimited.
>> They educate both the Understanding and the Reason.
>>> Every property of matter is a school for the Understanding, —its solidity or resistance, its inertia, its extension, its figure, its divisibility.
>>>> The Understanding adds, divides, combines, measures, and finds nutriment and room for its activity in this worthy scene.
>>>>> Meantime, Reason transfers all these lessons into its own world of thought, by perceiving the analogy that marries Matter and Mind.

The topic is restricted four times by a method that might be called variations on a theme.

Varieties. Some paragraphs gain development through only one device: definition, anecdote, example, or whatever. But as the many examples examined so far have demonstrated, the normal paragraph is a combination of two or even more methods of development. The writer uses the devices that do the job he wants done. If the survey of methods of development has given the idea that a writer chooses one method for paragraph one, another method for paragraph two, and so on, that impression is false. Writing is so organic a process and so utterly unpredictable in the ways by which it develops that the attempt to describe an essay by any kind of schematization must lead to a degree of distortion. You can turn back to the examples cited so far (more than forty of them!) and demonstrate to yourself that the "pure" paragraph is a somewhat rare bird.

RECAPITULATION

Methods of development that we have examined are: (1) examples, (2) logic, (3) data, (4) enumeration, (5) analogy, (6) anecdote, (7) cause and effect, (8) comparison and contrast, (9) definition, (10) description, (11) details, (12) metaphor, (13) restatement. This list of methods does not represent mutually exclusive items; for instance, supplying data is also supplying details. Nor should we expect to find that only one of the methods is used in each paragraph. Most paragraphs use a variety of means for development.

Writing is an organic process, and each idea needs its own kind of development. The important point to remember is that a bare idea, standing alone and unsupported, may serve as a good indicator toward a course of action or possible belief—"Thou shalt not kill!"—but it is not this sort of idea that serves as the stuff for the essay. If, in fact, someone were to write an essay on "Thou shalt not kill!" he would need to qualify, illustrate, develop, and control. For instance, does the injunction against killing apply in a just war? Answering that question, indeed, might demand a great number of subsidiary ideas, each of which would gain its development in a paragraph.

Exercise. Analyze specifically and in detail the methods of development used in the following paragraphs.

1. We shall define term simply here as a name capable of entering into a proposition. In our treatment of rhetorical sources, we have regarded the full predication consisting of a proposition as the true valida-

tor. But a single term is an incipient proposition, awaiting only the necessary coupling with another term; and it cannot be denied that single names set up expectancies of propositional embodiment. This causes everyone to realize the critical nature of the process of naming. Given the name "patriot," for example, we might expect to see coupled with it "Brutus," or "Washington," or "Parnell"; given the term "hot," we might expect to see "sun," "stove," and so on. In sum, single terms have their potencies, this being part of the phenomenon of names, and we shall here present a few of the most noteworthy in our time, with some remarks upon their etiology.

—Richard M. Weaver, "Ultimate Terms in Contemporary Rhetoric"

2. Literature, its exertions and objects, were now of little moment in my regard. I cared not, at this period, for books; they were apart from me. Nature,—except it were human nature,—the nature that is developed in earth and sky, was, in one sense, hidden from me; and all the imaginative delight, wherewith it had been spiritualized, passed away out of my mind. A gift, a faculty, if it had not departed, was suspended and inanimate within me. There would have been something sad, unutterably dreary, in all this, had I not been conscious that it lay at my own option to recall whatever was valuable in the past. It might be true, indeed, that this was a life which could not with impunity be lived too long; else, it might have made me permanently other than I had been without transforming me into any shape which it would be worth my while to take. But I never considered it as other than a transitory life. There was always a prophetic instinct, a low whisper in my ear, that, within no long period, and whenever a new change of custom should be essential to my good, a change would come.

—Nathaniel Hawthorne, "The Custom House"

3. In the realm of sound or rather *noise* it must be said that the offenses committed this way in the United States are unparalleled for sheer barbarism anywhere else in the world. Many years ago Schopenhauer wrote an essay "On Noise." It is many years since I read it, but I vividly recall how scorching Schopenhauer was on the sudden sharp brain-stopping, thought-killing explosive cracking of the whips of coachmen and others. What Schopenhauer would have had to say on the din and discord created by the automobile horns of today, the noises of starting and gear-shifting, the backfiring of trucks and buses, and the screeching and groaning of brakes and tires—all to the accompaniment of a perfusion of essence of gasoline exhaust fumes—can be guessed at.

—Ashley Montagu, "The Annihilation of Privacy"

4. Yet one cannot deny that there is an impersonal style:

The official announcements regarding the repayment of credits and the withdrawal of exchange regulations did not come early enough to have an important effect on Lombard Street. Nevertheless discount steadily declined under the pressure of demand from home and foreign buyers with increased reluctance of sellers.

Anybody might have written that: the voice is the voice of a tape-ma-chine. But the man who wrote it was not eager to tell his news, it was a matter of mechanical routine. He was not explaining anything, nor trying to arouse the emotions of his readers. He was not interested, so fell into the anonymous tone, which is the result of a long tradition. But the moment a man is really interested he speaks with his own voice; you are at once aware of a personality. Take the first sentence of Henry James' *The Death of the Lion*:

> I had simply, I suppose, a change of heart, and it must have begun when I received my manuscript back from Mr. Pinhorn.

At once we hear someone speaking, and recognize that we are listening to the speech of a man different from other men.

—Bonamy Dobrée, *Modern Prose Style*

5. Art becomes more or less infectious in consequence of three con-ditions: (1) in consequence of a greater or lesser peculiarity of the sen-sation conveyed; (2) in consequence of a greater or lesser clearness of the transmission of this sensation; and (3) in consequence of the sincerity of the artist, that is, of the greater or lesser force with which the artist himself experiences the sensations which he is conveying.

—Leo Tolstoy, "What Is Art?"

PARAGRAPH UNITY

We demonstrated at the first of this chapter that the paragraph is a convention, just as the sentence is a convention (even though the para-graph may not be so clearly defined and severely delimited as the sentence). In other words, as our experiment showed, people tend, in general, to agree on the concepts paragraph and non-paragraph. This idea may sound strange, but it is really simple. For instance, large groups of people recognize and differentiate cows, horses, and goats without stopping to define any of them. Somehow, the mind becomes prepared to recognize general "patterns" if they are prevalent.

It is quite obvious that if we recognize "paragraph," we are not re-ferring to any certain paragraph, just as when we state that we can recog-nize clouds, we are not referring to any particular cloud or to any particular type of clouds. It seems that the human mind is capable of generalizing forms so that a great number of individuals will fit into that general form. And this is precisely what we are talking about when we say that the paragraph is a convention. In order to illustrate the point further, we can perform a simple trick.

Is the following a paragraph?

> A noun is the name of a person, place, or thing. When the trout are not rising, it is advisable to fish with a wet fly. Cycling is good exercise, but jogging is better. He is unscrupulous.

And is the following a paragraph?

> Even though a noun is the name of a person, place, or thing, when the trout are not rising, it is advisable to fish with a wet fly. Furthermore, cycling is good exercise, but jogging is better. Because of all this, he is unscrupulous.

Most readers, if forced to choose which of the two examples more nearly approximates a paragraph, would opt for the second. They might not be able to tell exactly why the second example is more like a paragraph than the first, but they would agree that such is the case.

Again, we can ask, "Which of the following two examples is most nearly a sentence?"

> are of some coming people the
> the flestrotion of a loceness is whirting firly grobs

Most people would say that the second example is the sentence. But "the flestrotion of a loceness is whirting firly grobs" does not seem to be "the expression of a complete idea," which is the traditional definition of "sentence." Though we "feel" that the sequence constitutes a sentence, we cannot tell what that sentence might mean. And that is just the point! We can recognize a sentence without understanding its meaning. Noam Chomsky gives this famous example of a nonsense sentence:

> Colorless green ideas sleep furiously.

And everyone is familiar with Jabberwocky.

> 'Twas brillig, and the slithy toves
> Did gyre and gimble in the wabe;
> All mimsy were the borogroves,
> And the mome raths outgrabe

> —Lewis Carroll, "Alice In Wonderland"

It seems that we can recognize the *form* sentence independently of meaning. We sense that "the flestrotion" is a noun phrase because definite articles commonly precede nouns, and *-tion* is a nominal ending (beauti-fic*ation*, destruc*tion*). We know what "of" is because it belongs to a brief list of words (like *to, in, over*) that are called "prepositions," and prepo-sitions are followed by noun phrases (of a man, to the store, over the roof). The indefinite article *a* precedes nouns, and *-ness*, like *-tion*, is a nominal ending (loose*ness*, kind*ness*). *Is whirting* is a typical verb form in the present progressive: is thinking, is doing, is making. *Firly* is like an adjective (pretty, silly), and *grobs* seems to have the *-s* plural that is typical of nouns. All of this we, as native speakers of English, recognize intuitively. (See the chapter on Grammar.) Furthermore, we see that the whole series of nonsense words fits a pattern that is common for sentences in English:

> the flestrotion of a loceness is whirting firly grobs
> the destruction of a kindness is killing pretty trees.

Are there, then, such structural signals in the paragraph? Look again at the "nonsense" paragraph that was cited above:

> EVEN THOUGH a noun is the name of a person, place, or thing, when the trout are not rising, it is advisable to fish with a wet fly. FURTHERMORE, cycling is good exercise, but jogging is better. BE-CAUSE OF ALL THIS, he is unscrupulous.

Here is another example paragraph, this one "cemented" together by three simple words:

> Next, what happens to the verbally bright who have no zeal for a serviceable profession and who have no particular scientific or artistic bent? For the most part THEY make up the tribes of salesmanship, entertainment, business management, promotion, and advertising. HERE of course there is no question of utility or honor to begin with, so an ingenuous boy will not look here for a manly career. NEVERTHELESS, though we can pass by the sufferings of these well-paid callings, much publicized by their own writers, they are important to our theme because of the model they present to the growing boy.
>
> —Paul Goodman, *Growing Up Absurd*

Now read Goodman's paragraph *without* the three capitalized words. What happens?

We have said that an essay is a series of related paragraphs, and a paragraph is a series of related sentences. The problem of getting from paragraph to paragraph in the essay is analogous to the problem of getting from sentence to sentence in the paragraph.

We will now systematically explore the ways whereby paragraph unity comes about.

Transitional words and phrases. Three devices for joining sentences are *coordinating conjunctions* (*and, but, yet, or, for, etc.*), *subordinating conjunctions* (*because, although, whenever, etc.*), and *transitional adverbs* (*however, moreover, thus, etc.*).

> I went to college, *for* I wanted an education.
> I went to college *because* I wanted an education.
> I went to college; *moreover,* I wanted an education.

But as the passage by Paul Goodman illustrated, this kind of word can function at the paragraph level as well as at the sentence level. Here is another example, with all of the transitional words in capitals:

> The Spaniards refused the post-Renaissance liberty of Europe. AND the Spaniards filled most of America. The Yankees, TOO, refused, refused the post-Renaissance humanism of Europe. First and foremost, they hated masters. BUT under that, they hated the flowing ease of humour in Europe. At the bottom of the American soul was always a dark suspense, at the bottom of the Spanish-American soul the same. AND this dark suspense hated and hates the old European spontaneity, watches it collapse with satisfaction.
>
> —D. H. Lawrence, "The Spirit of the Place"

Look through any collection of essays, and you will find that coordinating conjunctions as transitions are extremely common, a fact about modern writing which contradicts the venerable schoolmarmish admonition, "Don't start sentences with conjunctions." Of course no good writer would want to start every sentence or even most sentences with coordinating conjunctions, but virtually all professional writers use these to make clear the relationships in their paragraphs, to serve as transitions between sentences.

Transitional adverbs are perhaps the second most common transitional device:

> It is attention to practice and indifference to overarching beliefs that guarantees our innocence, but our critics are sodden with ideology and cannot take this in. NONE THE LESS [normally written "nonetheless"] this nonsectarianism is one clear sign of superiority over Russia. . . .
>
> —Jacques Barzun, "Innocents at Home"

> Greek tragedy and the detective story have one characteristic in common, in which they both differ from modern tragedy, namely, the characters are not changed in or by their actions: in Greek tragedy because their actions are fated, in the detective story because the decisive event, the murder, has already occurred. Time and space THEREFORE are simply the when and where of revealing either what has to happen or what has actually happened. . . .
>
> —W. H. Auden, "The Guilty Vicarage"

A more general category of transitions is phrases that make the proper tie-ups in paragraphs. They are difficult to classify, but a few examples will illustrate their nature.

of course	If questioned closely enough, the fuming conservative will admit that he is really against capital punishment. *Of course* he clings tenaciously to the notion that wrongdoers should get the full works.

| *on the other hand* | The price of liberty is eternal vigilance. The price of eternal vigilance, *on the other hand,* is sore eyes. |
| *at the same time* | To most general observers, modern art seems like aberration. *At the same time,* no one can ignore what is happening in painting, the cinema, and music. |

There are other such conventional phrases that serve as transitions.

Time sequences. Observe how the following paragraph gains unity through the chronological sequence set up in it:

> THIRTY YEARS AGO only one out of every eight Americans at work had been to high school. TODAY four out of every five of the young people of high school age in the United States attend high school. TWENTY YEARS HENCE, when today's middle-aged will have retired, practically every working American will be a high school graduate. We have ALREADY passed the half-way mark.
>
> —Peter F. Drucker, "The Educational Revolution"

In the time orientation of paragraphs, the adverb "then" performs journeyman service. Analogous to the time sequence is, of course, the space sequence, in which the most common adverb is, as you might guess, "there."

Equivalence chains. At a somewhat deeper and less obvious level of structure are the equivalence chains. By "equivalence chain" is meant a series of words or phrases that are roughly equivalent to one another and that hence have nearly the same signification. An example of such a chain occurs in the following paragraph:

> LOGIC is the SCIENCE of correct reasoning. Like other sciences—chemistry, linguistics, astronomy—IT is best studied in and for ITSELF, for IT is a vast SUBJECT and a complicated ONE. However, any treatment of rhetoric that ignored LOGIC would be incomplete. The TWO SUBJECTS are intimately associated; rhetoric uses LOGIC, just as it uses (though at a different level) grammar and punctuation; and LOGIC in ITS turn acts as a control over rhetoric.

The most common aspect of equivalence chains is the pronoun-antecedent relationship:

> All during the reading for a biography, SUBJECTS for future books suggest THEMSELVES, stepping from the records with a brave refusal to rest quietly in their past. In my experience THESE are apt to be engaging personalities, handsome men, busy in doubtful enterprises. It is hard to resist THEM; their speech is witty and their manners invite. Sin is more dramatic, certainly, than a state of innocence or stubborn virtue.
>
> —Catherine Drinker Bowen, "The Search for a Subject"

When the pronoun in one sentence refers back to its antecedent, a unity is inevitably established.

Recapitulation. Paragraphs have form, just as sentences do—and that form can be analyzed with some exactness. Hence, the building of good paragraphs should not be a mystery. In a short time, the beginning writer ought to be able to construct paragraphs that do not leave the reader unsatisfied, paragraphs that fully and clearly handle their ideas, paragraphs that are unified, organic structures.

The methods of paragraph development that we have reviewed are helpful, but the writer will not run down the list and choose this device for one paragraph, that device for another paragraph, and a third device for yet another. The process of composition does not work that way. The skilled writer builds his structure almost automatically; the devices are part of his repertory, and he calls on them without thinking, in almost the same way that a violinist does not cogitate in advance about the fingering for a certain passage. The point, of course, is to become skillful enough that one can use all of the devices automatically and organically.

Exercise. (1) Turn back to "The Young American: Affluent and Unfulfilled." You will recall that you made a decision as to where the essay should be paragraphed. Now look closely at the paragraphs you discovered. How is each developed? What devices bring about unity in each paragraph? (2) Analyze the following paragraphs. Be prepared to discuss the methods of development, the relationships among the ideas, the transitions, the equivalence chains—and whatever else might appear significant.

   a. Or take the five-year-old, faced with two equal beakers, each filled to the same level with water. He will say that they are equal. Now pour the contents of one of the beakers into another that is taller and skinnier and ask whether there is the same amount to drink in both. The child will deny it, pointing out that one of them has more because the water is higher. This incapacity to recognize invariance of magnitude across transformations in the appearance of things is one of the most striking aspects of this stage.

   —Jerome Bruner, *Toward a Theory of Instruction*

   b. The wines of this country have won numerous medals and grand prizes in international competitions and at world and California fairs. American wines have been shipped to Europe to sell in competition with, and at higher prices than, similar European wines. Although a few Old World wines, some of which are so rare that only a few hundred gallons are grown annually, are renowned, the standard wines of the United States average higher in quality than those of any other country. The proportion of top-quality wines in comparison to the total production is higher here than in European wine growing countries. Even the average age of the wines is higher.

—Wine Institute, *The Story of Wine and Its Uses*

c. Entering that gable-ended Spouter-Inn, you found yourself in a wide, low, straggling entry with old-fashioned wainscots, reminding one of the bulwarks of some condemned old craft. On one side hung a very large oil-painting so thoroughly besmoked, and every way defaced, that in the unequal cross-lights by which you viewed it, it was only by diligent study and a series of systematic visits to it, and careful inquiry of the neighbors, that you could any way arrive at an understanding of its purpose. Such unaccountable masses of shades and shadows, that at first you almost thought some ambitious young artist, in the time of the New England hags, had endeavored to delineate chaos bewitched. But by dint of much and earnest contemplation, and oft repeated ponderings, and especially by throwing open the little window towards the back of the entry, you at last come to the conclusion that such an idea, however wild, might not be altogether unwarranted.

—Herman Melville, *Moby Dick*

d. The sign which segregates true art from its adulterations is this indubitable one—the infectiousness of art. If a man without any activity on his part and without any change of his position, in reading, hearing, seeing the production of another man, experiences a state of mind which unites him with that man and with others who, like him, apperceive the subject of art, then the subject which evokes such a state is a subject of art. No matter how poetical, how seemingly real, how effective or entertaining a subject may be, it is not a subject of art, if it does not evoke in man that sensation of joy which is distinct from all other sensations, that union of one's soul with another (the author) and with others (the hearers or spectators) who perceive the same artistic production.

Leo Tolstoy, "What Is Art?"

III ✍ The Grammars of English

An essay consists of paragraphs, and a paragraph consists of sentences. Therefore, in the development of a discussion of the essay, one might expect that a chapter on the sentence would follow the chapter on the paragraph, but there are good reasons for interpolating a theoretical discussion of the grammars of English. Grammar, after all, is the science that classifies, analyzes, and explains sentences and that (even more important) speculates about the processes whereby sentences are generated. Thus there is a practical reason for a lengthy consideration of grammar that precedes the chapter on the sentence.

But the main reason for studying grammar is not "practical" at all, any more than a knowledge of astronomy or psychology or history or mathematics is mainly practical. All of these subjects have their practical applications (as does grammar), but they are not in the curriculum for the same reasons that, say, driver education might be. That is, some academic disciplines are valuable in and of themselves. In *The Idea of a University*, Cardinal Newman put it this way:

> I am asked what is the end of University Education, and of the Liberal or Philosophical Knowledge which I conceive it to impart: I answer, that what I have already said has been sufficient to show that

65

it has a very tangible, real, and sufficient end, though the end cannot be divided from the knowledge itself. Knowledge is capable of being its own end. Such is the constitution of the human mind, that any kind of knowledge, if it be really such, is its own reward.

If knowledge in general should be its own reward, then knowledge of the processes of that most human of human characteristics, language, should be rewarding indeed.

There are several initial hindrances to writing a chapter on grammar. The so-called "new" grammar is developing at such a rapid pace that theories are out of date almost as soon as they get into print. Furthermore, students have widely varying backgrounds in the subject; some have been introduced to the old and the new, some have studied just the old or the new, and some have studied no grammar at all. But even those students who have spent three or four years with the new grammar probably have not been introduced to the theory behind it— and the present chapter will be concerned not so much with the nice details as with general principles that cast light in many directions.

The field of grammar can be roughly broken down into three areas: traditional, structural, and generative. We will deal with the theories and operations of each of the three.

TRADITIONAL GRAMMAR

The kind of grammar that most of us learned is now called "traditional," and some knowledge of that tradition is not only interesting, but also necessary for an understanding of the schism between old grammar and new grammar. There is no need here to become highly technical or deeply involved, but it is necessary to understand why the grammar that we inherited is what it is, and, furthermore, why it ranks with God, Mother, and Country as a cherished part of our heritage.

In the first place, traditional grammar is basically modelled on Latin grammar. This is a completely understandable and even salutary aspect of the development of language study. During the Middle Ages and through the Renaissance, Latin was the universal language of the learned; it was the language that received serious study at all levels in the schools; it was the language of learned writing. The medieval scholar felt that Latin somehow was a better, purer, and more expressive language than English or other modern languages. Man and his language constitute such a close emotional tie that attitudes toward language often mirror man's attitude toward his universe and his ultimate destiny. And the historical allegiance to Latin (and Greek) reflects the close tie. The argument runs something like this. Since God created a perfect universe, he must originally have created a perfect language for Adam. In the Garden of Eden, it is inconceivable that anything could be less than ideal. But in Adam's fall, we sinnèd all—and the world began its topsy-turvy course of degeneration to its present sad state. Language, like everything else, became impure and corrupt. But Latin was nearer to the pristine original than the corrupt modern languages; hence, it must have been a "purer," better language than, say, English or French.

There are other reasons for the prëeminence of classical languages. The literature of Greece and Rome was rich and meaningful. In fact, it was the major portion of medieval man's literary possessions. Therefore, the languages of these literatures were extremely important. Latin was an international language such as the world has not known since medieval times. With Latin as its common language, the learned world could be a real community of scholars of many countries. The classical tradition ran very deep; it is only in modern times that the accomplishments of Greece and Rome have become relatively meaningless to the great masses of literate people.

But it is also perfectly obvious that English is not Latin, and any attempt to adjust English grammar to Latin grammar would falsify both languages. One simple example illustrates this. In Latin, the single word *amo* is translated into two English words: *I love.* There is a tremendous difference between the structures that Latin and English use to express meanings. Latin was a *synthetic* language; in it, relationships were expressed by changes in word form. But from about 1400, English became an *analytic* language, that is, a language in which relationships were expressed largely by word order. Old English (the language up to about 1100 A.D.) was a synthetic language like Latin. For instance, all of the following meant "The man killed the king," because word form showed what we call subject and object relationship:

> Se man sloh thone kyning.
> Se man thone kyning sloh.
> Thone kyning sloh se man.
> Thone kyning se man sloh.
> Sloh thone kyning se man.

The definite article *se* (comparable to modern "the") meant that the noun following it was the subject. The definite article *thone* meant that the noun following it was the object. So word order in Old English—as in Latin—was not of primary importance. But note what happens when the Old English sentences above are translated, *word for word,* into modern English:

The man killed the king.
The man the king killed.
The king killed the man.
The king the man killed.
Killed the king the man.

Obviously the grammar of a synthetic language would be far different from the grammar of an analytic language. This means that applying Latin grammar to English would require major adjustments in the Latin grammar. These adjustments were made, so that traditional grammar worked relatively well and provided a relatively accurate description of the language. But the question arises: Why adjust Latin grammar to English? Why not write a grammar of English?

OUR "PROPER" ANCESTORS STEP IN

The study of language has always had one disadvantage—or advantage, depending on how one views it—compared with the study of science. There is nothing proper or improper about a mathematical equation or a chemical formula. Either it is right or wrong. But good manners, morality, patriotism, and kindness to dumb animals do not enter the question. Decisions about "right" and "wrong" and "proper" and "improper" in language somehow hit people at their deepest emotional springs, so that new language theories get associated with moral turpitude, communism, promiscuity, and atheism. (I personally remember a childhood in which "damn" and "hell" were current around the house, but a single "ain't" was worth at least a stern reprimand.) Whether we like it or not, we generally have a real hang-up on propriety in language.

Since the best definition of man is "the talking animal," it is clear that the language one uses is somehow going to get associated, rightly or wrongly, with his basic character—and more strangely and importantly, with his social status. The most significant historical phenomenon of modern times—*i.e.*, since the late Renaissance—is the emergence in Western civilization of a great middle class, an enormous mass of people who stand halfway between nothingness and eminence. This phenomenon became most marked in the eighteenth century. Four or five hundred years ago, society could be divided roughly but with some accuracy into nobility and learned on the one hand (a small minority) and illiterate lower classes on the other. But with the Social Revolution of the eighteenth century, an entirely different stratum of civilization gained new importance: the merchant, the banker, the broker, the entrepreneur —all with growing financial and political power. Gradually, there was a new mobility in society. The industrious craftsman could become a merchant, and the merchant could become a tycoon. But between the tycoon and the aristocracy there often stood a terrible barrier: "correct" use of language. During the Middle Ages, only some aristocrats and clergy were literate (either bilingual or polylingual); the lower class was illiterate. During subsequent eras, literacy spread, but the gap between the "correct" and "polite" user of language and the "incorrect," "impolite" user of language remained—as it does today.

Obviously, one way to gain admittance to polite society (providing one was wealthy enough in the first place) was to dress, act, and, most important, speak like the upper classes. Therefore, the great emerging middle classes (and indeed all literate persons) demanded to be told what was correct and what was incorrect, what was polite and what was rude.

> *Exercise.* Does "propriety" in language have any importance in the modern American social pecking order? Have you had any personal experiences with discrimination based on your own or someone else's use of language? Be prepared to answer in detail and with specific examples.

Interestingly enough, such questions would never have entered the minds of Shakespeare or Bacon. They had not yet discovered the *doctrine of correctness,* which was the main eighteenth-century contribution to the study of language.

In answer to the demand to know what was "right," "correct," and "proper," eighteenth-century grammarians produced treatises, grammar books that did not make much attempt to describe the language as it was, but which set down the laws for correctness and decency. These books had a terrific impact on the great masses—in "polite" society, in the schools, in learned circles.

In the eighteenth century, for the first time, the idea of absolute correctness entered the study of language. Listen to Robert Lowth, the high-priest of eighteenth-century grammar:

> The principal design of a Grammar of any Language is to teach us to express ourselves with propriety in that Language; and to enable us to judge of every phrase and form of construction, whether it be right or not. The plain way of doing this is, to lay down rules, and to illustrate them by examples. But, beside shewing what is right, the matter may be further explained by pointing out what is wrong. I will not take it upon me to say, whether we have any Grammar, that sufficiently instructs us by rule and example; but I am sure we have none, that, in the manner here attempted, teaches what is right by shewing what is wrong; though this may perhaps prove the more useful and effectual method of instruction.

Such absolute certitude was bound to make the weak tremble and to influence linguistic sinners to mend their ways.

Since the eighteenth century, school grammars have been rule-bound. The desirability of rules is a subject in itself. For the present, it is enough to know that the traditional grammar we have inherited is based firmly on the doctrine that in language there is an absolute right and an absolute wrong and almost as firmly on Latin, rather than English. (There is no intention here of oversimplifying. The great traditional scholarly grammars of English are magnificent works that show a very great deal indeed about the nature of our language, and within certain limits, traditional grammar is endlessly useful.)

COMMON SENSE AND TRADITIONAL GRAMMAR

The human quest for knowledge is paradoxical. We know a great deal indeed about the basic structure of the physical universe; we are conquering outer space; we have developed a technology that defies the ordinary intellect and the tool-kit in even the well equipped home.

But a widespread, serious effort to investigate language has begun only in recent years. (Naturally, there have always been serious scholars of language, from the earliest times on. These investigators, however, made isolated efforts as compared with the great impulse toward inquiry about the physical universe.) Much of what we find in our textbooks relies on unverified, untested common sense, and as modern skepticism often points out, common sense is a shaky basis for knowledge. In fact, our world and its inhabitants appear more and more to defy the laws of common sense; nothing is more uncommonsensical, for instance, than the notion that energy and matter are one and the same.

In language, it seems only commonsensical that one should thoroughly master the grammar—the rules of the game—before starting to learn the language itself. And it was on the basis of this common sense proposition that language was taught for hundreds of years. The eighteenth-century education of Samuel Johnson was typical. As we have seen, Latin formed the core of curricula up to the eighteenth century and beyond, and the way in which students were taught Latin reflects the linguistic theory that prevailed then—and that still prevails in the traditional English textbooks. The young Sam Johnson, entering the school at Lichfield when he was seven, began the arduous task of memorizing the rules of Latin grammar. The text that he used was undoubtedly that of William Lyly, a book that set the rules forth in doggerel verse, on the theory that verse is more easily remembered than prose. Once the boy had mastered the rules, he was set to parsing and construing and was allowed to read simple fables and tales in the Latin. As the student's mastery grew, he went on to the more substantial Latin authors, to Horace and Virgil and Livy and Ovid.

After all, it does make some sense to learn the basic rules of a *foreign* language, if the rules are used in conjunction with direct practice in reading, writing, and speaking that language. In German, for instance, it is useful for the beginner to know the general rule that the verb comes last in a subordinate clause or, in French, that the colloquial spoken past tense and the formal written past tense are different. But surely everyone would agree that learning all the rules *before* starting to learn the language is sheer madness.

The common sense proposition that one must know grammar in order to use his native language is strange indeed, one of the many unquestioned ideas that are part of our heritage from ages past. We need only observe language acquisition in children to realize that they hardly need to study grammar in order to use language adequately, even eloquently. And it is interesting that no "classic" writer has ever been a grammarian, if indeed any of our most revered authors were even barely competent grammarians. We must, then, conclude paradoxically that it is possible to use the language precisely, beautifully, and eloquently without knowing grammar—and this paradox directly contradicts the common sense proposition that one must know grammar to use a language. Confusion upon confusion! Mark Twain, Ernest Hemingway, Nathaniel Hawthorne, Herman Melville, Henry David Thoreau, F. Scott Fitzgerald, Robert Frost—all more or less ignorant of grammar.

Something must be wrong with linguistic common sense.

Exercise. Comment on the common sense of the following dicta about language:

1. You should not end a sentence with a preposition.

2. Don't use double negatives, for two negatives make a positive. Thus the sentence "I haven't got no money" must mean "I have *some* money."

3. The first step in learning to write sentences is to define the word "sentence."

4. "I *shall* go" just implies that something will happen in the future, but "I *will* go" implies resolution and determination.

5. French is a better language for love than is English.

WHAT IS A SENTENCE?

Since the sentence is the basic unit in language, reason tells us that a discussion of grammar should begin with a definition of "sentence." For purposes of this definition and other concepts of traditional grammar, we will use *Advanced English Grammar*, by George Lyman Kitt-redge and Frank Edgar Farley (1913), an old book, to be sure, but one that fully and intelligently expresses the traditional viewpoint that has come down to us in the school grammars of today. Kittredge and Farley tell us that "a sentence is a group of words which expresses a complete thought." According to that definition, are the following complete sentences?

1. "Did the Lions or the Oilers win the basketball game?"
2. "The Oilers. 3. They played a better game than they have all season."
4. "Oh?"
5. "Yes, it was most exciting."

Sentence 1 would probably fit our old definition (if we could first agree on the definition of "complete idea"). But what about sentence 2? By no stretching of the imagination is it a complete idea—*except in context*. In other words, sentence 1 is necessary for the "complete" idea of sentence 2. Of course, one might argue that sentence 2 is not a sentence at all, but that would be arguing against the reality of language, for everyone knows that *in the context given,* sentence 2 could be nothing but what it is. (If sentence 2 were "complete," *The Oilers won the basketball game,* we would feel that it was somehow strange or out of place.) And what about sentence 3? Is it "the expression of a complete idea"? Perhaps—and yet significant questions can be raised. Does the pronoun "they" have any significance unless it can be referred back to sentence 2? If your answer to this question is "no," then, according to the old definition, sentence 3 becomes a non-sentence. And sentence 4? It is a typical kind of locution in English. Shall we call it a non-sentence because it does not express a complete idea? According to the traditional definition, we encounter problems even with sentence 5, for the "it" in that sentence has no meaning except as it refers back to "game" in sentence 3.

Enough, then. It is apparent that forming a definition of "sentence" on the basis of idea would involve us in futile speculation and controversy. This is not to say, however, that native speakers do not know what a sentence is. Obviously they do. Later in this book, we will explain further; for the moment we will rest on the proposition that the *notional* definition of "sentence" is faulty and inoperable as a grammatical concept.

But the traditional definition of sentence is illustrative of at least two common sense propositions: (1) that we must define an entity before we understand it; (2) that since language conveys meaning, we should explain its elements in terms of meaning.

No science would insist on definition prior to investigation; it is not necessary, for instance, to define "cell" prior to actual cytological studies. One can know full well what something is without being able to propound a formal definition of it. The noun is a good example. Every native speaker of English handles nouns with amazing skill (even speakers of "substandard" English), but arriving at a definition of "noun" is a terribly difficult process. Kittredge and Farley tell us, "a noun is the name of a person, place, or thing." Thus we have nouns in

> *Washington* was the father of the nation.
> *Los Angeles* is on the Pacific coast.
> A *hammer* is a useful tool.

Clear enough, to be sure. But what about *love* in *Love is a many splendored thing*? Is love a person, a place, or a thing? Perhaps we need an expanded definition, to read, "a noun is the name of a person, place, thing, or *emotion*." But then what about *red* and *black* in *I like the red better than the black*? Should we expand our definition thus: "A noun is the name of a person, place, thing, emotion, or color"? The word *goodness* in *His goodness amazes me* forces another expansion: "A noun is the name of a person, place, thing, emotion, color, or quality." The point should be clear by now: the notional definition of noun (*i.e.*, definition on the basis of idea) is inaccurate and unworkable. Trying to formulate an adequate notional definition would involve one inextricably in an epistemological tangle. Such is precisely the case with many other aspects of language. We may "know" very well what we are doing, but we may not be able to explain or define.

Which brings us to our second point: that since language conveys meaning, we should explain its elements in terms of meaning. The notion implicit here is that language is perfectly logical. Thus, Kittredge and Farley say,

> Since language is the expression of thought, the rules of grammar agree, in the main, with the laws of thought. In other words, grammar is usually logical,—that is, its rules accord, in general, with the principles of logic, which is the science of exact reasoning.

And all of this, of course, is commonsensical enough. For example, it is just plain logic to say that two negatives make a positive; thus

> He does*n't* have *no* money

with its two negatives must mean "He does have some money"—except that we know very well the contrary is true. The proscription in English against the double negative has nothing to do with logic and little to do with meaning, for both

He doesn't have no money

and

He doesn't have any money

mean precisely the same thing. It is a good idea, at this point, to differentiate between an acceptable sentence, an unacceptable sentence, a "logical" sentence, and an "illogical" sentence:

A well-formed, logical sentence:

Jane stayed home because she didn't want to go.

A well-formed, illogical sentence:

Tiny giants roared silently at sour sweetness.

A badly-formed, logical sentence:

Jane done stayed to home seeings as how she didn't hanker to go.

A badly-formed, illogical sentence:

Them there tiny giants roared something fierce at sour sweetness.

This is the kind of differentiation that traditional grammar often fails to make.

AND THEN WE DIAGRAMMED

Much of what we associate with traditional grammar got picked up along the way in a fairly haphazard fashion. And much stems from long tradition. The countless hours spent in conjugating verbs obviously goes back to theories of Latin grammar and teaching outlined above:

I	see	the girl
	saw	
	will see	
	have seen	
	had seen	
	will have seen	

I	am seeing	the girl
	was seeing	
	will be seeing	
	have been seeing	
	had been seeing	
	will have been seeing	

The girl	is seen	by me
	was seen	
	will be seen	
	has been seen	
	had been seen	
	will have been seen	
	is being seen	
	was being seen	
	will be being seen	
	has been being seen	
	had been being seen	
	will have been being seen	

But interestingly enough, native speakers virtually never make errors in verb tense, so the countless hours spent on conjugations are therapy for the wrong disease.

And then we diagrammed. The system of diagramming with which a vast segment of the American public is familiar (or to which a vast segment of the American public was subjected) goes back to 1877, when Alonzo Reed and Brainerd Kellogg published *Work on English Grammar and Composition*. What the two originators of diagramming were after was a graphic method of analyzing and illustrating the relationships of English sentences. A popular text that is based entirely on diagramming is *Descriptive English Grammar* (1931), by Homer C. House and Susan Emolyn Harmon. In the second edition (1950), House explains:

> Most of the teachers using this book will find the diagramming a visual aid in objectifying the sentence units. The diagrams will show which are major and which are minor (modifying) elements of each sentence. It is important, however, to remember that *the diagram can only approximate the complete analysis,* and often needs to be supplemented by parsing (oral or written) and by some explanatory notation.

The underlined clause is the tip-off telling us that even Susan Emolyn Harmon senses problems in the analytical system that she developed so elaborately. The purposes of diagramming were (1) to aid students in learning grammar and (2) to give a graphic representation of sentence relationships.

Let us see, then, how well diagramming aids students in learning grammar. House and Harmon say,

> The *objective complement* is an adjective or a noun which completes the action expressed in the verb and refers to the direct object. The objective complement, if an adjective, describes or limits the object; if a noun, it is in a sense identical with the direct object.

In the first place, this explanation of "objective complement" is so terribly complex in itself that even the experienced grammarian must pause to unravel the meaning. But then the diagram "clarifies."

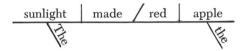

Now, if one does not understand the explanation of "objective complement"—and I am not at all sure that I do—how does one go about applying explanation to diagram or vice versa? The answer to the basic questions about the relationship of knowledge of language to description of language must wait; for the moment, diagramming as a pedagogical method or a descriptive system must come under serious questioning. Consider for example these two different sentences, both of which would take the same diagram form:

The dog chased the cat down the street

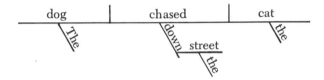

In the morning this child eats his cereal

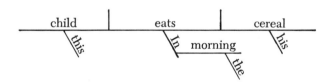

Even if diagramming gives a "rough" idea of the relationships in sentences, it obviously tends to obscure a great many differences among sentences. To put both of the example sentences above in the same diagrammatic framework defies common sense.

We could go on and on. The grammar that most of us learned is rife with paradox, fuzziness, and frustration.

GRAMMAR AS DESCRIPTION

There is nothing wrong with a prescriptive grammar *per se*. It is obviously a social advantage to be able to speak and write the language that educated people accept. This is merely a fact of life. Thus, any pedagogical grammar, any grammar used in the schools, must be, in part at least, prescriptive. It must admonish students not to use the double negative, not to use "ain't," not to use the objective case where educated people would normally use the subjective, and so on. But this kind of prescriptive grammar would never proscribe ending a sentence with a preposition, for in the educated dialect, prepositions frequently migrate to the ends of sentences; and sometimes the split infinitive is absolutely preferable to the unsplit. That is, prescriptiveness in a pedagogical grammar attempts to give the student the rules whereby he can form his language after the manner of educated and hence socially prestigious speakers and writers. For better or worse, this is a fact of life.

But a scholarly grammar, one that attempts to be complete and accurate, will be exclusively descriptive: it will be an anatomy of the language. An anatomy would not declare that the human torso contains no appendix merely because the appendix happens to be a useless and frequently annoying or dangerous organ. Like the anatomy, the descriptive grammar will set forth in detail what is, not what the grammarian thinks ought to be. And, after all, before anyone can make a value judgment about "good" or "bad," "effective" or "ineffective," "proper" or "improper," "ugly" or "beautiful," he must know the facts of the case. A descriptive grammar sets forth the facts about language.

The trouble with school grammars is that they confuse prescription and description and hence confuse students. To say that "ain't" is not English is to contradict the facts that students can observe all about them; to say that "It's me" is not used by educated people is to falsify reality.

A FIERCE COMPLEXITY

Everyone knows what language is: it is the series of verbal or written signals that convey meaning. Language is so simple that even three-year-olds use it with a high degree of sophistication—and so complicated that researchers have really just begun to unravel its basic processes. In many ways, the bases of language are more mysterious than the bases of physical nature, the atoms and subatomic particles that make up the universe. Consider the fierce complexity of the simplest kinds of talking or writing. For one to utter even the most rudimentary kind of sentence, the human brain, that most intricate of all computers, must make literally thousands of choices almost instantaneously. This process goes on as long as discourse is being produced, either in speaking or in writing. The speaker or writer is not aware of the awesome nature of the process; the computer on his shoulders does the job with no whirring of wheels, no hum of electronic circuitry, no blinking of lights. And yet even the most complicated problem turned out by the most advanced computer is a primitive exercise compared to what happens when two people casually discuss the weather.

The best reason for studying grammar is that it begins to unravel the complexity of language; ideally, grammar should provide the clearest insights into the workings of the human mind, for language is the characteristic product of the mind. The ramifications of grammar, then, are wide indeed; they are of tremendous importance to the psychologist, to the builder of mechanical brains (computers), to the anthropologist, to the philosopher. The layman should also find the study of grammar fascinating.

We must, however, be very clear about what grammar does and does not do, about what it describes and what it does not describe.

Everyone who uses a language in either speaking or writing has a grammar of that language—otherwise, he could not articulate. The four-year-old has command of a relatively sophisticated and terribly complex grammar. The illiterate hillsman who must sign his name with X nonetheless commands a grammar of English, for he speaks in sentences that are recognizably English. Since the great majority of users of English—from the illiterate to the highly educated—know very little about "grammar" but nonetheless have a highly complex grammar, we must conclude that the word *grammar* can be used in two ways.

In fact, everyone who uses the language has an internal, intuitive grammar that allows him to speak or write. He may not be able to describe that grammar, he may not know about nouns, verbs, prepositions, sentences, or clauses, but he does possess a grammar.

The other kind of grammar comes after the fact. It describes the language that the internal grammar produces, attempts to show the manifold complex relationships that exist in, say, the sentence after it is spoken or written. A simple diagram will make this clear:

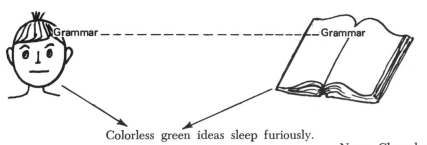

Colorless green ideas sleep furiously.

—Noam Chomsky

The individual's internal, intuitive grammar produces discourse; the grammar that we usually think of as grammar—the one in the book—attempts to describe the relationships that the internal grammar produced. But note also that a broken line runs between the book and the mind. Because the external grammar studies the relationships produced by the internal grammar, it is possible to draw some inferences from the external grammar about the nature of the internal grammar, that is, about the working of the human mind.

But if one hopes to understand the nature of grammar or of language in general, it is necessary to keep sharply separated the concept of the internal, intuitive grammar that produces discourse and the external grammar that describes discourse as produced.

GRAMMATICALITY

Traditional grammar was hazy about what constituted a grammatical utterance and what constituted an ungrammatical utterance. Before we proceed, we must clear up this haziness. In the following list, all ungrammatical utterances are preceded by an asterisk:

> Who did you go to the movie with?
> *With whom you did go to the movie?
> *He no money has.
> He ain't got no money.
> *Over the fence to the cow some hay I threw.
> We seen our friends last night.
> *We see our friends last night.

Now perhaps we are ready for a somewhat strange definition of grammaticality. We will define as grammatical all those utterances that would be produced by native speakers of the language, whether literate, illiterate, or in between. We will define as ungrammatical all those utterances that would not be produced by native speakers of the language. In the above list, we feel that the sentences preceded by asterisks are somehow "foreign"; the other sentences, though they may grate on our nerves as impolite and ignorant, are nonetheless immediately recognizable as homegrown products. A grammar of a language ideally should describe the whole language and hence should adopt the definition of *grammaticality* that is advanced above.

Caution: *grammaticality* is not a term of approval or disapproval; it is a label used to separate that which is in the English language on any level, for better or for worse, from that which is not in the English language.

Exercise. Now is the time to stop and summarize. The following questions should help you summarize and review some key ideas.

1. What part did Latin play in the formation of traditional English grammar?

2. Explain *synthetic* and *analytic* language.

3. What is "the doctrine of correctness"? When did it develop, and why?

4. State the most common "notional" definition of "sentence." Is the notional definition valid? Why?

5. In general, explain the reason behind diagramming. Explain the weaknesses of diagramming as a method of grammatical analysis.

6. Use your own words to express your own candid thoughts on the problem "Why learn any grammar?"

7. Explain "the doctrine of usage."

8. When we use the word "grammar," we are speaking of one of two things. What are those things?

9. Explain "grammaticality."

STRUCTURAL LINGUISTICS: GENERAL PRINCIPLES

Prior to the Second World War, a few scholars in American universities became interested in the languages of the American Indians, the so-called *Amerind* languages. Now these languages were not related to English as are the members of the *Indo-European* family like French, German, Russian, and a number of others. So different were the Amerind groups from the Indo-European that a completely new kind of grammatical analysis was required, and it was in response to this need that structural linguistics began to develop. With the coming of the War, another necessity developed: suddenly there was terrific demand for speakers of a great variety of languages. In order to train the requisite number of people, linguists were forced to develop new materials and new methods that would do the job rapidly and efficiently. The War, then, was the second impulse toward the development of structural linguistics.

What is the foundation of structural linguistics? Suppose you were assigned to record the language of a Northwestern Indian tribe, the Salish. A number of problems immediately arise. First and foremost, you do not know the language at all. Second, the language has no writing system; it has been preserved orally, as is the case with a great many languages. Your job will involve the following steps: (a) analysis of the sounds that go to make up the language, (b) transcription of those sounds into some kind of adequate alphabet, (c) discovery of the way the sounds fit together into "segments" of words and ultimately into words, (d) working out the *syntax* or the way words and phrases go together to make sentences. This, of course, is an oversimplification of the process, but it does indicate the main problems facing the structuralist.

Structual linguistics works from the smallest element of language up to the largest. The smallest meaningfully significant unit in the language is the *phoneme*. The concept of the phoneme is more easily illustrated than defined. For instance, the letters *b* and *p* are essentially the same in pronunciation, except that *b* is pronounced with *voicing*, that is, when one utters a *b*, the vocal cords vibrate, which is not the case with *p*. You can easily demonstrate this principle for yourself if you will lightly touch your throat and alternately utter *b* and *p*. But it is not the mere difference in sound that makes *b* and *p* separate phonemes; rather the point is that that difference in sound brings about a difference in meaning: bit/pit, but/putt, bat/pat. Some differences in sound are not significant so far as meaning is concerned. For instance, in the pair top/pot, the *t*'s are demonstrably different in their sound, but both *t*'s are the same phoneme. In pronouncing *pot,* one lets out a little puff of air after the *t*, a characteristic that is not typical of other *t*'s, such as the one in *top.*

The alphabet is an inadequate representation of the phonemes of a language, for the alphabet does not begin to show different pronunciations for the same phoneme or even the variety of phonemes. Think of the word "bird." A speaker with a Boston accent would probably say something like *bŏd,* with the German umlaut O. A native of Brooklyn might say *boyd.* But in writing, the word is spelled invariably b-i r-d. In my particular dialect, *Mary, marry,* and *merry* all sound exactly alike, but some speakers pronounce each of the three in a different way. And in the subdialect of my wife's native central Utah, *horse* is pronounced *harse,* and her name, Norma, comes out *Narma.*

> *Exercise.* How do the members of the class pronounce the following: orange, coffee, Barry/bury, Nevada, greasy, buoy, creek? Are the *n*'s in *inch* and *ran* pronounced in exactly the same way?

We have said that the phoneme is the smallest *meaningfully significant* unit of language. That means that a change in phoneme—but not necessarily a change in sound—brings a change in meaning. The voicing of the *s* in *greasy* does not bring about a different word: greazy (a pronunciation typical of the Southern states). Thus we can see that *p* and *b* are different phonemes, but the two pronunciations of the *s* in the environment of the word "greasy" do not constitute separate phonemes, for the meaning of the word remains the same regardless of which of the two pronunciations one chooses. We conclude that the phoneme can have variations, in just the same way that handwritten *r*'s and *v*'s differ and yet remain recognizably the same letter. The variations of a phoneme are called *allophones,* and each phoneme may have several allophones.

The alphabet system is an inadequate way to represent the actual sounds and phonemes of a language; there is simply too much data for the twenty-six characters to handle. For this reason, linguists have devised *phonetic alphabets* with sufficient characters to record the pronunciations and phonemes of languages. (But it must be stressed that individual phonemes can have a variety of pronunciations; only when a change is meaningfully significant does the phoneme alter.) The study of the sounds in a language, *phonology,* is too intricate for anything but the briefest outline here. Nonetheless, it is worthwhile to know something about the alphabet and its limitations.

The next largest unit of language after the phoneme (and, of course, after the syllable) is the *morpheme*. This unit is difficult to define, but fairly easy to illustrate. First and foremost, "morpheme" and "word" are not synonymous, even though sometimes a word consists of only one morpheme. "Nice" is both a morpheme and a word, but "nicely" is a word made up of two morphemes. "Ungrateful" is a word made up of three morphemes: un-grate-ful. Notice that none of these morphemes can stand alone; they are all *bound* morphemes. In nice-ly, there are a bound morpheme and a *free* morpheme, for "nice" can stand alone. In "boys" there are two morphemes, one bound and one free, for the plural indicator in English is, of course, a morpheme. Morphemes, then, are the characteristic units of which words are made.

> *Exercise.* What are the morphemes in the following words? Are they bound or free? beautiful, unlikely, modish, democracy, lighthousekeeper, sharper, seventy, one-fourth, waded.

After this brief introduction to the concept of phonemes and morphemes, we can turn to the sentence, the structural level of greatest interest to us.

In 1952, C. C. Fries published a most important book, *The Structure of English*. In this work, Professor Fries set out to take a fresh look at English; he decided to cut free of accepted doctrine and Latinate grammar, to investigate empirically and draw conclusions on the basis of the data. In a scientific age, such a procedure should not seem startling, but the study of language had been terribly bound by tradition. Fries's findings are not nearly as important to us as his methods, for they act as a guide to inquiry about language.

In Ann Arbor, Michigan, Fries recorded some 250,000 words of telephone conversations, and with this data as a basis, he set out to discover what the unprejudiced investigator could conclude about the English language. He did not assume that he could recognize sentences or the parts of speech; he did not rely on the grammatical tradition that was available to him. Calling upon the work that had been done in structural linguistics during the war, he attempted to analyze the English language as if it were an "exotic" language of which he knew nothing. (Remember that the same sort of thing had been done in the social sciences. Before it could make significant progress, psychology had to divest itself of centuries of preconceptions about the human mind and begin to investigate experimentally, empirically.)

Fries's first job was to isolate the basic structural unit of language, the sentence. He could not rely on the old definition: a sentence is the expression of a complete thought. But he did need some working hypothesis, and he drew this from Leonard Bloomfield, who had said that "Each sentence is an independent linguistic form, not included by virtue of any grammatical construction in any larger linguistic form." That is, Bloomfield's definition concerned the sentence's grammatical independence and hence was a definition based on structure, not on meaning.

Fries had additional concepts that helped him. Kenneth L. Pike had published *Intonation of American English* in 1945, a study of the sound patterns of the language. It was Pike's contention that there are four significant tone levels in everyone's speech; these tone levels signal the "grammar" of the sentence. The four levels are *extra high* (*hh*), *high* (*h*), *normal* (*n*), and *low* (*l*). It is by various combinations of these levels that speakers signal the grammar of their sentences. For instance, the sequence *h-l* signals completion of an independent grammatical unit:

I want my break ⌐ fast.

On the other hand, the sequence *h-n* signals that more is to come:

I want my break ⌐ fast   (but I can't have it.)

An intonation of *n-h* tells the listener that more is to come in a series:

one   two   three   four

Rising intonations also signal questions:

You are here?

This brief outline illustrates one of the criteria that Fries used to isolate sentences. But there were other precise ways to segment discourse. For instance, every time there was a change of speaker, one could assume that the chunk of discourse isolated by the change was

    1. A single *minimum* free utterance.
    2. A single free utterance, not minimum but expanded.
    3. A sequence of two or more free utterances.[1]

With these criteria (plus, admittedly, a native speaker's intuition), Fries began to isolate the structural units of English, units which he could then describe on the basis of their form, not their meaning—for it was one of Fries's main purposes to get away from a meaning-based analysis of language.

What might be the most logical and accurate method for investigating the form of sentences? Systematic trial and error with a wide variety of types seems to be the answer. In other words, Fries had to determine "What goes where when?" Suppose we have isolated the following unit: The movie is good. The unit has four "slots" into which we can place other words to see if they still add up to a locution that would be likely to occur in the language:

The	man	is good.
	car	
	taste	
	job	
	coin	
	country	
	mother	

All of the words that fit in the second slot in the frame sentence we can group together and call words of Class 1. Then we can try the third slot:

---

[1]Charles C. Fries, *The Structure of English* (New York: 1952), p. 37.

The   _____   seems   good.
    feels
    smells
    tastes
    becomes

All of the words that fit the third slot we can group together as words of Class 2. And we can do the same thing with the fourth slot:

The   _____   is/ are   good
    bad
    happy
    indifferent
    efficient
    pretty
    ugly

The words that fit the fourth slot we can call words of Class 3. And, in fact, there is another important class of words:

The   _____   run/runs   quickly
    quietly
    lithely
    fast
    easily
    wearily
    slowly

This is the slot-filler technique that Fries used. Of course, in order to make his analysis meaningful, he needed a great many more frames than have been illustrated here. For instance, he needed a frame that would isolate what we call transitive verbs:

The   _____   remember(s) the _____
    see(s)
    meet(s)
    like(s)
    love(s)
    know(s)
    hit(s)

After painstakingly thorough work, Fries concluded that the language has four _parts of speech_—generally what we would call nouns, verbs, adjectives, and adverbs—and fifteen categories of _function words._ The parts of speech are _open classes;_ they can and do constantly gain new members. For instance, every time DuPont invents a new fabric, the firm coins a new word of Class 1 as a name for it: Dacron, Nylon,

Orlon. The other three classes of parts of speech also gain new members and lose old ones. Such is not the case with function words.

> *Exercise.* You might like to investigate language with the slot-filler technique. In order to do so, devise frames, and then for one slot in the frame, substitute as many other words as you can. For instance: The girl *may* go to the movie. How many words can you substitute for "may" in the frame sentence? Try this technique with other classes of words.

Function words belong to closed groups; they are limited in number; they do not become more or less numerous. Here are some lists of the groups of function words that Fries isolated:

> Group F: at, by, for, from, in, of, on, to, with, over, up, across, after
> Group G: do, did
> Group I: when, why, where, how, who, which, what

The way words can be used in sentences is not the only criterion for putting them in one class or another. Words have certain *formal* characteristics that categorize them as belonging to one group or another. For example, nouns can be pluralized: boy/boys, man/men, medium/media (but sheep/sheep). Also, nouns can be preceded by articles: *the* man, *a* medium, *an* ox. Adjectives can be compared: good/better/best, pretty/prettier/prettiest, intelligent/more intelligent/ most intelligent. Adverbs frequently end in *-ly*: quick*ly*, sure*ly*, proper*ly*.

> *Exercise.* Point out the formal and syntactical characteristics that allow you to identify the parts of speech in the following non-sense sentence:
>
> A klorby dorbness dersated the umpth phlogracy gridically.

Someone in the class might like to investigate Fries's discussion of the formal characteristics of parts of speech and report to the class. The discussion is on pages 110-141 of *The Structure of English*.

The most disappointing aspect of structural linguistics has been its handling of *syntax*, the study of how words and phrases go together to make sentences in a language. Structural work on syntax has bound itself pretty much to the analysis of *immediate constituents*. The immediate constituent is one of the two or sometimes more elements of which a structure is formed. For instance, in *He sings*, we find two immediate constituents:

With *He sings in the bathtub,* the situation becomes more complex:

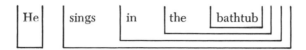

This diagram is a graphic representation of the structural levels in the sentence. The diagram tells us something like this:

> The sentence in question is made up of two primary structural elements, a subject ("He"), and a predicate.
>
> The predicate is made up of a verb and a prepositional phrase.
>
> The prepositional phrase is made up of a preposition and a noun phrase.
>
> The noun phrase is made up of an article and a noun.

All of this works at the structural levels illustrated in the diagram. The diagram attempts to illustrate the "Chinese box" nature of language, wherein a structure can contain another structure and that structure can contain another. . . . The purpose of immediate constituent analysis is to show the layers of syntactical relationships. The usefulness of this kind of analysis is illustrated by the following chart:[2]

The	old	man	who	lives	there	has	gone	to	his	son's	house
The	graybeard		who	survives		went		to	that		house
The	graybeard		surviving			went		to	Boston		
The	survivor					went			there		
He						went					

With the chart, we can see the syntactic similarity among five different sentences, and we can see the layers of structure in all five. Another kind of diagram is used for this type of analysis:

---

[2]H. A. Gleason, Jr., *An Introduction to Descriptive Linguistics* (New York: 1961), p. 130.

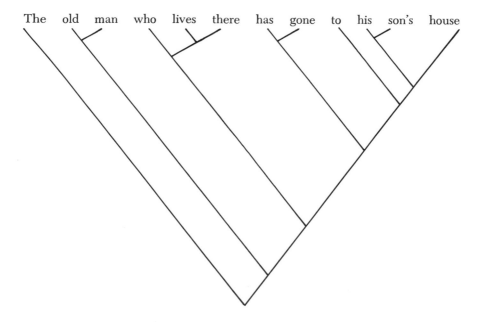

The old man who lives there has gone to his son's house

This upside-down "tree" diagram shows the syntax of the sentence and which items are included in which other items. For instance, "who lives there" is an included sentence (i.e., a relative clause); it therefore is set off by its own tree, the main line of which runs directly to the main sentence line.

If you will look at these diagrams, you will see that they provide a graphic representation of the relationships of items in a sentence. Yet one cannot help asking: "To what purpose?" Once one has discovered the immediate constituent structure of a sentence, what does one have? Very little—in my opinion at least. Immediate contituent analysis does not in itself provide enough data to be of great value.

Structural linguistics has made its greatest contribution in the analysis of phonemes, morphemes, and the sound system of language. It has firmly turned the attention of scholars and teachers to the formal characteristics of language and hence has precipitated a minor revolution in the teaching of grammar and languages.

STRUCTURAL LINGUISTICS: USES

In the schools, structural linguistics began to overcome the entrenched, old-fashioned ideas about language and grammar. Very little had happened in the teaching of grammar since the eighteenth century; the work of nineteenth-century linguistics and of the early structuralists simply did not penetrate the schools or the lower reaches of colleges and universities. The result was a dry sterility in many classes. All of us remember the tedious hours of grammar drill, the Mosaic injunctions about good grammatical morality, and the long lists of rules (many of which had little relation with practice).

But not every student should become a structural linguist (though there is ample reason for every liberally educated man to understand what structural linguistics is about in general). Nonetheless, the attitudes and procedures of structural linguistics can be valuable to everyone.

Remember that the structuralist, like a botanist or zoologist, goes into the field to collect his data and makes his generalizations on the basis of his observations. If the evidence indicates that educated speakers make no distinction between "shall" and "will" except in first person interrogative ("Shall we go?"), the structuralist reports his findings and lets others make value judgments about whether this fact of language is good or bad. Every educated man needs to develop the same kind of impartial awareness about language. In fact, every native speaker of English has the equipment to become a perceptive observer of his language.

The work of the structuralists was the major factor creating a new attitude toward correctness in language. No longer is it possible to think in terms of absolute right and wrong. As in the new situation ethics, propriety is determined by circumstances: what is good in one language situation may be bad in another. The question of whether "it is me" is correct or incorrect English is now meaningless. The answer will have to be: that depends on when and where the expression is used and who uses it. The more formal "It is I" certainly is not correct *per se*, would be, in fact, completely out of place in some instances. Even the most traditional of grammarians must now admit that there are varying levels of usage and that not every level is appropriate in every situation.

Prose style has always been a concern of the truly educated man. At the very least, no one would attempt to write awkward, hazy prose. But until the 1940's or so, all discussions of style were frustratingly vague. They talked about ease, balance, clarity, precision, passion, sublimity, and so on. But the analyst had precious little to say about the "how" and the "why" of this or that admirable prose style and almost as little to say about how the student could develop his own style.

With the advent of structural linguistics, it became clear that style has two elements: the thoughts expressed and the structures that express the thought. In other words, it was possible to speak of structural style independent of meaning and to analyze that style. Very recently, tremendously exciting work on style has emerged, and the germs for this work lay in the theories and technique of structural linguistics.

We know that an idea can be expressed in a variety of ways; if this were not so, translations and paraphrases would not be possible. The language offers options. It is in these options that style lies. When one makes a choice, either conscious or unconscious, the result is style. Put another way: one's style is the choices he makes in the language that he uses. For instance, this sentence from *Moby Dick*:

> We then turned over the book together, and I endeavored to explain to him the purpose of the printing, and the meaning of the few pictures that were in it.

The English language gave Melville a number of different possibilities for expressing his ideas; among them:

> We then turned over the book together. I endeavored to explain to him the purpose of the printing. I also endeavored to explain to him the meaning of the few pictures that were in it.

> We then turned over the book together, I endeavoring to explain to him the purpose of the printing and the meaning of the few pictures that were in it.

> As we then turned over the book together, I endeavored to explain to him the purpose of the printing, and the meaning of the few pictures that were in it.

> We at that time leafed through the tome together, and I attempted to make him understand the intent of the lines of characters, and the purport of the few lithographs that were in it.

Although the four variations say practically the same thing as the original, the styles differ more or less markedly, and these variations can be analyzed and described in formal terms. When we talk about "proper words in proper places" as constituting style, we are saying that the places in which words are placed in sentences can be precisely described, as can the grammatical devices that make for the syntax of a given sentence, and, indeed, as can the vocabulary.

If nothing else, the section on structural linguistics should make the student conscious of the formal considerations of grammar and of the difference between form and meaning. Objectivity in one's attitude toward language is just as valuable as objectivity in any other learned inquiry. It was system and objectivity that structural linguistics brought to the study of grammar.

GENERATIVE GRAMMAR: GENERAL PRINCIPLES

The latest development in grammar began about 1957 with the publication of Noam Chomsky's *Syntactic Structures*. This new system is sometimes called *transformational grammar,* sometimes *generative grammar* and sometimes *transformational generative grammar.* We will opt for *generative grammar.* Chomsky's explanation of generative grammar is in these two sentences from *Syntactic Structures*:

> The fundamental aim in the linguistic analysis of a language L is to separate the *grammatical* sequences which are the sentences of L from the *ungrammatical* sequences which are not sentences of L and to study the structure of the grammatical sequences. The grammar of L will thus be a device that generates all of the grammatical sequences of L and none of the ungrammatical ones.

And, undoubtedly, this important passage needs a great deal of explanation and illustration. We will reserve the details for later. At present, we should understand what Chomsky is saying, for it is important to have a grasp of the theoretical differences and similarities among traditional grammar, structural linguistics, and generative grammar.

The first step toward understanding what Chomsky says is to turn right back to the concept of grammaticality. At the risk of being repetitious, we can take a further look at grammaticality. Traditional grammar would very likely label the following sentences as ungrammatical:

> He ain't been here since March.
> Him and me done the job.
> Who did you go with.

The "grammatical" forms of these sentences would be

> He hasn't [has not] been here since March.
> He and I did the job.
> Whom did you go with? [With whom did you go?]

But compare the following:

> He ain't been here since March.
> He no have been here since March.
>
> Him and me done the job.
> He and I, we do the job.
>
> Who did you go with?
> You go with someone?

Of each pair, we would say that the first item "sounds like English," but the second item sounds like a foreigner trying to talk English. In other words, a native speaker (perhaps uneducated) would be perfectly capable of saying unself-consciously: He ain't been here since March. But only a person who had not grown up with the English language and who had not mastered it would say: He no have been here since March.

It is possible, then, to separate utterances into two categories: those that we sense as grammatical (i.e., those that we feel a native speaker from any class might utter) and those that we sense as ungrammatical. But now a question arises: How do we sense that some utterances are grammatical and some are ungrammatical?

In answering this question, the grammarian must differentiate between *competence* and *performance,* two fairly complicated concepts. Since any ten thousand speakers could identify those utterances that are native to the language and those that are not native, we must assume that competence exceeds performance. That is, even an illiterate will be likely to recognize the ungrammatical even though his own performance does not enable him to produce all of the possible sentences in all of the possible dialects of English. The speaker of a "substandard" dialect might not be able to speak like a college professor, but he will recognize whether or not that college professor is speaking "native" English.

Therefore, we can conclude that there is a hypothetical construct called *the English language.* And note that *the English language* is nothing but a hypothetical construct. In this sense, you and I do not speak the English language, but only variations thereof. Both of our variations go together with millions of other variations to make up what we call *the English language.* The technical term for the individual use of the whole is called *parole;* the hypothetical construct that· is the whole is called *langue.* Everyone has mastered *parole;* no one has mastered *langue.*

All of this probably sounds highly abstruse, interesting enough, to be sure, but not very practical. And yet it is this very theory that determines the practice of generative grammar.

The generative grammarian feels that his work should be concerned with the hypothetical construct called *langue,* not with the individual and partial version thereof called *parole.* The structuralist starts with the analysis of individual use or uses. The transformationalist starts with "the whole picture." To oversimplify a bit: the structuralist begins with the empirical data of individual usage and works upward; the transformationalist begins with *langue* and tries to develop the rules whereby *parole* evolves from *langue.* Two examples will make this distinction clear:

The structuralist's first job is to discover the significant sounds of a language—that is, to discover the smallest parts of any language.

The transformationalist's first task is to discover the underlying principles that generate language. Thus, the first rule of generative grammar tells us that a sentence is made up of a noun phrase and a verb phrase.

But there is an important corollary to generative grammar theory. The generativist believes that man has an inborn capacity for language, much as he has the innate, intuitive ability to walk. But there is a difference between one's ability to walk and one's ability to talk. Barring physical or motor handicaps, every child will learn to walk— presumably even a child who has never seen anyone walk, though, of course, such a child is only a theoretical possibility. We say, then, that *homo sapiens* is destined to walk. He is also destined to talk, but he will not do so unless he is in contact with the social situation that triggers talking; that is, talking is imitative, comes about only when the child hears others of his species talking. Language, then, seems to be an inherent ability that needs the catalyst of a social situation.

To extend the analogy between walking and talking a bit further: theoretically the child is born with the *competence* not only to walk, but to run, high jump, and dance. We know, however, that not everyone, in actual *performance,* will be able to run the four-minute mile or to star in the New York City Ballet. The theoretical *competence* is inherent in every human being, but the actual *performance* will vary widely among humans. Such is the case with language; there is a wide difference between theoretical competence and actual performance.

Nonetheless, there is every reason to base language theory on the abstraction competence rather than on actual, observable performance. One reason for this is that language theory needs to be general enough to explain basic processes and at the same time include countless variations. For instance, Freud's effort was to develop a general theory of mind that would embrace the normal and the pathological, that would accomodate both neurosis and psychosis, that would explain both love and hate. If his theory of mind had been limited to, say, the schizoid personality, its usefulness would have been severly limited. In fact, a theory of schizophrenia had to be merged into or, on the other hand, to develop from a general theory of mind. Put another way: the theory that is not broad enough to include explanations for all phenomena in its province will be severely limited in its usefulness and because of its fragmentary nature may actually mislead the investigator.

Generative grammar, then, will proceed from a theory of language competence as opposed to a theory of the individual's language performance. This distinction can be simplified. Of this sentence

He done got his-self into a pickle

we would say, "It is not *good* English." But of this sentence:

Him no know who comings

we would say, "It is not English." In other words, native speakers have the competence to recognize their language and what is not their language. Hence, we can infer that native speakers have some kind of general sense for their language, what the Germans call *Sprachgefühl*.

Generative grammar will be a series of rules which applied automatically and systematically will produce all of the possible grammatical combinations in a language and none that are ungrammatical. The reader is undoubtedly one step ahead of the author at this point. As everyone has suspected, generative grammar will be the kind of digital system that could be adapted to use in a computer for translating from one language to another.

That is, generative grammar will be a finite set of rules that will produce an infinite set of results.

This is the house that Jack built.
This is the malt that lay in the house that Jack built.
This is the rat that ate the malt that lay in the house that Jack built.
This is the cat that chased the rat that ate the malt that lay in the house that Jack built.
This is the dog that worried the cat that chased the rat that ate the malt that lay in the house that Jack built.
This is the cow that tossed the dog that worried the cat that chased the rat that ate the malt that lay in the house that Jack built.
And so on.

It is easy to demonstrate that there is no theoretical limit to the length of any English sentence. It is equally easy to demonstrate that there is no limit to the number of possible different sentences, in just the same way that there is no limit to number:

1000000000000000000000000000000000000000000000000000000000

or to the application of mathematical functions:

2	4	8	16	32	64	128	256	512
+2	+4	+8	+16	+32	+64	+128	+256	+512
4	8	16	32	64	128	256	512	1024

In mathematics, then, there is no limit to the totals that can be obtained by any process, but the process itself is recurrent. That is, we derive 10 by adding 0 to 1; we derive 100 by adding 0 to 10; and so on. The sum of 512 plus 512 is derived by the same process as is the sum of 2 plus 2. We can apply the same rules over and over again to derive an infinite number of conclusions. The rules themselves are limited in number; the products of the rules are unlimited or infinite. Such would be the case with the rules in a complete generative grammar.

One might say that the whole task of generative grammar is to explain *linguistic novelty*: the simple fact that you and I can produce and understand completely unique sentences. At first glance this capability might not seem extraordinary at all; *homo sapiens* is the talking animal. Consider, however, that as you read this book, you encounter sentence after sentence that you have never seen before. Probably you have not seen even one per cent of the sentences in this book before. Furthermore, in your everyday conversation, you produce sentences that have never been uttered before. In spite of this principle of linguistic novelty, *we* are able to understand one another—quite a remarkable fact if you think about it.

The explanation of our ability to communicate in spite of—or perhaps because of—linguistic novelty must have something to do with our understanding of the words in the vocabulary and our ability to put those words into grammatical structures. That is, it seems that our ability to understand must hinge upon our knowledge of the meanings of words and our ability to use and understand the structures that the language affords us. (This bears repeating: without hesitation, we recognize sentences that are "native" English and that are not "native" English.) It would seem, then, that the grammar of a language must be an affair involving two separate segments: words and structures. Learn the words, learn the structures, put them together, and *voila!* English sentences. But the intricate minuet of language does not allow us so neatly to separate the dancer from the dance.

NOUN PHRASES

A common English sentence pattern is *noun + transitive verb + noun*. Simple enough. Once we have formulated this simple diagram ($N + VT + N$), we should be able to use it to describe a great number of *grammatical* English sentences: *Boys hate baths, Girls love curls, Cats like fish, Children watch TV*, all of which seem perfectly grammatical and natural. It might appear that we can take any word from the large barrel marked *noun,* any word from the equally large barrel marked *transitive verb,* and any other word from the *noun* barrel and place them (in that order) on a line to derive a perfectly grammatical, natural English sentence. But suppose we choose the noun *likeness.* (We're sure it's a noun because it has the nominal suffix-*ness.*) If we attempt to make it the subject of the verb *know,* we will encounter just a bit of difficulty: **Likeness knows Chicago.* The sentence sounds strange, perhaps figurative or metaphorical. Analogous sentences appear to work: *Jones knows Chicago, Conventioneers know Chicago, Bootleggers know Chicago.* It appears that not every noun will function as the subject of every transitive verb.

The objects of verbs have the same kinds of limitations. We can say *The children liked swimming* or *The children liked to swim.* We can say *The children refused to eat,* but not *The children refused eating.* In American English, the verb *seem* will take an adjective as its complement, but not a noun: *He seems happy, *He seems a man.* (American English would demand *He seems to be a man.*)

In short, the language contains an intricate system of *selectional restrictions* that limits the functioning of words in syntactic slots. The verb *love* will take only an animate subject: *Men love women, Dogs love bones, Worms love loamy soil.* When we say *Misery loves company,* we are clearly in the realm of the figurative. As a matter of fact, much of the effect of poetry depends on the conscious violation of selectional restrictions. In one stanza from "The Waltzer in the House" by Stanley Kunitz are numerous poetical violations of selectional restrictions:

> A sweet, a delicate white mouse,
> A little blossom of a beast,
> Is waltzing in the house
> Among the crackers and the yeast.

Mice don't waltz. Mice are not blossoms. Except in poetry, which uses language for its own ends. But if the reader did not sense the violation of the "rules," there would, after all, be no poetry.

Words and structures are not two separate compartments of language that can be studied independently of each other. This is an important point to keep in mind, for the ensuing discussion will concentrate on structures.

Traditional grammar says that sentences consist of *subjects* and *predicates*

Cats	purr.
The children	are playing in the yard.
The author	wrote the book.
With the fishermen and the life on the river, the beautiful barges with their own life on board, the tugs with their smokestacks that folded back to pass under the bridges, pulling a tow of barges, the great elms on the stone banks of the river, the plane trees and in some places the populars, I	could never be lonely along the river.—Hemingway
I	smile to myself in putting the following to the honorable members of the Court, prompted as I am to take the bull by the horns.—Henry Miller

Generative grammar starts from exactly the same premise: that *every* sentence is (or is derived from) a two-part structure. One way of stating this principle is to work from the most general concept (that of sentence) toward the more specific or the layers of structures that go to make up the sentence. Thus, we might say that a sentence consists of a subject and a predicate. Or we might also use the more suitable terminology of generative grammar and say that *a sentence consists of a noun phrase and a verb phrase*. A convenient shorthand method of stating this "rule" is the following:

$$(1) \quad S \rightarrow NP + VP$$

To be read: Sentence (S) is rewritten as ($\rightarrow$) Noun Phrase (NP) plus Verb Phrase (VP). In other words, the arrow which is so common in the formulae of generative grammar can be read simply as "consists of" or "is rewritten as."

Generative grammar uses a shorthand notation that may appear formidable, but that actually is simple and that saves much space and a great deal of time. (The grammarian uses formulae and notations for the same reason that the mathematician does: merely because a special "language" is the most convenient way of stating concepts. It is much easier to write $3,333,333 \div 3 = 1,111,111$ than to write "three million three hundred and thirty-three thousand three hundred and thirty-three divided by three equals one million one hundred and eleven thousand one hundred and eleven.") Rule 1 illustrates one of the methods that generative grammar uses to state its principles. The other common method is the *branching tree diagram,* thus:

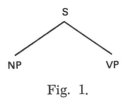

Fig. 1.

As we shall see, the branching tree diagram has the advantage of showing graphically the constituents that go to make up sentences and the way in which those constituents fit together syntactically.

We have said that the sentence consists of a noun phrase and a verb phrase (or, roughly, a subject and a predicate). This general rule would seem to contradict some of the observable facts of language. The following sentences seem not to contain NP's (subjects):

> Come here!
> Get on the beam!
> Straighten up and fly right!

And the following sentences seem not to be NP + VP, but something else:

> Are we going?
> Seldom were they at home.
> Did you ring the bell?

It might be suspected, then, that the rule S→NP + VP applies only to sentences like *Cats purr* or *The children are playing in the yard* or *The author wrote the book,* not to sentences like *Come here* or *Seldom were they at home.* As a matter of fact, our grammar assumes (and our discussion will later demonstrate) that sentences like *Come here* and *Seldom were they at home* are merely systematic variations of sentences that develop from S→NP + VP:

> (You) come here.
> They were at home seldom.

Later on, we will examine the rules whereby sentences get rearranged from their basic forms. At present, we must investigate what can come from NP, the noun phrase side of the branching tree diagram. In this discussion, the objective will be to illustrate some general principles and to give the student enough knowledge of language to enable him to find answers to the questions that he might want to ask. Nothing approaching a complete grammar of NP will be attempted.

We know that certain kinds of words can serve as the subjects of sentences:

$$\left\{\begin{array}{l} \text{John} \\ \text{The boy} \\ \text{He} \\ \text{Someone} \end{array}\right\} \text{called my name.}$$

In our notational system, the brackets { } mean that one item must be chosen, and only one. Thus,

$$\left\{\begin{array}{l} A \\ B \\ C \end{array}\right\} D \rightarrow \left\{\begin{array}{l} E \\ F \\ G \end{array}\right\} H$$

means either AD *or* BD *or* CD is rewritten as either EH *or* FH *or* GH. And the brackets containing the four NP's mean that the sentence can appear *John called my name* or *The boy called my name* or *He called my name* or *Someone called my name.* And we need to discover whether or not these four kinds of subjects represent the possibilities for NP's in basic sentences.

This thought has probably occurred to someone: Many sentences have clauses as subjects:

Whoever called my name knew me.
That he is brilliant is obvious.
Wherever you are is where I want to be.

In order to simplify and systematize our inquiry, we will ignore such sentences for the time being and deal only with those that have subjects like *John, The boy, He, Someone.* There is good reason for using this procedure, for it turns out that sentences like *That he is brilliant is obvious* are derived from two sentences that are put together by the rules of grammar, rules that we will deal with in the discussion of embedding. Another sort of subject that we will ignore for the moment is illustrated in the following sentences:

His being brilliant is easy.
For him to be brilliant is easy.

The following series of rules tells a great deal about the NP. Look carefully at the series, and follow the explanations of it:

$$(2)\ \text{NP} \rightarrow \begin{Bmatrix} \text{Prop} \\ \text{Det + N} \\ \text{Pers} \\ \text{Indef} \end{Bmatrix}$$

The rule tells us that NP must be rewritten as either Prop(er Noun), Det(erminer) plus (Common) N(oun), Pers(onal Pronoun), or Indef(inite Pronoun), and we will find the definitions for these terms in the rules that follow. (Note well that the terms and concepts of generative grammar are self-defining.)

(3) Prop→John, Chicago, Germany, Mr. Smith, January . . .

Proper noun (Prop) is a word like those listed. The three dots indicate that the list could go on indefinitely.

(4) N→boy, dog, love, money, earth, work, brick, tree . . .

Common noun (N) is a word like those listed. The three dots indicate the list could go on indefinitely.

(5) Pers→I, you, he, she, it, we, they

Personal pronoun (Pers) is one of the words listed. Absence of three dots indicates that the list is complete.

(6) Indef→every-, some-, no-, any- + -body, -one, -thing

Indefinite pronoun (Indef) is *everybody, somebody, nobody, anybody; everyone, someone, no one, anyone; everything, something, nothing, anything.*

Our explanation of Det(erminer) in Rule 2 will be complicated and hard to follow, but taking the trouble to unravel the mystery will be worthwhile for at least two reasons: (1) the development of the rules that define Det illustrates how generative grammar works; (2) these rules show how drastically incomplete traditional grammar is. So, the rules for Det:

$$(7)\ \text{Det} \rightarrow (\text{Predet})\ (\text{Preart}) \begin{Bmatrix} \text{Art} \\ \text{Dem} \\ \text{Gen} \end{Bmatrix} (\text{Postdet})$$

A word of explanation and a reminder. Parentheses mean that an item is optional; it may occur in the structure, but it need not. Thus A→(B)C means A is rewritten either as BC or as C. The brackets mean that one of the items in them, but only one, must be chosen.

(8) Predet→several of, many of, few of, a box of, a stack of . . .

(9) Preart→just, merely, only . . .

(10) Art→ $\begin{Bmatrix} \text{Def} \\ \text{Nondef} \end{Bmatrix}$

And now we must pause a bit to do some thinking, for Rule 10, when interpreted, will seem strange, and Rules 11 and 12 will seem even stranger. Traditional grammar tells us that there are two kinds of articles, definite and indefinite, but Rule 10 above has said that Art(icle) is rewritten as either Def(inite) or Nondef(inite). That is, the new grammar has introduced a strange term for one of the two kinds of articles. There are theoretical reasons for this new terminology, reasons that we need not explore. Just remember that Indef(inite) is a kind of pronoun and Nondef(inite) is a kind of article. (By the way, just in case you haven't thought about it, Predet means, of course, *predeterminer,* and Preart means *prearticle.*) You will note that Rule 11 is easy enough:

(11) Def→the

exactly as in traditional grammar, but

(12) Nondef $\begin{Bmatrix} a(n) \\ \text{some} \\ \varnothing \end{Bmatrix}$

What is Rule 12 telling us? Actually it is doing two simple, logical things. First, it adds to the list of articles the word *some,* as in *Some people like violence.* Since *some* in this kind of use functions exactly like the other nondefinite articles, there is no reason why it should not be grouped with them; in fact, there are compelling reasons why it should be so grouped, not the least of which is that it has the same nondefinite meaning as *a(n).* But what about the *null:∅?* That symbol never occurs as an article in written English. Is it merely a figment of some grammarian's warped imagination? There are, in fact, two very good reasons for including the ∅. The first is this: it is much easier to make a rule which says every common noun must be preceded by a determiner (Det + N) than it is to say: almost every common noun must be preceded by a determiner, but there are the following exceptions. . . . In fact, we know that in writing and speaking many common nouns are not preceded by any apparent determiner:

> *Boys* like *candy.*
> *Rice* provides cheap *nourishment.*
> *Love* conquers all.
> Give me *liberty,* or give me *death.*
> *Men* are what they eat.

Notice the semantic shift that comes about in the following variations:

The boys in my family like candy.
The rice that we eat provides cheap nourishment.
His love conquers all.
Give me the liberty to vote, or give me the death of a hero.
Those men who overindulge are what they eat.

These two lists of sentences should demonstrate that there are indeed features of meaning that can be termed definite and nondefinite. The null (Ø) in the rewrite of Nondef symbolizes a real semantic feature, then.

To finish our definition of Det, we need only the following rules:

(13) Dem→this, these, that, those
(14) Gen→my, your, his, its, her, our, their
(15) Postdet→(Ord) (Card)
(16) Ord→first, second, third, fourth . . .
(17) Card→one, two, three, four . . .

(Dem, demonstrative; Gen, genitive; Postdet, postdeterminer; Ord, ordinal number; Card, cardinal number.)

This series of seventeen rules is not exactly like the rules in a typical generative grammar. For one thing, the scientific grammar will separate *lexical* entries from rules like 2 and 7. That is, rules 3 through 6 (defining Prop, N, Pers, and Indef) would come in a section of their own, a section that would supply the actual words to go into structures. But for our purposes, the list of seventeen rules serves nicely to show quite a lot about the nature of the noun phrase as well as a bit concerning the functioning of grammar.

There is much more that could be said. For instance, any complete grammar must have several rewrite rules for N. We have already encountered the concept of selectional restrictions; our rules for rewriting N would need to reflect those restrictions. There are count nouns (tree, three trees), noncount nouns (flour, mush); abstract nouns (love, hate) and concrete nouns (gold, hair); animate nouns (girl, worm) and inanimate nouns (rock, lake). All of these features are significant to the grammar. However, since we are interested in the system not as scientific linguists attempting to construct a complete and acurate grammar, but as informed laymen who want to know the general principles of language, our inquiry concerning NP can end at this point.

Exercise. By way of summary and review, answer the following:

1. In your own words, state the concepts in Chomsky's explanation of generative grammar.

2. Define "grammaticality." Give examples to illustrate.

3. Explain *competence* and *performance*.

4. Explain *langue* and *parole*.

5. In your own words, explain the following: "Generative grammar will be a series of rules which applied automatically and systematically will produce all of the possible grammatical combinations in a language and none that are ungrammatical."

6. In your own words, explain the following: "That is, generative grammar will be a finite set of rules that will produce an infinite set of results."

7. In your own words, explain "linguistic novelty."

8. In your own words, explain "selectional restrictions." Give examples.

9. The following rule means what?

$$A(B) \rightarrow C(D)(E)$$

10. The following rule means what?

$$H \begin{Bmatrix} I \\ J \end{Bmatrix} \mapsto \begin{Bmatrix} X \\ Y \end{Bmatrix} Z$$

11. The following series of rules can be stated in a branching tree diagram as illustrated below.

(1) A→B + C
(2) B→D + E
(3) C→F + G

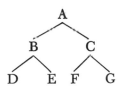

Draw a branching tree diagram that illustrates the following rules:

(1) A→B + C
(2) C→D + E
(3) E→F + G

12. NP→

13. Applying Rules 1 through 15 of this chapter can produce a variety of branching tree diagrams. Here is one of them:

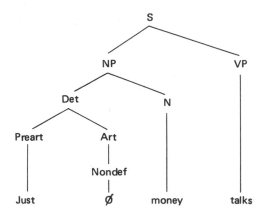

Since we have as yet developed no rules for VP, that element of the above derivation was inserted merely to make a sentence. Use Rules 1 through 15 to develop at least three unique branching tree diagrams of sentences. You may use your powers of invention to fill in the VP.

14. Draw branching tree diagrams that show the derivation of the following sentences:

The earth turns.
Several of the good men left.
A pile of only the first three tons vanished.

VERB PHRASES

Traditional grammar identifies three kinds of verbs: *transitive*

The boy *kisses* the girl.
The policeman *gives* the driver a ticket.

intransitive

Dogs *bark*.
The soprano *is singing*.

and *linking*

The weather *is* nasty.
The steak *smells* good.
Your proposal *seems* fair.

Just a bit of investigation will reveal that this rough-and-ready classification overlooks much and hides more concerning the verb.

Linking verbs, for instance. Traditional grammar would put *to be*, *seem*, and *become* all in the same barrel, in spite of obvious selectional restrictions that differentiate them in usage. Carefully note the following:

$$\text{He } \textit{is} \begin{cases} \text{a man (NP)} \\ \text{handsome (Adj)} \\ \text{here (Adv of place)} \end{cases}$$

$$\text{He } \textit{becomes} \begin{cases} \text{intelligent (Adj)} \\ \text{an expert (NP)} \end{cases}$$

$$\text{He } \textit{seems} \text{ happy (Adj)}$$

In other words, there are significant differences in the selectional restrictions of verbs that are traditionally classed as linking. The verb *to be* will take NP, Adj, or Adv of place as a complement; verbs like *become* will take either Adj or NP; and verbs like *seem* will take only Adj in modern American English. **He seems a man* is ungrammatical; American grammar would demand *He seems to be a man*.

These are only some of the niceties of the verb system that a complete grammar must take into account.

The first rule of generative grammar tells us that S→NP + VP. In the last section of this chapter, we investigated the nature of the NP when the NP is either Prop, Det + N, Pers, or Indef. Now we need to get some idea of the possibilities of VP, the second half of our two-part sentence division.

In a sentence such as *The elephant eats the peanut*, we can see that VP must branch into two components, thus:

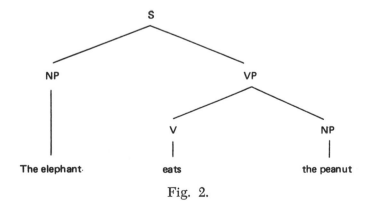

Fig. 2.

But in sentences such as *Elephants dance*, the VP is apparently one unit:

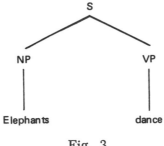

Fig. 3.

However, if we think for a moment, we will realize that these branching tree diagrams must grossly oversimplify the nature of the sentence. One characteristic of the sentence is that it has *tense*; it is placed in time. If our diagram is to be accurate and completely useful, it must show that essential sentence characteristic. The next question, then, is this: How many tenses are there in English. The answer depends on how one defines tense. Traditionally we talk about six tenses:

present:	go
past:	went
future:	will go
present perfect:	have gone
past perfect:	had gone
future perfect:	will have gone

But there is a significant difference among these tenses. Some of them are absolute, as when *go* changes to *went* to indicate past, and some of them are periphrastic, as when we add *will* to *go* to produce future. Another fact of language becomes apparent also: sometimes the complete verb is one word (go, went), but sometimes it is a series of words (will go, will have gone). Surely we want our grammar to specify exactly how these words can be combined, for they cannot be combined at random: *have will gone, *gone have.

Furthermore, we can see now that our branching tree diagram must accomodate (and graphically illustrate) more features than just the principal verb. Suppose tentatively that we say in a sentence every verb must have at least tense and may have other features such as words like *may, can,* and *will* (may go, can go, will go). We will classify tense and several other features as *auxiliary* (Aux). Our diagram, then, will look like this:

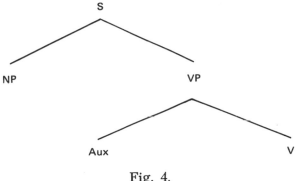

Fig. 4.

And we conclude that Aux must at the very least contain tense, because without tense, there can be no sentence:

*The elephant to eat the peanut
*Elephants to dance

But we can conclude also that tense does not appear alone in the sentence; it becomes a feature of a word:

go + past tense = went
walk + past tense = walked

Since tense is a feature of a word, we can conclude that English has only two absolute tenses, past and present, for no single word can appear in any other tense.

Now, if we look at the following verbs, we discover a series of features that must be explained.

can go
is going
has gone

Perhaps the easiest way to explain how the simple verb *go* can pick up so many diverse features is simply to present a rule and then justify the individual parts. The rule is this:

(18) Aux→Tense (M) (have + part) (be + ing)

This is quite a remarkable rule, for in the shortest of compasses it explains all of the elements of any *active voice verb* in any sentence. It says this:

Auxiliary consists of *tense* and may contain a *Modal, have* or *has* plus a *past participle* (part) and a form of *be* plus a *present participle* (ing). Remember that parentheses indicate that an item is optional.

Two more rules give us the information we need to understand any *active voice verb* in English. These rules are

$$(19) \quad \text{Tense} \rightarrow \begin{cases} \text{Present} \\ \text{Past} \end{cases}$$

(20) M(odal)→can, may, must, shall, will

These three rules (18, 19, and 20) tell us that the complete verb (1) must have present or past tense; (2) may contain a modal; (3) may contain either *have* or *has* plus a past participial form; (4) may contain a form of *be* plus a present participial form. In practice, all of this works out with extreme elegance and simplicity. For instance, it explains the so-called progressive form of the verb: I *am talking*. Here we have simply

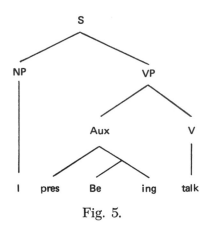

Fig. 5.

A glance at the diagram shows that the units must combine and work together. For instance, the sequence I + pres + be must result in *am*, for the first person present of *to be* is *am*. And ing + talk equals *talking*. It may seem strange that the sequence is I + pres + be + ing + talk rather than I + be + pres + talk + ing. But a little thought makes the reason for the first sequence apparent. It is simpler to list all of the elements of the verb in a series of rules and then rearrange those elements after they have been expressed in the diagram than it would be to construct rules that would put all of the elements in their natural order. Such a series of rules would be terrifically complex, and it is easy to flip-flop elements so that they get rearranged into their natural order. In other words, our present method is much simpler than a sequence of rules that would result in a series of units in their final

order. (We could very easily construct another rule that would show
how the elements of Aux must be arranged in the sentence.)

Here is another example:

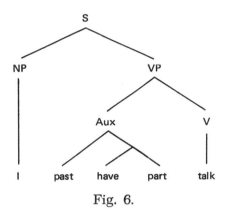

Fig. 6.

Again, we know that the sequence I + past + have must equal *I had,*
and part + talk must equal *talked,* for the past participle of *talk* is
talked, just as the past participle of *go* is *gone.*

Our logic tells us, then, that

pres + may + have + part + talk

must be grouped to produce

pres + may   have   part + talk

and rearranged to produce

may + pres   have   talk + part

to result in

may   have   talked

Here is an example of all possible forms of the verb *see* in active
voice:

I *see*

> pres + see
>
> see + pres
>
> see

I *saw*

```
past + see

see + past

saw
```

I *will see*

```
pres + will      see

will + pres   +  see

will             see
```

I *would see*

```
past + will      see

will + past   +  see

would            see
```

I *have seen*

```
pres + have      part + see

have + pres   +  see + part

have             seen
```

I *had seen*

```
past + have      part + see

have + past   +  see + part

had              seen
```

I *will have seen*

pres + will		have		part + see
will + pres	+	have	+	see + part
will		have		seen

I *would have seen*

past + will		have		part + see
will + past	+	have	+	see + part
would		have		seen

I *am seeing*

pres + be		ing + see
be + pres	+	see + ing
am		seeing

I *was seeing*

past + be		ing + see
be + past	+	see + ing
was		seeing

I *will be seeing*

pres + will		be		ing + see
will + pres	+	be	+	see + ing
will		be		seeing

I *would be seeing*

past + will		be		ing + see
will + past	+	be	+	see + ing
would		be		seeing

I *have been seeing*

pres + have		part + be		ing + see
have + pres	+	be + part	+	see + ing
have		been		seeing

I *had been seeing*

past + have		part + be		ing + see
have + past	+	be + part	+	see + ing
had		been		seeing

I *will have been seeing*

pres + will		have		part + be		ing + see
will + pres	+	have	+	be + part	+	see + ing
will		have		**been**		seeing

I *would have been seeing*

past + will		have		part + be		ing + see
will + past	+	have	+	Be + part	+	see + ing
would		have		been		seeing

What all of this demonstrates is the basic regularity of the system of verbs. But if you have followed closely, you have also discovered another important concept: the grammar of English can be described much more briefly, simply, and coherently than has hitherto been supposed. The last few pages have contained a very great deal of information, much more than could be expressed in dozens or hundreds of pages in traditional grammar.

The English verb in active voice can have only these elements: tense, modal, *perfective aspect* (have + part), and *durative aspect* (be + ing). Rules 18, 19, and 20 are quite remarkable for the great amount that they say in so little space.

> *Exercise.* By way of summary and review, analyze the elements that go to make up the following verbs. Example: the verb *had been working* contains the elements past + have + part + be + in + work; the verb *see* contains the elements pres + see.
>
> 1. He *worked* until dawn.
> 2. The boys *have been hitting* the girls.
> 3. No one *would like* that movie.
> 4. What *can be* the matter?
> 5. He *will be gone* by this time tomorrow.
> 6. Nowadays everyone *is doing* his thing.
> 7. The movie *will have been playing* for a week now.
> 8. You *would have done* what I did.
> 9. He *wants* the best.
> 10. No one *has asked* my permission.
> 11. The boys *will be playing* the game.
> 12. I *am* a man.
> 13. The guests *were making* the best of a bad dinner.
> 14. A trick question: I *won't.*
> 15. I *will.*

It is well to remember that VP contains not just the verb, but also the elements that *predicate* contains in traditional grammar. So that sentences such as those in Figures 7 and 8 are extremely common.

This discussion of VP is far from complete. It ignores a great number of important matters, and it truncates the discussion of others. For instance, What about the verb *look* in a sentence such as *The librarian looks up the reference*? Is the word *up* a part of the verb? If so, how does it function? We know that we can say *He looks the reference up* or *He looks up the reference,* but we cannot say **He looks up it,* although we can say *He looks it up.* We might also ask how it comes

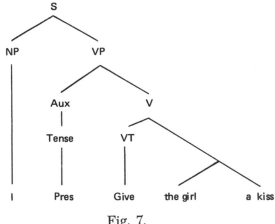

Fig. 7.

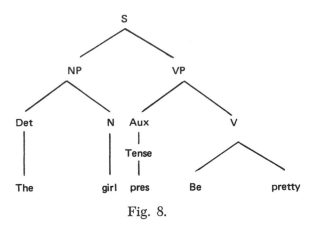

Fig. 8.

about that some transitive verbs can be followed by two noun phrases, while others must be followed by only one:

> The nurse tells *the children the story.*
> The nurse tends *the children.*

Furthermore, we might ask how many separate and distinct classes of verbs there are in the language, for there are certainly more than the traditional three that the old grammar lists.

   The whole point of the discussion of VP was to open up new vistas of understanding and speculation, new ways of looking at that old subject, language.

Exercise. By way of summary and review, answer the following:

    1. Traditional grammar lists three kinds of verbs. What are they? Use one of each in a sentence.

    2. How can we differentiate between a verb like *seem* and a verb like *become?*

    3. What is *absolute tense?* What is *periphrastic tense?* Give examples of each.

    4. The modals are _____.

    5. Aux→

TRANSFORMS

So far, our inquiry has concerned sentences like the following:

> The man catches the ball.
> A car is skidding.
> Some people seem lazy.
> The child is naughty.

but not sentences like these:

> The ball is caught by the man.
> Is a car skidding?
> Some people do seem lazy.
> The child is not naughty.

In the language, there are basic sentence forms (in the jargon of grammar they are called *kernels*), and there are systematic rearrangements of these basic sentence forms. By definition, any sentence that is not a kernel is a *transform*. We have investigated the kinds of rules from which kernels develop (rules for structuring NP and VP), and now we will take a brief look at the ways in which single kernels are rearranged. (In the next section, we will discuss the processes whereby two or more kernels are put together.)

    Nothing, apparently, is easier than changing a declarative sentence (such as *He is here*) into an interrogative sentence that will bring an answer of either "yes" or "no" (*Is he here?*).

Jeff is reading.	Is Jeff reading?
Mary can go to the show.	Can Mary go to the show?
Tony has arrived.	Has Tony arrived?

In other words, when the verb includes either modal or aspect (have + part, be + ing), we can create the interrogative apparently by a simple flip-flop of words: *Mary can go, Can Mary go?* But actually two sentence elements are moved in front of the NP, not just one. The clue is this: *Mary could go, Could Mary go?* Both tense and modal are moved. Now look at the following:

Mary	past + can	go
past + can	Mary	go
can + past	Mary	go
Could	Mary	go?

Jim + pres + be + ing + run		
pres + be	Jim	ing + run
be + pres	Jim	run + ing
Is	Jim	running?

Bob + past + have + part + leave		
past + have	Bob	part + leave
have + past	Bob	leave + part
Had	Bob	left?

In other words, if the VP begins with Tense + be, Tense + have, or Tense + Modal, constructing the yes/no question is only a matter of flip-flopping those elements with NP: I + pres + be + ing + sing becomes pres + be + I + ing + sing, for instance. But what about the following?

They + pres + sing (They sing.)

We know that the yes/no question corresponding to *They sing* is *Do they sing?* Thus, we know that we interrogate by adding *do* to the front of the sequence, but is any other rearrangement necessary? Here is the clue: *Did they sing.* In other words, *do* carries tense. (To state the principle another way, NP and Tense are flip-flopped and *do* is added as a tense carrier, since tense must be expressed by a word.)

They + past + sing		
past + they + sing		
do + past + they + sing		
Did	they	sing?

In fact, *do* is a most useful word in English. It carries tense in both the negative and the emphatic forms of sentences.

They sing.	Yes, they do sing!
	They do not sing.

Once we understand the use of *do,* the whole matter of negation is clarified.

I	pres + be	ing + run	
I	am	running	
I	pres + be	not	ing + run
I	am	not	running

I	past + can	run	
I	could	run	
I	past + can	not	run
I	could	not	run

I	pres + have	part + run	
I	have	run	
I	pres + have	not	part + run
I	have		not	run

I	pres + run		
I	run		
1	pres	not	run
I	do + pres	not	run
I	do	not	run

When the negative separates tense and a word to which it can attach itself (be, have, modal, verb), do is inserted to carry tense. Exactly the same situation prevails in the emphatic. Let A symbolize the stress in a spoken emphatic sentence. Then

He + pres + may + hit + it
He + pres + may + A + hit + it (spoken with stress on *may*)

he + pres + be + ing + hit + it
he + pres + be + A + ing + hit + it
he + pres + have + part + hit + it
he + pres + have + A + part + hit + it

he + pres + hit + it (He hits it.)
he + pres + A + hit + it
he + do + pres + A + hit + it (He does hit it!)

The so-called wh questions (those with words like *who, what, which*) are nothing more than rearrangements of yes/no questions. Once we have derived *Has the plumber cleaned the drain?* it is easy to rearrange the NP + VP sequence and substitute an interrogative word to derive *Who has cleaned the drain?*

He may see you. May he see you? Who may see you? Whom may he see?

He has seen you. Has he seen you? Who has seen you? Whom has he seen?

He is seeing you. Is he seeing you? Who is seeing you? Whom is he seeing?

He sees you. Does he see you? Whom does he see?

Another example of the regularity and simplicity of the language system is the *passive transformation*:

The cow kicks the milkmaid.
The milkmaid is kicked by the cow.

The Jets played the Colts.
The Colts were played by the Jets.

Justice has conquered injustice.
Injustice has been conquered by justice.

We gave him a hand.
He was given a hand by us.
A hand was given him by us.

If you look at these examples, you will see that in the passive a noun phrase that, in active, followed the verb (was direct object or indirect object) has been placed in front of the verb as its subject. The original subject has become the object of a preposition, a process that we might symbolize thus:

$$NP_1 + VT + NP_2 \rightarrow NP_2 + VT + (by + NP_1)$$

Notice that in passive, the by + NP_1 can be deleted:

You see the movie. The movie is seen by you. The movie is seen.

But something else happens in passive. The following strings indicate what that something is:

He + pres + love + candy
Candy + pres + be + part + love (by him)

The passive verb always picks up a *be* and *part*. (In fact, the best definition of passive is this: any form of the verb *be* plus a past participle.)

Joe felt the wind.
Joe + past + feel + the wind

The wind was felt by Joe.
the wind + past + be + part + feel + by Joe

The team has won the game.
the team + pres + have + part + win + the game

The game has been won by the team.
the game + pres + have + part + be + part + win + by the team

There are many other ways of rearranging kernels into transforms.

A crowd was there.
There was a crowd there.

The crowd was big.
There was a big crowd.

Children like ice cream.
What children like is ice cream.

The last example is of the so-called *cleft sentence* transformation, in which *what* and *be* are inserted into a sentence: He argued the point/ What he argued was the point. And so on. We have not begun to exhaust the possibilities for examples of the transformations that a single sentence can undergo. The attempt has been to illustrate some general principles and, even more important, some ways of thinking about language that will help the student better to understand the grammar of English.

EMBEDDING

So far we have dealt with sentences having NP's that consist of Prop, Det + N, Pers, and Indef, but we know that such sentences as the following are common:

Students who are interested	study grammar
Few men	know what is good for them
The team that wins the game	will play in the Rose Bowl.

Simplified diagrams of these three sentences look like this:

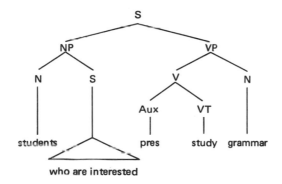

Fig. 9.

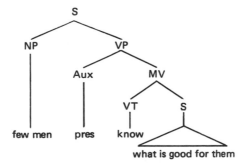

Fig. 10.

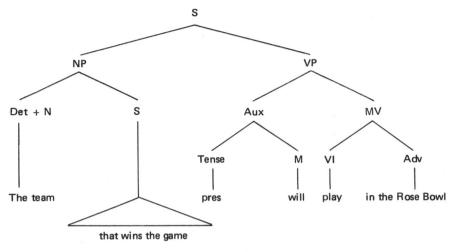

Fig. 11.

Language is like a Chinese box. We can put sentences within sentences within sentences within sentences. . . .

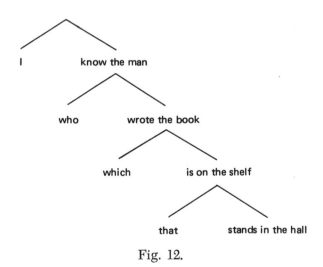

Fig. 12.

This ability of a *matrix sentence* to absorb other sentences by *embedding* is certainly one of the most important aspects of language. The ramifications of embedding will concern us for the next few pages.

The *relative* embedding is the most easily recognized and understood. Two sentences *with identical nouns* can be joined by a relative transformation. Thus

> I know THE MAN. THE MAN owns the house. I know the man WHO owns the house.

> THE CLASS is interesting. THE CLASS meets at noon. The class WHICH meets at noon is interesting.

> The professor advanced an IDEA. The IDEA was brilliant. The professor advanced an idea THAT was brilliant.

Of more interest than relatives themselves, however, are the structures that develop from relatives. It might seem surprising but it is true nonetheless that attributive and appositive adjectives derive from relatives, or at least from the same grammatical principles. We can demonstrate this easily enough. Suppose two sentences,

> I have a house which is white.
> I have a white house.

If the two sentences are synonymous (as indeed these two are), we must conclude that at some level of structure they must be identical, for identical meanings come from identical *deep structures*. Since we can easily diagram the deep structure of the first example sentence, we can discover where the meaning of both sentences must derive from:

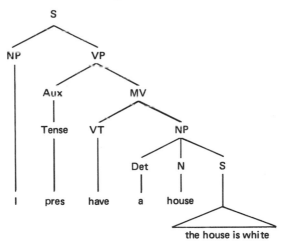

Fig. 13.

If you agree that Figure 13 represents the deep structure of the sentence *I have a house which is white,* and if you agree that that sentence and the sentence *I have a white house* are synonymous, then you must also agree that *I have a white house* has the same deep structure as *I have a house which is white.* Therefore, without going into the details of the process, we can assume that our derivation will go something like this:

1. Given: the two kernels with identical nouns:
   I have a house. The house is white.
2. A relative transformation combines them:
   I have a house which is white.
3. A deletion transformation omits everything but the adjective:
   *I have a house white.
4. Another transformation flip-flops the sentence elements so that they appear in their grammatical order:
   I have a white house.

This principle might seem unduly complex. Why not simply devise a rule that says, "Every noun can be preceded by an adjective"? (Thus: (Adj) N.) The answer is that such a rule fails to explain the synonymy that has just been pointed out, and it also fails to explain such constructions as

A girl *sweet and pretty* lives in the city.

The river, *lazy in the morning sunshine,* rambled through the valley.

If we view these two sentences from the standpoint of the four-part derivation outlined above, we have the explanation for the *appositive* position in which the adjectives appear:

A girl lives in the city. A girl is sweet and pretty.
A girl who is sweet and pretty lives in the city.
A girl sweet and pretty lives in the city.

The river rambled through the valley. The river was lazy in the morning sunshine.
The river, which was lazy in the morning sunshine, rambled through the valley.
The river, lazy in the morning sunshine, rambled through the valley.

Another example:

Dogs don't bite. Dogs are barking.
Dogs which are barking don't bite.
Dogs barking don't bite.
Barking dogs don't bite.

The ways in which embeddings come about are various, and not always discernible at first glance. The sentence

It is hard for him to concentrate

comes from *It is hard* and *He concentrates,* as does the variation *For him to concentrate is hard.* A sentence such as *It is good that he concentrates* is obviously a close relative, as is *His concentrating is good.* Such constructions may not appear to be the combination of two sentences through embedding, but undoubtedly they are. Take *For him to concentrate is hard* as an example. It is easy enough to see that *for him to concentrate* could derive from the sentence *He concentrates,* but what about *is hard?* If this at some point in the total derivation was a sentence, what was the subject? The clue comes when we realize that *It is hard for him to concentrate* and *For him to concentrate is hard* are synonymous and thus must have the same deep structure, which we can represent like this:

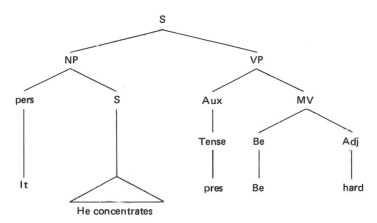

Fig. 14.

Similar are such pairs as

> It is fortunate that he is honest.
> That he is honest is fortunate.

and

> His understanding the problem is miraculous.
> It is miraculous, his understanding the problem.

even though the last sentence above would be more likely to occur in informal speech than in writing.

It is this ability of language to compact the meanings of two or more sentences into one sentence that makes for density in prose, but also for economy. For instance, here is a sentence from Conrad's "An Outpost of Progress":

Kayerts and Carlier walked arm in arm, drawing close to one another as children do in the dark; and they had the same, not altogether unpleasant, sense of danger which one half suspects to be imaginary.

Into this one sentence are compacted the meanings of the following

Kayerts and Carlier walked arm in arm.

1. Kayerts and Carlier drew close to one another.
2. Children draw close to one another in the dark.
3. They [Kayerts and Carlier] had the same sense of danger.
4. The sense of danger was not altogether unpleasant.
5. One half suspects (something).
6. The sense of danger is imaginary.

Now it must be stressed that every shred of meaning found in the matrix and six inserts listed above is also found in the sentence as Conrad wrote it, which is quite an amazing thing if you think about it.

Here are some examples of how sentences get built through embedding:

He got the basket and began to pick up the other chicks, picking each one up slowly by a foot and then flinging it into the basket with a nasty, snapping motion.—Robert Penn Warren

He got the basket.

1. He began (something).
2. He picked up the other chicks.
3. He picked each one up slowly by a foot.
4. He flung it into the basket with a motion.
5. The motion was nasty.
6. The motion was snapping.

During the year 1817, little Abe Lincoln, eight years old, going on nine, had an ax put in his hands and helped his father cut down trees and notch logs for the corners of their new cabin, forty yards from the pole-shed where the family was cooking, eating, and sleeping.—Carl Sandburg

During the year 1817, Abe Lincoln had (something).

1. Abe Lincoln was little.
2. Abe Lincoln was eight years old.
3. Abe Lincoln was going on nine.
4. An ax was put in his hands.
5. He helped his father cut down trees.
6. He helped his father notch logs for the corners of their cabin.
7. Their cabin was new.
8. Their cabin was forty yards from the pole-shed.
9. The family was cooking in the pole-shed.
10. The family was eating in the pole-shed.
11. The family was sleeping in the pole-shed.

When the Inquisitors summoned Galileo before them, they told him he must not find that the earth revolves around the sun.—Walter Lippman

> They told him (something).
>> 1. The Inquisitors summoned Galileo before them.
>> 2. He must not find (something).
>> 3. The earth revolves around the sun.

The prose of immature writers (sometimes caller "primer prose") is characterized by its failure to use the devices of embedding:

> My hobby is my favorite pastime. My hobby is fishing. It is an inexpensive and healthy way to relax.
>
> My hobby, fishing, is my favorite pastime, an inexpensive and healthy way to relax.
>
> Last summer we travelled to Montana. We stayed there for a week. We enjoyed the scenery.
>
> Last summer we travelled to Montana, where we stayed for a week because we enjoyed the scenery.

and so on.

Exercise. By way of summary and review:

1. What are the three kinds of verbs identified by traditional grammar. Explain and illustrate why the traditional classification is inadequate.

2. What are the absolute tenses in English? How can you prove your answer?

3. Aux→

4. Show the elements that go to make up the following complete verbs:

> worked might have been will go is twisting
> had been living did travel will have been done

5. Explain how we derive *Do you want some?* from *You want some.*

6. Explain how we derive *He did not come* from *He came.*

7. Explain how we derive *He did come* from *He came.*

8. Explain how we derive *What did you want?* from *You wanted something.*

9. Explain how we derive passive voice from active voice.

10. Whenever possible, change the following verbs to passive:

> am hits had understood is studying had been visiting
> needs has won read had overlooked

11. Apply the cleft sentence transformation to the following sentences: (Examples: He sits on a chair—What he sits on is a

chair; The class discusses Shakespeare—What the class discusses is
Shakespeare.) My manuscript is in my file cabinet. I live in a
house. USC is a university. Los Angeles is in California.

12. Embed the second of the following pairs of sentences in
the first. Use a variety of embedding devices. The mare ain't what
she used to be/The mare is old and gray. It is easy/My son studies.
He stopped smoking a pipe/Smoking a pipe is a bad habit.
I know (something)/My mood depends on the weather. It is
funny/No one saw you. The children played/The children were
laughing at their funny toys.

GENERATIVE GRAMMAR: USES

A subject need not have practical usefulness in order to be justified.
All knowledge might be divided into pure and servile: that which is
its own end and that which serves some other end. Surely the best
motive for learning about grammar is the quest for pure knowledge
about the nature of language, the curiosity that leads one to ask questions and seek answers. As pure knowledge, grammar is certainly as
intriguing and fruitful a subject of inquiry as any other discipline in
the academic spectrum, but generative grammar in particular holds
promise of a great deal of practical usefulness in a variety of areas:
pedagogy, stylistic analysis, creativity theory, and psychology, among
others.

There is some evidence that a knowledge of generative grammar
improves students' writing. A study by Donald Bateman and Frank
Zidonis concludes: "Statistical analysis suggests, but does not prove,
that there is a relation between a knowledge of generative grammar
and an ability to produce well-formed sentences of greater structural
complexity." Be this as it may, generative grammar is of more use
to the teacher than to the student, for it is more complete and more
systematic than other grammars and hence allows the teacher to make
finer discriminations about language. It is not only possible, but probable that courses in both English and foreign languages—for grade
schools, high schools, and universities—will gain their method, thrust,
and organization from generative grammar. Which is not to say that
students will necessarily be learning the grammar. The grammar will
give teachers the whereby to organize and teach more effective courses.
Since generative grammar is a series of rules which, when automatically
applied, will produce well formed sentences, the system should be of
value in the planning of exercises for "sentence building," i.e., as a

guide to the sequence in which grammatical devices should be presented to students. The student who wrote the following paragraph could greatly profit from learning how to use various sorts of embedding devices:

> My greatest love is the love of my possessions. I feel like a king when I am amongst my posessessions. But my possessions are not material possessions such as a beautiful new automobile or an enormous new house. Rather, my possessions are the wonders of nature, the beautiful snow-capped mountains, the deep, crystal-clear lakes.

The reason for choppiness and immaturity of this prose is that the writer has not learned the grammatical devices whereby he can put his ideas together into compact units. A series of exercises based on the principles of generative grammar could give him that ability rapidly. (But to repeat: the student need not learn the rules. The teacher needs to know the grammar in order to structure the work; the student will work with actual sentences. Many of the exercises in this discussion of generative grammar are illustrative of the principle being discussed.)

A great social problem today is the number of speakers who have mastered only a non-standard dialect and hence are, in effect, foreign speakers in the schools of our cities. Applied generative grammar will be of great value in remedying this situation.

Finally, the very nature of generative grammar will make it relatively easy to program, so that teaching machines will be able to relieve teachers of much of the burden of repetitive drill.

The problem of style in language has *always* concerned theorists and critics, but even the most fundamental questions about style have been subjects of dispute until recently. The advent of generative grammar with all that it implies about language systems has clarified much and settled many disputes. It now seems possible to identify the prose of a given writer as surely as his fingerprints can be identified. Of the thousands of choices that the language system offers the writer, he will characteristically opt for a fairly narrow range, and the options of one writer will be different from those of all other writers. Using generative grammar, analysts can now give a precise description of the structural style of this or that author. Before the coming of generative grammar, it was possible to talk in only the most superficial and impressionistic terms about the structural style of writers; it is now possible to be a good deal more accurate and searching.

As to generative grammar's bearing upon theories of creativity and psychology, the water gets deep. Nonetheless, estheticians and psychologists are turning more and more to generative grammar for insights into the way the mind produces discourse. The assumption is that the rules of generative grammar are analogous to the mental processes whereby discourse is produced (i.e., that the rules of the external grammar are similar to the "rules" of the internal grammar). If such is indeed the case, then we can conclude that generative grammar provides a rough schematic model of the working of the human mind. As Jerome Bruner says in *Toward a Theory of Instruction,* "The shape or style of mind is, in some measure, the outcome of internalizing the functions inherent in the language we use." If this is the case, then a precise description of language should be a step toward a precise description of mind, and certainly generative grammar is the most precise of all descriptions of language.

IV ✒ The Sentence

The discussion of grammar was highly theoretical; it shot off in many directions, for instance, toward the whole theory of how the human computer (the brain) produces discourse and toward producing an abstract model of language against which every individual's use of his own language can be measured. A knowledge of the theory of grammar (like a knowledge of the theories of human behavior) may or may not have practical applications, but, in any case, the educated man should know something about the nature of language.

In the present chapter, we will turn from theory to practice. Grammar is a theoretical explanation of how sentences are produced; now the discussion will look at sentences (good ones and bad ones) and give some hortative advice about how to write good ones and avoid bad ones.

The sentence may or may not be the expression of a complete idea. In any case, that is a bad definition because it presupposes a definition of "idea," and the definition of idea propels us out of grammar and into an epistemological morass. In fact, we need not define sentence in order to see how sentences work.

All sentences in the language are either kernel sentences or kernel sentences that have been added to or transformed by systematic processes. All sentences in the language are created by regular processes that modern grammar can more or less adequately describe. If this were not the case, we could not identify such a thing as a grammatical English sentence or an ungrammatical English sentence.

We can look at the situation in this way: *a limited number of rules allows us to produce an unlimited number of sentences.* So we can state the rules whereby we produce sentences, but we can never hope to describe each individual sentence. This must be true, because we continually encounter sentences that we have never seen before and probably will never see again, yet we recognize that they are English sentences. That is, we intuitively recognize that they have been produced by the rules of English grammar.

Exercise. In your own words, summarize the points made in the preceding three paragraphs.

In the last chapter, we discovered that a *kernel sentence* is a sort of minimal utterance, a sentence that has no additions and that is not transformed. In fact, just a bit of simplification allows us to say that the following are the basic English sentence types:

Type

	Subject		Complement	(Adverb)
to be	*Subject*	*Be verb*	*Complement*	*(Adverb)*
	The boy	was	good	(all the time)
I	*Subject*	*VI*		*(Adverb)*
	The boy	ran		(down the street)
II	*Subject*	*VT*	*Object*	*(Adverb)*
	The boy	hit	the girl	(viciously)
III	*Subject*	*Linking Verb*	*Complement*	*(Adverb)*
	The boy	became	ill	(at the fair)

Exercise.
1. What do the parentheses around the adverbs mean?
2. List six more linking verbs. Use each in a sentence.

The chart could be refined to include, for instance, different kinds of *VI* and *VT*. But the four kinds of sentences listed above represent the basic patterns from which all English sentences, no matter how complex, grow.

The processes by which sentences grow are systematic. We will now take a brief look at those processes.

SIMPLE SENTENCES

Simple sentences consist of one independent clause, but they can have any number of modifiers, and there is no theoretical limit to their length. That is, a simple sentence could, in theory, be infinitely long:

> The meal was good.
> The meal was very good.
> The meal was very very good.
> The meal was very very very good.
> The meal was very very very very good.

> Joe ate the meal.
> Joe ate the good meal.
> Ravenously hungry, Joe ate the good meal.
> Ravenously hungry, Joe ate the good meal in the greasy spoon.

> And so on.

The ways in which sentences get expanded is most interesting. You might want to use your intuition to discover some of the systematic processes of language. The following questions should remind you of principles developed in the chapter on grammar.

Exercise.

1. If *I see the man* and *The man was old* can generate *I see the old man*, then *I see the house* and *The house is white* will generate _____.

2. If *The dog growled* and *The dog is vicious* will generate *The vicious dog growled*, then *The horse galloped* and *The horse is gentle* will generate _____.

3. If *I kissed the girl* and *The girl is beautiful* will generate *I kissed the beautiful girl*, then *I climbed the mountain* and *The mountain is high* will generate _____.

4. Can we generalize by saying that one systematic way of explaining the insertion of adjectives into a base sentence is to conclude that they enter via an included sentence that is abbreviated?

> Base: I saw a movie.
> Insert: The movie was exciting.
> Process:
> > Combining: I saw a movie (the movie was exciting).
> > Deleting: I saw a movie exciting.
> > Ordering: I saw an exciting movie.

This explanation may, of course, seem roundabout and unnecessarily complicated. Perhaps there is a simpler systematic way of explaining the inclusion of adjectives in base sentences. But the method developed here has stood many tests; the reasons for its utility will become clear hereafter. What we are saying, then, is that any sentence with an adjective in it is actually at least two sentences combined. And that leads us to the rule about English grammar that says

N (S)

This means that any noun may be followed by a sentence. Of course, the sentences that sometimes follow nouns are not independent constructions. Sometimes, as we have seen, they result in adjectives.

I bought a necktie.
The necktie was red.
I bought a red necktie.

Sometimes the optional sentences that follow nouns may result in *verbal constructions*.

I saw a boy.
The boy was eating candy.
I saw a boy (the boy was eating candy).
I saw a boy eating candy.

Exercise. Indicate the base and the insert from which the following simple sentences resulted.
1. Good books are hard to find.
2. Beware of Greeks bearing gifts.
3. The Constitution is the basis of our fundamental liberties.
4. Sitting on the bank, he dabbled his feet in the water.
5. True love is never at a loss for words.

There are many ways in which kernels grow into full-fledged sentences. For instance, carefully analyze the following:

It is easy. I speak English.
It is easy for me to speak English.

It is easy. I ride bicycles.
It is easy for me to ride bicycles.

Exercise. Does the following rule make sense to you? If so, explain it. Does it hold true for all English sentences that fit the patterns of the base and the insert?

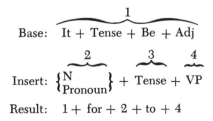

1
⎴
Base: It + Tense + Be + Adj

2   3   4
Insert: {N / Pronoun} + Tense + VP

Result: 1 + for + 2 + to + 4

In the result, what happens to element 2 if it is the pronoun "I" since it follows "for"? What is left out of the insert sentence in the result?

To repeat a point: language is completely systematic. Language processes are of the same order as mathematical processes: a finite number of rules will produce an infinite number of sentences.

To assume that a simple sentence is also simple-minded is to make a mistake.

COMPLEX SENTENCES

A complex sentence has one independent clause and any number of dependent clauses.

> The idea *that the private and public realms are coexistent* and *that the real problem is a right relationship between them rather than the disproportionate elevation of one or the other,* we owe to a remarkable study *that has been published within the year.*
>
> —August Heckscher

Or

> No solution is sound
> if it merely deals with the problems of today,
> if it merely feeds the hungry today in the hope
> that tomorrow they will not be so tactless as to starve in our sight.
>
> —Alice Mary Hilton

Complex sentences come into being through two of the systematic rules of language: N(S) says that any noun or noun equivalent can be followed by a sentence, and (Sub)S says that any sentence can be subordinated. N(S) explains such sentences as our old friend

> This is the house that Jack built.
> This is the malt that lay in the house that Jack built.
> This is the rat that ate the malt that lay in the house that Jack built.
> This is the cat that chased the rat that ate the malt that lay in the house that Jack built.
> This is the dog that worried the cat that chased the rat that ate the malt that lay in the house that Jack built.
> This is the cow with the crumpled horn that tossed the dog that worried the cat that chased the rat that ate the malt that lay in the house that Jack built.

In other words

> N (S)
> This is the house (Jack built the house)
> This is the house *that Jack built.*

Exercise. Into what sentences may the following be combined by the rule N(S)?

1. I know a man. The man is a millionaire.

2. My uncle is singing in the bathtub. My uncle is always happy.

3. Human beings are never happy. Human beings don't find their vocation.

The rule (Sub)S says merely that a word such as *because, if, when, although* may be placed before any sentence, and when that happens, the subordinated sentence may be connected to any other sentence:

> We have discussed the meaning of symbols generally. As we said, man's ultimate concern must be expressed symbolically.
>
> We have discussed the meaning of symbols generally *because,* as we said, man's ultimate concern must be expressed symbolically.
>
> —Paul Tillich

> Neither should any word be said to them of the wars in heaven, and of the plots and fightings of the gods against one another. . . . We mean our future guardians to regard the habit of quarreling among themselves as of all things the basest.
>
> Neither, *if* we mean our future guardians to regard the habit of quarreling among themselves as of all things the basest, should any word be said to them of the wars in heaven, and of the plots and fightings of the gods against one another. . . .
>
> —Plato

RELATIVE PRONOUNS

The *definite* relative pronouns are

who　　The man *who* came to dinner was Uncle George.

whom　The teacher *whom* the students liked best was Mrs. Bates.

which　The game *which* the children played most often was Monopoly.

that　　The wine *that* I drank was burgundy.

Notice that a definite relative pronoun always has a clear *antecedent* to which it refers:

> The team *that* wins this game will go to the Rose Bowl.
>
> The idea of *which* I am fond is the concept of freedom.
>
> Everyone likes the notion *that* love is free.

Exercise. Define antecedent.

Indefinite relative pronouns are *whose, whom, which, what,* and *who* and their compounds with *-ever* and *-soever*. Indefinite relative pronouns do not have antecedents. They appear in sentences such as the following:

> I know *what* I want.
> I will be ready for *whatever* happens.
> The girl did not know *whose* was the best.

Exercise. Use each of the indefinite relative pronouns in a sentence.

RELATIVE ADJECTIVES

Relative adjectives are *whose* and *which*. They function like adjectives in modifying nouns, and they function like relative pronouns in linking a clause to an antecedent:

> The railroad *whose* fares are lowest will carry the most passengers.
> At midnight, by *which* time I was exhausted, the last guest left.

Indefinite relative adjectives are *whose, which, what,* and their compounds with *-ever* and *-soever.*

> I know *whose* dog bit the postman.
> I know *which* dog bit the postman.
> I know *what* dog bit the postman.
> *Whatever* dog bit the postman, justice must be done.

RELATIVE ADVERBS

Relative adverbs, like relative pronouns and relative adjectives, may be either definite or indefinite:

def.   The park was a place *where* he could feel free.

indef.   The park was *where* he could feel free.

def.   There was a time *when* I could dance all night.

indef.   That was *when* I could dance all night.

Exercise. Underline all of the relatives in the following passage, and explain how they function.

> Under a government which imprisons any unjustly, the true place for a just man is also a prison. The proper place to-day, the only place which Massachusetts has provided for her freer and less desponding spirits, is in her prisons, to be put out and locked out of the State by

her own act, as they have already put themselves out by their principles. It is there that the fugitive slave, and the Mexican prisoner on parole, and the Indian come to plead the wrongs of his race should find them; on that separate, but more free and honorable ground, where the State places those who are not *with* her, but *against* her,—the only house in a slave State in which a free man can abide with honor.

—Thoreau

EXPRESSING RELATIONSHIPS

Sentences should be structurally accurate, logical, and effective. But, as we have seen, structurally acceptable sentences may be completely illogical, and, conversely, logical sentences may be structurally unacceptable. Some aspects of English structure have no connection with logic; they are simply structural conventions—the way we say things in English. (The double negative, once again, is a good example; educated English does not use it: He doesn't get no dinner tonight.) And we can recall the following: *Colorless green ideas sleep furiously.* We could argue for weeks over its meaning and its logic, but we must admit that it is a structurally acceptable English sentence.

The English language provides a number of simple ways to express the relationships among ideas. Note the following three sentences:

He wanted to go, *and* he had enough money to buy the ticket.

He wanted to go *because* he had enough money to buy the ticket.

He wanted to go; *moreover,* he had enough money to buy the ticket.

Obviously, each of the sentences contains two ideas. (Note that each idea could well be expressed in a sentence by itself: He wanted to go. He had enough money to buy the ticket.) And just as obviously, each of the sentences employs a different method of combining those ideas structurally and logically.

As they function in the structure, the three words *and, because,* and *moreover* are quite different. They belong to different word-groups, and they show different relationships among ideas.

First, we should look at the differences in the way they function structurally:

He wanted to go, *and* he had enough money to buy the ticket.

but not

And he had enough money to buy the ticket, he wanted to go.

He wanted to go *because* he had enough money to buy the ticket.

or

Because he had enough money to buy the ticket, he wanted to go.

He wanted to go; *moreover,* he had enough money to buy the ticket.

or

He wanted to go; he, *moreover,* had enough money to buy the ticket.

or

He wanted to go; he had, *moreover,* enough money to buy the ticket.

or

He wanted to go; he had enough money, *moreover,* to buy the ticket.

or

He wanted to go; he had enough money to buy the ticket, *moreover.*

The alternatives among these sentences are not equally effective and graceful, but they are all structurally possible.

From the examples, we can see that *and* must stand between the elements joined. It can join

words

Jonson *and* Shakespeare (were dramatists).

phrases

(We went) into the building *and* up the stairs.

clauses

We went into the building, *and* they went up the stairs.

a series of words, phrases, or clauses

(I like) coffee, tea, *and* milk.

(We went) into the building, up the stairs, *and* out on the roof.

We went into the building, they went up the stairs, *and* the workmen went out onto the roof.

We can see that schematically *and* patterns like this when it is in a sentence:

—————————— + — ———— —

Jonson and Shakespeare were dramatists.

or like this:

————————————— , ——————————— , + ——— ————————

We went into the building, up the stairs, and out onto the roof.

or

I like coffee, tea, *and* milk.

or

We went into the building, they went up the stairs, *and* the workmen went out onto the roof.

and so on. *And* must stand between the elements joined.

But *because* patterns differently. It joins clauses, and it stands either between the clauses or at the beginning of the first clause, thus:

—————————— + ——————————————————————

He wanted to go *because* he had enough money to buy the ticket.

or

   + ——————————————————————— , ——————————

Because he had enough money to buy the ticket, he wanted to go.

And *moreover* is a movable modifier; that is, it may be placed in a number of positions in its clause, thus:

He wanted to go; *moreover*, he had enough money to buy the ticket.
He wanted to go; he, *moreover*, had enough money to buy the ticket.
He wanted to go; he had enough money, *moreover*. . . .

and so on.

Words that pattern and function like *and* are called coordinating conjunctions. There are only seven words that function in the way that *and* does:

<table>
<tr><td></td><td>and</td><td>he didn't study</td></tr>
<tr><td></td><td>or</td><td>he didn't study</td></tr>
<tr><td></td><td>nor</td><td>*did he study*</td></tr>
<tr><td>He failed the course,</td><td>but</td><td>he didn't study</td></tr>
<tr><td></td><td>yet</td><td>he didn't study</td></tr>
<tr><td></td><td>so</td><td>he didn't study</td></tr>
<tr><td></td><td>for</td><td>he didn't study</td></tr>
</table>

Not all of these alternatives are logically possible, and with the use of *nor*, the second clause must be changed slightly. Nonetheless, all of these words are structurally possible in the place of *and* in the pattern sentence which we use here. But not all of them can substitute for *and* in every construction. For instance,

                Jim, Joe, *and* Jack must go.

or

                Jim, Joe, *or* Jack must go.

but not

                Jim, Joe, *but* Jack must go.

Another group of words function as coordinating conjunctions:

but not and *yet not*
    Jim, Joe, *but not* Jack must go.
    Jim and Joe must go, but not Jack.
    Jim and Joe must go, yet not Jack.

either . . . or
    Either Jim, Joe, *or* Jack must go.

neither . . . nor
> *Neither* Jim *nor* Joe must go.

not . . . but
> *Not* Jim *but* Joe must go.

both . . . and
> *Both* Jim *and* Joe must go.

Words that function like *because* are called *subordinating conjunctions*. There are sixteen of them: *after, although, as, as if, because, before, if, since, so that, than, unless, until, when (whenever), where (wherever), whether, while.* They always join one clause to another, and, remember, they pattern like this:

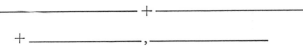

Further examples of the functioning of subordinating conjunctions:

after
> *After* we left the house, we walked downtown.
> We walked downtown *after* we left the house.
> (Note the following: *After* the show, we had a Coke.
> *After* in this instance is not a conjunction. The conjunction subordinates a clause; *after the show* is a prepositional phrase.)

although
> *Although* it was snowing, we took a long hike.
> We took a long hike *although* it was snowing.

so that
> *So that* we understand one another, I will repeat the instruction.
> I will repeat the instructions *so that* we understand one another.

than
> I can swim better *than* you can [swim].
> John knows him better *than* you do [know him].
> (Note that the subordinate clause introduced by *than* does not normally change position in the way that other subordinate clauses do. That is, in English we would not normally say *Better than you do, John knows him.*)

unless
> You cannot join the fraternity *unless* you maintain a "C" grade point average.
> *Unless* you maintain a "C" grade point average, you cannot join the fraternity.

A third method of showing the relationships among ideas in a sentence is the use of *transitional adverbs.* The thirteen most commonly used are *nevertheless, however, moreover, hence, consequently, nonetheless, accordingly, then, besides, likewise, indeed,* and *therefore.* Once again, *transitional adverbs are movable modifiers.*

> He wanted to see it; *however,* he didn't have time.
> He wanted to see it; he, nonetheless, didn't have time.
> He wanted to see it; he didn't have time though.

Notice that in the example sentences, the two clauses are joined by a symbolic conjunction, the semicolon (see "Punctuation"). The transitional adverb, unlike subordinating and coordinating conjunctions, does not serve as a conjunction joining two clauses; rather, it functions as a transitional element, showing the idea relationships between two clauses. Note the following series of sentences:

> I want to study painting. I have the talent.
> I want to study painting; I have the talent.
> I want to study painting, and I have the talent.
> I want to study painting, for I have the talent.
> If I want to study painting, I have the talent.
> I want to study painting; moreover, I have the talent.

Most readers will feel that something is missing in the first three examples, that something is wrong with them. Their fault is their failure to show the relationship between the two ideas that they express. Furthermore, notice this:

> structurally unacceptable in English
> > Although I want to study painting. I don't have time.

> structurally acceptable in English
> > I want to study painting. However, I don't have time.

Transitional adverbs do not provide structural links between clauses in a sentence; hence, the structural link must be expressed by a symbolic conjunction (;) or sometimes by a true conjunction, thus:

> I want to study painting, and, moreover, I have the talent.

The structural relationship that comes about through subordination is clear. The logical or *semantic* relationship is naturally more complex and at times even ambiguous. However, since structure expresses meaning—even though it does not always depend on meaning—the writer must concern himself with the ideational relationships that he can achieve through the use of subordination. Subordination can be used to express the following kinds of relationships:

> concessive
> > Although he came late, he arrived in time for the main feature.

temporal
> While I did the dishes, she vacuumed the floor.

adversative
> Whereas Bill was brilliant, John was industrious.

causative
> Because Bill was brilliant, he was a good student.

Subordination expresses other kinds of relationships, and since meaning is such a tenuous consideration, perhaps no list of the possible semantic relationships expressed by subordination can be either complete or absolutely clear. While acceptable structure (not necessarily effective structure) on any level of usage is normally a black and white matter, meaning relationships and their interpretation often fall into areas of gray.

Though they differ in structural function from subordinating conjunctions, coordinating conjunctions frequently express the same kinds of meaning relationships that subordinating conjunctions do. For instance,

concession
> *Although* he came late, he arrived in time for the main feature.
> He came late, *yet* he arrived in time for the main feature.

adversativity
> *Whereas* Bill was brilliant, John was industrious.
> Bill was brilliant, *but* John was industrious.

cause
> *Because* Bill was brilliant, he was a good student.
> Bill was a good student, *for* he was brilliant.

Transitional adverbs also express these relationships:

concession
> He came late; *however,* he arrived in time for the main feature.

adversativity
> Bill was brilliant; *however,* John was industrious.

cause
> Bill was brilliant; *therefore,* he was a good student.

Some of these examples illustrate how difficult it is to discuss the differences or similarities in meaning that one achieves through the use of coordinating and subordinating conjunctions and transitional adverbs. For instance, the difference between this concessive use of *however*

> He came late; *however,* he arrived in time for the main feature.

and this adversative use of the same word

> Bill was brilliant; *however,* John was industrious.

becomes nearly a metaphysical consideration. Fortunately, we need not concern ourselves with such problems. Our purpose is to discuss and learn the structural possibilities of the language, not to split semantic hairs.

Exercise.

1. Join the following clauses with the appropriate conjunctions or transitional adverbs; use at least three different ones for each pair of clauses.

(a) The radical may be uncomfortable in today's society _____ he is in the minority.

(b) Politics is the art of the possible _____ the possible is frequently a stopgap.

(c) _____ Harry Truman was elected president, the real age of the common man had begun.

(d) The family went on a picnic _____ it rained.

2. Discuss the use of coordinating and subordinating conjunctions and transitional adverbs in the following sentences. Are the usages appropriate? Why? If not, why not? Which words would be more appropriate?

(a) In this myth-making process the radicals inevitably suffer a serious handicap, for the audacious reformer of a century ago is likely to appear today as a man of orthodox ideas, and latter-day conservatives, with any appreciation of the earlier clash of ideas, are likely to claim him as their own.

—Arthur M. Schlesinger

(b) The story, though it may read as a cautionary tale, deals with real human passions, sexual and aggressive; it certainly does not present rewards of virtue in any unambiguous form or show the adult world in any wholly benevolent light.

—David Riesman

(c) The president of the firm wanted to negotiate, and he realized that a strike would be disastrous.

3. Write sentences using *for, moreover, while, so, because, yet.*

4. Supply the missing links in the following sentences so that they become both structurally accurate and meaningful.

(a) The prince knew that ultimately he would have to take revenge, and he awaited the right moment, and in the meantime Claudius was apprehensive about his situation.

(b) He may indeed act, as I said. He acts, so to speak, by accident. The redblooded may reflect. He reflects by accident.

(c) There is some hesitancy over my title. It will involve a radical change in the format of the title.

CUMULATIVE SENTENCES

So far, so good. Sentences gain texture through the addition of clauses, and clauses gain their syntax through relative words, subordinating and coordinating conjunctions, and transitional adverbs. We might conclude, then, that sentences which do not contain these elements would seem anemic and underdeveloped. But look at the following examples from modern prose:

> Going to the First Class bar, Hillier expected the last word in cushioned silk walls, a delicious shadowless twilight, bar stools with arms and backs, a carpet like a fall of snow.
> —Anthony Burgess
>
> I smile to myself in putting the following to the honorable members of the court, prompted as I am to take the bull by the horns.
> —Henry Miller

Neither of these sentences contains a subordinate or a coordinate clause, though each might:

> *When* he went to the First Class bar, Hillier expected the last word. . . .
>
> I smile to myself in putting the following to the honorable members of the court *since* I am prompted to take the bull by the horns.

There must be some methods of "sentence building" that our discussion has not so far explored.

> *Exercise.* It might be instructive for *you* to explore a bit. Without using conjunctions of any kind or relatives, "build" the following seven sentences. Example:

I was dejected.
Standing in the cold autumn rain, I was dejected.
Standing in the cold autumn rain drizzling from a murky sky, I was dejected.
Standing in the cold autumn rain drizzling from a murky sky, I was dejected, a lost soul crying for succor.
1. The horse trotted.
2. The banner flew.
3. In the distance, firing was heard.
4. The afternoon was monotonous.
5. Man is the talking animal.
6. The cigar smoke curled toward the ceiling.
7. The little boy sobbed.

What we need to do now is look at the ways in which sentences from the best modern prose grow from "kernels" into mature structures packed with ideas. In order to make this investigation, we will rely upon the work done by Professor Francis Christensen of the University of Southern California. Christensen speaks of *cumulative sentences,* that is, sentences that grow by the addition of elements to a base, and it is on the possible kinds of additions that we must focus.

NOUN CLUSTERS

Note the following additions:

> Good taste and bad taste cannot be explained by wealth or education, by breeding or background.

> Good taste and bad taste, *adventurous taste and timid taste,* cannot be explained by wealth or education, by breeding or background.
> —Russell Lynes

> They had the normal confidence of their years in their ability to remake the world and the opportunity.

> They had the normal confidence of their years in their ability to remake the world and, *unlike less fortunate generations,* the opportunity.
> —John Kenneth Galbraith

> It was Sunday.

> It was Sunday—*not a day, but rather a gap between two other days.*
> —F. Scott Fitzgerald

> Her cheeks were sunk slightly, her lips were partly open, and on the young face there was the ominous and fixed expression—*the absorbed, contemplating expression of the unconscious who are going to die.*
> —Joseph Conrad

The additions in the example sentences are all built on the principle of adding a noun and its modifiers. Graphically, what does this mean?

base
> The time had come.

noun addition
> The time—the moment—had come.

noun-plus-modifier additions
> The time—the moment of triumph—had come.

> The time had come, the moment of triumph over the forces of evil.

> The moment of triumph over the forces of evil—that time had come.

The grammatical principle of the noun-cluster addition goes back to the general rule N(S), but we need not follow that tortuous trail again. It is, however, important to note that the ideas of more than one sentence can be packed into one sentence via the noun-cluster addition:

The old women screamed around the corpse. The old women were harpies who fed on death.

The old women, harpies who fed on death, screamed around the corpse.

The urge to *love* is always ignored, save briefly or locally. The urge to love is the real message of every sincere, sane Messiah.

The urge to *love*—the real message of every sincere, sane Messiah—is always ignored, save briefly or locally.

—Philip Wylie

The mobs were maniacs. The mobs were raging animals who knew no reason. The mobs were madmen propelled by their own frenzy.

The mobs were maniacs, raging animals who knew no reason, madmen propelled by their own frenzy.

She turned again to the lady on her left who was somebody in the New Deal and carried about with her a typewritten report of the hearings of some committee which she was anxious to discuss. The lady was her *vis-à-vis* at breakfast. The lady was a person with dangling earrings, a cigarette holder, and a lorgnette.

She turned again to the lady on her left, her vis-à-vis at breakfast, a person with dangling earrings, a cigarette holder, and a lorgnette, who was somebody in the New Deal and carried about with her a typewritten report of the hearings of some committee which she was anxious to discuss.

—Mary McCarthy

Francis Bacon asserted, no doubt as one of the ripe lessons of experience, that "Knowledge is power." Francis Bacon was a man who rose to eminence by betraying his friends.

Francis Bacon, a man who rose to eminence by betraying his friends, asserted, no doubt as one of the ripe lessons of experience, that "Knowledge is power."

Exercise. Combine the following sentences by inserting one of them into the other as a noun cluster.

1. We sensed the dilemma. It was a situation in which we could do no right.

2. The coed trembled at the thought of taking the test. The coed was an excessively timid girl who severely doubted her own abilities.

3. The Renaissance came late to Germany. Germany was a country isolated from the mainstream of European intellectual life.

4. The music gave the whole audience a strange feeling of disquietude, as though somehow the wailing violin had destroyed

all traditional expectations about harmony. The audience was at first a group of fashionable listeners out for an evening of diverson.

5. Tiny Tim is a quick blooming plant that will soon die in the glare of overexposure. Tiny Tim is a typical phenomenon of mass culture.

6. Though we admired the general, we feared him. He was a man of overwhelming personal conviction.

7. Our interests are dictated by our inner needs. Our real preoccupations are dictated by our inner needs.

8. All of the mice were placed in an enclosed chamber. Six hundred mice in all were used.

9. The true scholar is an ascetic. He is a hermit. He is a seer. He is, above all, a human being.

10. A good style results from sentences packed with meaningful relationships. A good style results from sentences packed with relationships which carry the reader's mind beyond the possibilities of a one-plus-one correlation.

VERBAL CLUSTERS

One of the most characteristic ways in which the modern sentence is built to maturity is through verbal clusters. The chapter on grammar has worked out the technical details of verbs and verbals, but, as a matter of fact, those technical details are not at all necessary to an understanding of the principle. Look carefully at the following sentences:

At noon a red and white range cow with one new calf, *shining and curled,* came slowly up from the desert, *stopping often to let the calf rest.*
—Walter Van Tilburg Clark

In a new fall suit she sat in the club car, *waiting.*
—Mary McCarthy

Their contributions were like delicate seedlings, *carefully nurtured,* and well-grown in March. . . .
—Lewis Mumford

The white man, *turning his back upon the setting sun,* looked along the empty and broad expanse of the sea-reach.
—Joseph Conrad

Baffled but quite caught, Howe read on.
—Lionel Trilling

And for a moment, *braced against the steadily approaching vibrations of the sound,* he had the fantastic notion that the plane was going to strike the hotel.
—Frank Rooney

An Arab navvy *working on the path nearby* lowered his heavy hoe and sidled slowly towards us.

—George Orwell

When I came out of the gap in the osage hedge into the road, I saw him *sitting on his mare* over the heads of the other men who were standing around, *admiring the flood.*

—Robert Penn Warren

The process whereby verbal clusters are added is basically simple:

A group of the townspeople stood on the station siding of a little Kansas town. They were awaiting the coming of the night train, which was already twenty minutes overdue.

A group of the townspeople stood on the station siding of a little Kansas town, awaiting the coming of the night train, which was already twenty minutes overdue.

—Willa Cather

The lowlands lay under five feet of water. The lowlands were flooded by the torrential downpour.

The lowlands lay under five feet of water, flooded by the torrential downpour.

He came up with long strides of his skeleton legs. He was swinging a staff as tall as himself. He was entering the common room of the station. He would squat on his heels to the left of the door.

He came up with long strides of his skeleton legs, swinging a staff as tall as himself, and, entering the common room of the station, would squat on his heels to the left of the door.

—Joseph Conrad

His aunts were two small old women. They were plainly dressed.

His aunts were two small, plainly dressed old women.

—James Joyce

Now carefully follow this series:

He sat on the floor. He was singing.
He sat on the floor, singing.

The old man walked along. The old man was bowed down by troubles.
The old man, bowed down by troubles, walked along.
The old man walked along, bowed down by troubles.

The breezes played a tune. It was uttering the sounds of spring.
The breezes played a tune uttering the sounds of spring.

In technical terms, there are two kinds of participles (fully explained under the discussion of verbs in the chapter on grammar): the present participle (seeing, doing, feeling, thinking, walking, rationalizing) and the past participle (seen, done, felt, thought, walked, rational-

ized). Either of these forms with their complements and modifiers can
come into a base sentence from an insert sentence:

> Base: The team advanced.
> Insert: The team was gaining ground inch by inch.
> Results: The team, gaining ground inch by inch, advanced.
> Gaining ground inch by inch, the team advanced.

> Base: He waited outside the drawing-room door until the waltz should
> finish.
> Insert: He was listening to the skirts that swept against it and to the
> shuffling of feet.
> Result: He waited outside the drawing-room door until the waltz should
> finish, listening to the skirts that swept against it and to the
> shuffling of feet.
> —James Joyce

> Base: He worried about the stability of the government.
> Insert: He was troubled by rumors of insurrection.
> Result: Troubled by rumors of insurrection, he worried about the sta-
> bility of the government.

> Base: He paid the newsboy.
> Inserts: He was rapidly taking a coin from his pocket.
> The newsboy was huddled against the building.
> Result: Rapidly taking a coin from his pocket, he paid the newsboy
> huddled against the building.

In other words, we can use the principle of the verbal cluster to combine

> He was a wreck of a man.
> He was given to drink early in life.
> He was trembling and palsied by age thirty.
> Given to drink early in life, he was a wreck of a man, trembling
> and palsied by age thirty.

or to combine the necessary elements to create this sentence:

> Again he could not see, *whirling;* there was a face in the red haze,
> moonlike, bigger than the full moon, the owner of it half again his
> size, *he leaping in the red haze toward the face, feeling no blow, feel-
> ing no shock when his head struck the earth, scrabbling up and leaping
> again, feeling no blow this time either and tasting no blood, scrabbling
> up to see the other boy in full flight and himself already leaping into
> pursuit as his father's hand jerked him back, the harsh, cold voice speak-
> ing above him. . . .*
> —William Faulkner

> I understood the reasons.
> I saw the point.
> Understanding the reasons, I saw the point.

> The plane descended to the airport.
> The airport was shrouded in smog.
> The plane descended to the airport shrouded in smog.

Exercise. By creating verbal clusters, combine the following groups of sentences.

(Example: *The runner saw his chance* and *The runner stole second* can be combined into either *Seeing his chance, the runner stole second* or *Stealing second, the runner saw his chance.* Which is the more probable and logical?)

1. The bird flies into the tree. The bird settles on its nest.

2. He went on slowly. He turned his face to the pane.

3. As few as 11 large earthworms can transfer a lethal dose of DDT to a robin. And 11 worms form a small part of a day's rations to a bird that eats 10 to 12 earthworms in as many minutes. (Rachel Carson)

4. To become aware of the problem is a condition of taking steps toward its solution. The problem is in part economic. (John Dewey)

5. The canon law of the Church, and the civil law of the State, owe to Justinian's lawyers their influence on the development of Europe. They established in the Western mind the ideal that an authority should be at once lawful, and law enforcing, and should in itself exhibit a rationally adjusted system of organization. (Alfred North Whitehead)

6. The coat was soaked. It had fallen into the river.

7. The way these comrades look at problems is wrong. They do not look at the essential or main aspects but emphasize the non-essential or minor ones. (Mao Tse-Tung)

8. Ideas come from heaven. They drop from the skies.

9. He was absolutely without fear. The man stood his ground against the charging bull.

10. The ego is hemmed in and cannot disport itself. It swings dissatisfied between antagonism and conformity, out of which one can fashion but few objects of delight: one imagines with difficulty a life's work wholly devoted to expressing rage or listlessness. (Jacques Barzun)

ADJECTIVE CLUSTERS

An extremely simple method of giving texture to sentences, without predicating (i.e., without adding complete clauses through relatives or conjunctions), is to add adjective clusters.

> The dog froze to a rigid point.
> The dog was wild with anticipation.
>> The dog, wild with anticipation, froze to a rigid point.
>> Wild with anticipation, the dog froze to a rigid point.

The class sat quietly, waiting for the teacher.
The class was wary and hostile as rattlers coiled to strike.
  The class, wary and hostile as rattlers coiled to strike, sat quietly, waiting for the teacher.
  Wary and hostile as rattlers coiled to strike, the class sat quietly, waiting for the teacher.

The old man stood there.
The old man was shabby in his secondhand clothes.
The old man was proud after a life of uncompromising honesty.
  The old man stood there, shabby in his secondhand clothes, but proud after a life of uncompromising honesty.
  Shabby in his secondhand clothes, but proud after a life of uncompromising honesty, the old man stood there.
  The old man, shabby in his secondhand clothes, but proud after a life of uncompromising honesty, stood there.

They went at a walk.
The walk was not very fast, but faster than they could imaginably enjoy.
  They went at a walk, not very fast, but faster than they could imaginably enjoy.

—James Agee

Harking back to our grammar, we can see the principle by which adjective clusters are derived. The base sentence (matrix) and the insert must have the same NP. And the insert sentence must have Be + Adj. Under these conditions, the two sentences can be combined. Some more examples:

The trout fought against the flexible tension of the rod.
The trout [or it] was dogged in its battle.
  Dogged in its battle, the trout fought against the flexible tension of the rod.

He is aggressive and blunt-spoken.
He makes it clear that no one is going to put anything over on him.
  Aggressive and blunt-spoken, he makes it clear that no one is going to put anything over on him.

Exercise. Using the principle of the adjective cluster, combine the following sentences.

1. The salesman is willing and eager. The salesman knocks on the door.

2. The woman sat on the bench. She was big with child.

3. Johnson gnawed his pencil. He was unwilling to make such a serious commitment.

4. The yard was sweet with the smell of blossoms. The yard was bathed by the morning sun.

5. The blond was proud, haughty, and selfish. The blond loved only herself.

6. The houses on the street had an air of elegance. The elegance was just slightly smug because of its overdone neatness.

7. The book is full of urbane irony. The book is a delight for the reader.

8. The students were frantic with registration. The students were rushing about the gymnasium.

9. The matchflame was bright in the total darkness. The matchflame gave off enough light to reveal Tom's features.

ABSOLUTES

Any sentence can be added to any other sentence in the following manner:

> A single original organic type can produce a group by branching into a number of distinct sub-types.
> The ramifications remain separate down to the level of species.
> A single original organic type can produce a group by branching into a number of distinct sub-types, the ramifications remaining separate down to the level of species. (Sir Julian Huxley)

> According to this second possible view, Christianity is, as it were, the egg, grub, and chrysalis between butterfly and butterfly.
> Christianity is a transitional thing which bridges the gap between one civilization and another. . . . (Arnold J. Toynbee)
> According to this second possible view, Christianity is, as it were, the egg, grub, and chrysalis between ,butterfly and butterfly, Christianity being a transitional thing which bridges the gap between one civilization and another. . . .

University of Southern California is in Los Angeles.
It is a major urban institution.
> University of Southern California being in Los Angeles, it is a major urban institution.

It is easy to see what happens to the insert sentence in the absolute addition: most simply stated, the verb is converted to a participle.

The guests *went.* We did the dishes.
The guests *having gone,* we did the dishes.

The clock *was broken.* We didn't know what time it was.
The clock *having been broken,* we didn't know what time it was.

The book *was* long. I read until dawn.
The book *being* long, I read until dawn.

I *was awed* by this system, I *believed* in it, I *respected* its force.
The alternative was "going bad." (Alfred Kazin)
> I *being awed* by this system, *believing* in it, *respecting* it, the alternative was "going bad."

Next day Jim Laird *was* drunk and unable to attend the funeral services. Steavens called twice at his office, but was compelled to start east without seeing him. (Willa Cather)

Next day Jim Laird *being* drunk and unable to attend the funeral services, Steavens called twice at his office, but was compelled to start east without seeing him.

Now carefully examine the next example:

The dogs were there first.
Ten of them *were huddled* back under the kitchen.
Himself [he] and Sam *were squatting* to peer back into the obscurity where they crouched, quiet.
The eyes *were rolling* and luminous, *vanishing*.
And no sound, only that effluvium which the boy could not quite place yet, something more than dog, stronger than dog and not just animal, just beast even.

The dogs were there first, ten of them *huddled* back under the kitchen, himself and Sam *squatting* to peer back into the obscurity where they crouched, quiet, the eyes *rolling* and luminous, *vanishing*, and no sound, only that effluvium which the boy could not quite place yet, of something more than dog and not just animal, just beast even. (William Faulkner)

Remember that there are two kinds of participles. *The past participle*:

The hymn was *sung*. The congregation sat down.
The hymn *sung*, the congregation sat down.

The work was *done*. I put away my tools.
The work *done*, I put away my tools.

The *present participle*:

No one was *coming*. The meeting failed.
No one *coming*, the meeting failed.

Everyone helped. The house was soon painted.
Everyone *helping*, the house was soon painted.

Exercise. Using the principle of the absolute, combine the following sentences.

1. John was unable to attend the meeting. He sent an emissary in his place.

2. The season was far advanced. It was too late to plant radishes.

3. The guide had been unable to locate the trail. We overnighted by the stream.

4. Those few years of dangerous passage are an ascent into unknown hills. They take the breath sometimes and bewilder the vision. (Tennessee Williams)

5. A door opened a few minutes after dawn. A bicycle wheel was thrust out, followed by a thin young Armenian boy. (Vahan Krikorian Gregory)

6. The world has been brought to the edge of destruction. It is now time for mankind to retreat.

7. It was late afternoon. This time tomorrow he would be somewhere on a good graveled road, driving his car past things that happened to people, quicker than their happening. (Eudora Welty)

8. Few graduates acknowledge their debts to *alma mater*. The alumni fund remains puny.

9. No challenge seemed too great. Alexander longed for new worlds to conquer.

10. The general populace did not think of the results of their decision. They voted for restrictive legislation. (Be careful with this one.)

PREPOSITIONAL PHRASES

Prepositional phrases are such common additions that we hardly need to discuss them, and probably need no practice in their use. It is enough to illustrate that they are important in building the texture of sentences.

> The first *in time* and the first *in importance* *of the influ-ences upon the mind* is that *of nature.* (Emerson)

> For it came about *in this way* that *for the past three hundred years* there has been growing up *in men's minds,* dominated as they are *by science,* a new imaginative picture of science. (W. T. Stace)

SUMMARY

In summarizing the discussion of sentence relationships, it might be well to analyze a few sentences from the prose of writers who are generally admired. If you follow the analysis carefully, you will begin to develop a sense of style that, hopefully, will aid you in working toward mature prose.

We will use the following system of notation: RC (relative clause); SC (subordinate clause); NC (noun cluster); VC (verb cluster); AC (adjective cluster); Abs (absolute); PP (prepositional phrase).

Joseph Conrad (simple sentence)

base	The steersman dug his paddle / 1— / and held hard / 2— /
PP	/1—into the stream/
PP	/2—with stiffened arms/
Abs	his body thrown forward

James Thurber (complex sentence)

NC	A vital and restless breed
PP	of men
VC	given
PP	to tapping our toes and drumming
PP	with our fingers
VC	infatuated
PP	with every new crazy rhythm
RC	that rears its ugly beat
base	we have never truly loved harmony
NC	the graceful structure
PP	of shapes and tones
base	and / 1— / we pay the awful price / 2— /
PP	/1—for this blindness and deafness/
PP	/2—of continuous cacophony/

Walter Lippmann (complex sentence; simple sentence)

PP	In government offices
RC	which are sensitive
PP	to the vehemence and passion
PP	of mass sentiment
base	public men have no sure tenure.
base	They are / 1— / perpetual office seekers
PP	/1—in effect/
AC	always on trial
PP	for their political lives
VC	always required to court their restless constituents

Loren Eiseley (complex sentence)

base	It is with the coming of man that a vast hole seems to open
PP	in nature
NC	a vast black whirlpool
VC	spinning faster and 'faster
VC	consuming flesh, stones, soil, minerals
VC	sucking down the lightning
VC	wrenching power
PP	from the atom

SC	until the ancient sounds of nature are drowned
PP	in the cacophony
PP	of something
RC	which is no longer nature
NC	something instead
RC	which is loose and knocking
PP	at the world's heart,
NC	something demonic and no longer planned
VC	escaped, it may be
VC	spewed
PP	out of nature
VC	contending / 1— / against its master
PP	/1—in a final giant's game/

Robert Penn Warren (complex sentence)

base	He had very big hands
AC	knotted and grayish
PP	in the joints
PP	with calloused palms
RC	which seemed to be streaked
PP	with rust
PP	with the rust coming up
PP	between the fingers
VC	to show
PP	from the back

James Baldwin

base	I read about it
PP	in the paper
PP	in the subway
PP	on my way
PP	to work
base	I read it
base	and I couldn't believe it
base	and I read it again
base	Then perhaps I just stared
PP	at it
PP	at the newspaper
VC	spelling out his name
VC	spelling out the story
base	I stared
PP	at it

PP	in the swinging lights
PP	of the subway car
PP	and in my own face
VC	trapped in the darkness
RC	which roared outside

James Joyce

base	The raisins and almonds and figs and apples and oranges and chocolates and sweets were now passed
PP	about the table
base	and Aunt Julia invited all the guests to have either port or sherry
PP	At first
base	Mr. Bartell D'Arcy refused to take either
base	but one of his neighbors nudged him and whispered something
PP	to him
RC	upon which he allowed his glass to be filled
base	Gradually / 1— / the conversation ceased
SC	/1—as the last glasses were being filled/
base	A pause followed
VC	broken only
PP	by the noise
PP	of the wine
PP	and by unsettlings
PP	of chairs
base	The Misses Morkan / 1— / looked down
NC	/1—all three/
PP	at the tablecloth
base	Someone coughed once or twice
base	and then a few gentlemen patted the table gently as a signal
PP	for silence

Ruth Benedict

base	A chief / 1— / / 2— / talked / 3— / a great deal
PP	/1—of the Digger Indians/
RC	/2—as the Californians call them/
PP	/3—to me/
PP	about the ways
PP	of his people
PP	in the old days

base	He was a Christian and a leader
PP	among his people
PP	in the planting of peaches and apricots
PP	on irrigated land
base	but / 1— / his hands trembled and his voice broke
SC	/1—when he talked
PP	of the shamans
RC	who had transformed themselves
PP	into bears
PP	before his eyes
PP	in the bear dance/
PP	with excitement

Now, for the sake of comparison, we will do the same kind of analysis on a passage from the student theme which appeared in Chapter II of this book.

base	Recently I returned
PP	from the island
PP	of Puerto Rico
RC	where I had been on a tour of duty
PP	with the Air Force
PP	During these two years
base	I acquired my greatest love
base	This love is not only my greatest love but the love
PP	of many
PP	of the people
PP	of the island
base	It is the sport
PP	of skin diving
base	I would venture to say
RC	that this is one of the most beautiful and adventurous sports
VC	known to man
base	Most of the diving / 1— / was at depths
RC	/1— that I did/
PP	from 30 to 40 feet
PP	At this depth
base	the waters / 1— / are of a dark blue
PP	/1—of the Caribbean/
NC	like the sky
PP	on a clear day
PP	at sunset

Exercise.

1. What would be the effect if the absolute in the sentence from Joseph Conrad were expressed in a complete predication? Would the style suffer or be improved?

2. How many words come before the base in the James Thurber sentence? How many additions? What would be the effect if all additions came after the base?

3. Lippmann's sentences are shorter than that by Thurber. What effect do the short sentences have?

4. What is the predominant stylistic feature of the Eiseley sentence?

5. Notice that all of the additions in the Robert Penn Warren sentence come after the base; all contribute to the description of "hands." Do you think that this kind of sentence movement is typical of descriptive prose? Find three or four other descriptive sentences that have a movement typical to that of Warren's.

6. Perhaps a good adjective to describe Baldwin's style in the sentences analyzed is "staccato." Explain.

7. Explain the ways in which James Joyce's sentences seem to accomplish the tasks that they apparently set out to do.

8. The sentences from the student theme are thin textured, "anemic." Does the analysis of the additions help explain why? Discuss in detail.

9. You might like to do a diagnosis of your own prose. Is its texture thin? Do you feel that it is mature? You can determine much by finding the kind and numbers of additions that you seem typically to use. Therefore, do an analysis of, say, a hundred words that you think are typical of the way you usually write. On the basis of this analysis, be prepared to characterize your prose.

THE VERB

We have already discussed the verb in some detail, but in connection with the effectiveness of the sentence, no consideration is more important than the verb. Some interesting things can be done with it. For instance,

he + present + eat + an apple (which you will recall are the elements of the sentence *He eats an apple*)

can be systematically transformed in this way:

an apple + present + be + en + eat (by + him), or *An apple is eaten (by him)*.

he + present + have + en + eat + an apple (He has eaten an apple)
can be systematically transformed to

an apple + present + have + en + be + en + eat +   (by + him),
or *An apple has been eaten (by him).*

She sings a song becomes *A song is sung (by her). The man bought a
new car* becomes *A new car was bought (by the man). The class has
already taken the test* becomes *The test has already been taken (by the
class). She is singing a song* becomes *A song is being sung (by her).*
And so on.

This transformation is known as the passive voice. The passive voice
can be defined as *any form of the verb Be plus a past participle.*

Exercise.   Underline only the verbs in passive:

is singing   was sung   will be done   has gone   will be making   will have been going   will have been seen   is chewing
has chewed   will be chewed   is written   can write
may be spoken

Change the following sentences into passive:

1. I need at least five dollars by tomorrow.
2. We are going to eat dinner at the Yee Mee Loo.
3. Roaring and snorting, the bull, head down, charged the
spectators.
4. The man bought a set of encyclopedias.
5. Place the substance in the centrifuge, and fasten it securely.

Some comments on these sentences will reveal much about the
passive voice. Notice what happens when (1) is changed to passive:
At least five dollars is needed (by me) tomorrow. The sentence becomes wordy, and it definitely loses straightforwardness. The case is
the same with (2): Dinner is going to be eaten (by us) at the Yee Mee
Loo. The third sentence becomes virtually impossible in the passive
voice: Roaring and snorting, head down, the spectators were charged
(by the bull). In this instance, the change to passive has ruined the
syntax of the sentence, for the passive construction brings about a
so-called dangling modifier: "Roaring and snorting" attaches itself to
"spectators" rather than to "the bull." Of course, one might write the
sentence this way: The spectators were charged by the bull, roaring
and snorting, head down. But that alternative is awkward at best.

Perhaps the fifth sentence is the only one that really seems natural
in the passive voice. Scientific writing and sets of instructions are often
in the passive voice, presumably to avoid the necessity of identifying
the doer and to achieve impersonality. In other words, passive has a

definite and useful function; but it should not be used indiscriminately. Some students seem to think automatically and naturally in passive voice, but this is a habit that the experienced writer overcomes. Indeed, it is almost a rule of thumb with beginning writers that they should consciously choose between active and passive. Many sentences that simply won't "come out" result from passive. So, if you are having trouble expressing an idea, check to see if your verb is passive; if it is, change it to active, and see if your problem is solved.

Another principle of good sentences is found in the kinds of verbs that writers choose. Some students habitually express their ideas with Be verbs: His running is fast vs. He runs fast; My arrival in Chicago was on the first of May vs. I arrived in Chicago on the first of May. The Be verb is like an equal sign. Its real function is to carry tense and fill a structural slot. Not all languages demand that this structural slot be filled when the idea to be expressed is equational: He is a boy, He = boy. In Russian, one would say: On malcheek (He boy). So the principle is that verbs other than Be fill structural slots that are necessary in the language, but they also carry meaning.

> *Exercise.* Eliminate the Be verbs in the following sentences, but do not alter the meaning.
> 1. His pleading of the case was eloquent.
> 2. The chef's Caesar salad was tasty.
> 3. The train's speed was eighty-five miles an hours.
> 4. Mothers normally are protective of their children.
> 5. The trouble is that we are seldom aware of the protection
>
> afforded by natural enemies until it fails. (Rachel Carson)

Sometimes Be verbs serve excellently. Sometimes they do not. Use proper verbs in proper places.

Closely allied with the tendency to use Be verbs where others would do a better job is the *there is/there are* circumlocution: There is a man in the backyard vs. A man is in the backyard; There are fifteen guests invited to the party vs. Fifteen guests are invited to the party. Obviously, there is/there are must be used with caution.

VARIETY

If variety is the spice of life, it is the ultimate seasoning for sentences. Nothing wears on the reader more annoyingly than sentence after sentence of the same pattern and the same approximate length. The prose that we like to read has great variety in sentence types and lengths. This principle is easily illustrated by analysis of a passage by George Orwell:

Sentence 1 (55 words) complex

adverb clause	When you walk
prep. phrase	through a town like this
appositive	two hundred thousand inhabitants
adj. clause	of whom at least twenty thousand own nothing
prep. phrase	except the rags
adj. clause	they stand up in
adverb clause	when you see
noun clause	how the people live
noun clause	and still more easily how they die
base clause	it is always difficult to believe
noun clause	that you are walking
prep. phrase	among human beings

Sentence 2 (10 words) simple

base	All colonial empires are / / founded
prep. phrase	/in reality/
prep. phrase	upon that fact

Sentence 3 (12 words) compound

base	The people have brown faces
coordinate clause	[and] besides, there are so many
prep. phrase	of them

Sentence 4 (8 words) simple

base	Are they really the same flesh
prep. phrase	as yourself

Sentence 5 (5 words) simple

base	Do they even have names

Sentence 6 (18 words) complex

base	Or are they merely a kind
prep. phrase	of undifferentiated brown stuff
appositive	about as individual
elliptical adverb clause	as bees or coral insects [are individual]

Sentence 7 (33 words) compound-complex

base	They rise
prep. phrase	out of the earth
coordinate clause	they sweat and starve
prep. phrase	for a few years
coordinate clause	and then they sink back
prep. phrase	into the nameless mounds
prep. phrase	of the graveyard
coordinate clause	and nobody notices
noun clause	that they are gone

Sentence 8 (11 words) simple

base	And even the graves themselves soon fade back
prep. phrase	into the soil

Sentence 9 (38 words) compound-complex

adverb	Sometimes
absolute	out for a walk
adverb clause	as you break your way
prep. phrase	through the prickly pear
base	you notice
noun clause	that it is bumpy underfoot
coordinate clause	and only a certain regularity / / tells you
prep. phrase	/in the bumps/
noun clause	that you are walking
prep. phrase	over skeletons

This lengthy analysis demonstrates the kind of variety that good writers achieve. Almost certainly they do not plan in advance to achieve variety, but their versatility and their writing habits lead them to it. All writers should develop such spontaneous habits.

> *Exercise.* Analyze two or three paragraphs of your own prose in the way that the Orwell passage was analyzed. Can you make any specific suggestions about improving your own prose?

UNITY

Good sentences stick to the point, make the point, and then drop the point. That is, good sentences are unified. They get where they're going, and they don't have fuzzy destinations or more than one destination.

The University of Southern California, whose team won the Rose Bowl this year, is located in downtown Los Angeles, a sprawling city that is troubled with smog, and we like living near the ocean as well as being associated with a university that has a fine school of medicine.

Admittedly the above example is extreme, but it illustrates what can happen to sentences that get out of control.

EMPHASIS

Sometimes the point of a sentence is obscured because the wrong element receives emphasis. Generally speaking, the last element in a sentence will be the most emphatic, so that the following

We waited and waited and waited in the meantime.

should be revised to read

In the meantime, we waited and waited and waited.

Exercise. Revise the following sentences to achieve better emphasis.

1. Students who discipline themselves can do better with few exceptions.

2. Particularly in California, motorcycle gangs are becoming a menace.

3. We tended to be in favor of Medicare, even if it did smack of socialism.

4. We never did—under any circumstances—approve of rote learning.

Sometimes one can achieve emphasis by changing the normal order of words in a sentence:

Provident Father never was, but delightful he was always.

Exercise. The following sentences from Thoreau's *Walden* have been changed to make them less emphatic. Revise them so that their emphasis is regained.

1. I have seen whence came the expression, "the glassy surface of the lake," standing on the smooth sandy beach at the east end of the pond, in a calm September afternoon, when a slight haze makes the opposite shoreline indistinct.

2. Its water is as cold as it is pure for four months in the year. . . .

3. The same is true of White Pond, as far as my observation goes.

4. I lay down on the ice and looked through the hole out of curiosity.

PARALLELISM

In grammar, parallelism means the connecting of like elements. Sometimes parallelism is optional, used for stylistic effects, as in the following sentences from Samuel Johnson's biography of Pope:

> Dryden knew more of man
>   in his general nature
> and Pope
>   in his local manners.

> The notions of Dryden were formed
>   by comprehensive speculation,
> and those of Pope
>   by minute attention.

> There is more dignity
>   in the knowledge
>   of Dryden
> and more certainty
>   in that
>   of Pope.

But often violation of grammatical parallelism constitutes a downright error. Coordinated verbals must be of the same type, so that we cannot say

> *Writing* novels and *to hunt* big game were Hemingway's passions.

One should not yoke a noun with an adjective:

> In the modern world, education is both a *necessity* and *pleasant*.

Phrases and clauses should not be coordinated:

> The professor is popular not only *in the salon,* but *because he is a brilliant lecturer.*

Sometimes the problem is more intricate. Look carefully at the following sentence from a freshman theme:

> Botany 101 meets at 8:00, English 102 meeting at 9:00 on the other side of the campus, and I don't have time to get from one class to another.

The muddle of this sentence results from an egregious lack of parellelism, but also from another fault. Both *meets* and *don't have* are finite verbs; *meeting* is a verbal (i.e., verb form that does not have tense). So the sentence might be revised in this way:

> Botany 101 meets at 8:00, English 102 meets at 9:00 on the other side of the campus, and I don't have time to get from one class to another.

But the best revision is this:

> Because Botany 101 meets at 8:00 and English 102 meets at 9:00 on the other side of the campus, I don't have time to get from one class to another.

Exercise. Explain why the final revision is the most satisfactory.

Now look at this sentence:

> The University expects the students to maintain a satisfactory GPA, wants them to participate in extracurricular activities, and the faculty gives huge assignments.

In other words, two verb phrases and a clause are coordinated. Earlier in this chapter, the nature of coordination was explained.. But briefly, here is the principle. We can say

> I like to swim. I like to eat pie. I like to watch movies.

or

> I like to swim, I like to eat pie, and I like to watch movies.

or

> I like
>   to swim
>   to eat pie
>   and to watch movies

or

> I like to
>   swim
>   eat pie
>   and watch movies

but not

> I like
>   to swim
>   to eat pie
>   and I like to watch movies.

Exercise. Eliminate the unparallel constructions in the following sentences.

1. To be well dressed, you should wear a dark suit, a red tie, and carry a clean handkerchief.

2. The group likes to sing motets and, most of all, playing recorders.

3. Integrity of understanding and to discern nicely were not allotted in a less proportion to Dryden than to Pope.

4. Man cannot live by bread alone, by love alone, and he needs many things.

After correlative conjunctions (either . . . or, neither . . . nor, not only . . . but also) forms must be parallel. Thus if the sentence contains *neither + noun,* it must also have *nor + noun.*

> We recognized neither James nor John.

Sentences such as the following violate parallelism:

> Either we must drive faster or take a room for the night.

> *Exercise.* How may the above sentence be rearranged so as not to violate parallelism?

SHIFTS

Shifts frequently involve parellelism—the shift, for instance, from a gerund construction to an infinitive construction: The girls in the class learned to knit and sewing. But the most annoying shifts are those that are not grammatically incorrect, such as a shift in subject:

> The *book* is interesting, *it* is informative, and *you* will like it.

Writers often shift from the impersonal third person into second person:

> When *one* has gone through classical logic, the next step is symbolic logic. Mastering symbolic logic is a difficult but rewarding task, for when *you* have conquered that subject, others, such as grammar, become easier for *you.*

> *Exercise.* Eliminate the shifts from the two example sentences.

Another kind of shift:

> The president knew *about the students cheating on their tests* and *that the honor system had failed.*

Here the shift is from a phrase to a clause. Another kind of shift is from active to passive:

> If you are fishing with a wet fly, a sinking line should be used.

> *Exercise.* Eliminate the shifts from the two example sentences.

The point is to join like with like, to avoid shifting from one type of construction to another.

AMBIGUITY

An ambiguous statement is one that is capable of two or more interpretations. For example,

> She told her friend that she had been away too long.

The ambiguity in this sentence arises from faulty pronoun reference; one does not know whether the second *she* refers to the first *she* or to *friend*.

Modifiers also cause ambiguity:

> The king beheaded those lords who had opposed him for good reason.

Here, *for good reason* could modify either *beheaded* or *opposed*.

> *Exercise.* Eliminate the ambiguity from the two example sentences. (You will need to rewrite the first one completely.)

He saw the man in the room is slightly ambiguous. Why?

Some ambiguity is intentional, as when a statement elicits the response, "Are you being facetious?" This kind of ambiguity usually arises from irony. For instance, I say, "My new car is really a gem," and the listener does not know whether I am pleased with the car or am ironically criticizing it.

AWKWARDNESS

Some sentences are simply ungainly—because of the way the elements are put together, because of the words used, because of the "movement" of the ideas. Most of the time, one must sense the awkwardness of locutions through his "ear for language."

> *Exercise.* Eliminate the awkwardness from the following sentences.
>
> 1. Rhetoric has been, from the fourth century, one of the important intellectual currents of Western man.
>
> 2. Throughout the middle ages and the Renaissance, higher education consisted of the *trivium* and the *quadrivium,* which were the two curricula of higher education.
>
> 3. The three liberal arts of grammar, rhetoric, and logic were what made up the *trivium,* while four liberal arts were included in the *quadrivium*—arithmetic, music, geometry, and astronomy.
>
> 4. The intellectual world, then, that we have inherited was shaped by the seven liberal arts, and rhetoric was a prominent member of the seven liberal arts.

5. We must inevitably take into account, when we think of the intellectual accomplishments of Bacon or the artistic accomplishments of Shakespeare, the milieu of ideas that produced them.

6. The history, for this reason, of rhetoric is an essential cultural subject.

WORDINESS

What is wrong with the following sentence?

Due to the fact that vacation intervened, I was not able to finish my lectures on Johnson.

The glaring problem is *due to the fact that,* which means nothing more than *because.* It is an invariable rule that good style uses as few words as possible to convey the entire meaning. Thus *become acquainted with* means *meet; attend an institution of higher learning* means *go to college; indulge in recreation* means *swim* or *play golf; the high-price spread* means *butter; keep up with correspondence* means *write letters.*

Good prose is direct and to the point; it is not loaded with *deadwood.*

Exercise. Prune the following sentences.

1. During the time that he was attending the university, he changed majors at least six times.

2. The yard is neat and trim in appearance.

3. Harvard is located in a city called Cambridge, Massachusetts.

4. Last summer, my family visited Paris, France.

5. The subject of the history of rhetoric has a logical consistency that makes an outline of main trends possible, feasible, and practicable.

6. In the centuries before the time that Aristotle lived, the subject of rhetoric flourished as a practical art necessary for coming out winner in law suits in the courts.

FINALLY

Good sentences make good style. Densely textured sentences bring meaningful relationships into being, relationships that make for subtlety and accuracy in the expression of ideas. Thinly textured sentences convey only thin ideas. Of course, there is no formula that will tell one how to write satisfactory sentences. The process is too infinitely complex to be boiled down to a set of rules that everyone can follow, step by step. If one is aware of the possibilities (and this chapter has attempted to bring about that awareness), he has a beginning. But success depends on practice. And practice involves not just writing, but also revising, a conscious effort to pack meaning into well constructed sentences. And practice involves another element as well: reading. Perhaps the process of learning to write mature sentences can be expressed by a cracked record: read write revise read write revise read write revise read write revise read write revise read write revise read write revise read write revise read write revise read write revise. . . .

V ☞ Punctuation

No aspect of English is more regular or more easily mastered than punctuation. But considering all of the time spent teaching it—and all of the futile results—one would think that punctuation is some kind of arcane mystery, revealed only to the select few, closed forever to the bemused layman. In the first place, a great many silly myths about punctuation have been promulgated, for instance, that the period represents a pause value of three, the semicolon a pause value of one, and the colon midway between. This is simply false. The system of punctuation presented in this chapter reflects modern *American* usage, but not necessarily modern British usage. The regularity of the system was first described by Harold Whitehall in his book *Structural Essentials of English* (New York: Harcourt, Brace and Company, 1951). All discussions of punctuation owe a debt to Professor Whitehall.

PUNCTUATION AND SPOKEN ENGLISH

Intonation—stress and pitch—in spoken English serve as a kind of oral punctuation. For instance, what mark of end punctuation should be used with the following sentence?

I am going to Chicago

The answer to that question depends on whether the sentence is spoken like this

ca
I am going to Chi
go.

or like this

go?
ca
I am going to Chi

A certain kind of intonation signals, "Coordination! More to come." Compare the way you say

ca
I am going to Chi
go.

with the way you say

cago, and   New
I am going to Chi   he is going to
York.

These transcriptions are not scientifically accurate, but they do illustrate the important point that intonation carries meaning in the spoken language and that there is some correspondence between intonation in the spoken language and punctuation in the written language. The advice that emerges from this principle is that the writer should rely in good part on his ear when he gropes for punctuation. He should read his sentences aloud, to hear how the "punctuation" sounds.

THE USES OF PUNCTUATION

In English, punctuation has four and *only* four functions. It

1. links
2. separates
3. encloses
4. shows omissions.

So we can speak of *linking, separating, enclosing,* and *omission* punctuation. Notice that the system of punctuation is contrastive; that is, one use does not overlap another. This makes for neatness, ease of explanation, and ease of understanding.

LINKING PUNCTUATION

The semicolon (;), colon (:), and dash (—) are what Whitehall calls symbolic conjunctions, for they can link clauses:

I saw the movie, and I liked it.
I saw the movie; I liked it.

The Use of the Semicolon.

(a) To link clauses that could be linked with conjunctions:

Nelly read *Bleak House;* she found it a bleak book.
No one volunteered; the task was too odious.

(b) To link items in a series that are themselves characterized by internal comma punctuation:

The candidates were James Smith, 25, Newport Beach; Jack Brown, 23, Huntington Beach; Mary Jones, 24, Costa Mesa; and Elizabeth Rex, 26, Westminster.

His favorite books were *Huckleberry Finn,* by Mark Twain; *Moby Dick,* by Herman Melville; *The Red Badge of Courage,* by Stephen Crane; and *The Scarlet Letter,* by Nathaniel Hawthorne.

The semicolon *always* comes outside of end quotation marks:

The chairman reported, "The treasury is utterly depleted"; however, the club had no need for funds.

The Use of the Colon. The colon is like an arrow pointing forwards; it directs attention to what follows it.

The punch included the following ingredients: gin, rum, brandy, bourbon, and a teaspoon of lemon juice.
There was only one way to describe the experiment: it was a failure.

The colon has certain conventional uses:

11:25 P.M.
Dear Sir:

The colon *always* comes outside of end quotation marks:

One thing is certain about "Byzantium": it is a masterpiece.

The Use of the Dash. The dash, one might say, is the opposite of the colon; the dash directs the reader's attention backwards, toward what precedes it:

Gin, rum, brandy, bourbon, and a teaspoon of lemon juice—these were the ingredients in the punch.

The dash shows unexpectedness, as when a surprise addition is made to a sentence:

She was beautiful—beautiful and utterly stupid.

The dash is used before the name of the author of a quote:

"Nothing can exceed the closeness with which the whole fits again into its germ."
—Henry James

The Use of the Hyphen. The hyphen links words and parts of words:

> the commander-in-chief
> a devil-may-care viewpoint.

The hyphen, of course, shows word division where part of a word is on one line and the other part on a following line, of which there are many examples in this book. The hyphen also

(a) links numbers from twenty-one to ninety-nine

> seventy-six trombones
> ninety-eight dollars

(b) links fractions

> one-half
> two-thirds

SEPARATING PUNCTUATION

The punctuation that separates sentences from each other—period, question mark, and exclamation point—needs little discussion. Perhaps the only confusion arises in the use of the question mark with direct quotations. Carefully study the following examples, and the problems of using the question mark will be solved:

> John said, "Are you going?"
> Did John say, "You are going"?
> Did John say, "Are you going"?

To summarize: If the interrogative element ("Are you going") is within the quotation marks, the question mark comes within them. If the interrogative element is in the introductory statement (Did John say), the question mark comes outside the quotation marks. If both the introductory statement (Did John say) and the quoted passage ("Are you going") are interrogative in form, the question mark comes outside the quotation marks.

The Use of the Separating Comma.

(a) To separate items in a coordinated series:

> The class studied Dryden, Swift, Pope, Gay, and Johnson.
> Either the first, the second, or the third must be the one.

(b) To separate coordinate clauses:

> Nothing came of his effort, but he tried again.
> Not only did we enjoy the concert, but the trip to town was beautiful.

(c) To separate initial adverbial modifiers from the rest of the sentence:

> After the ball was over, Mary took out her glass eye.
> (Mary took out her glass eye after the ball was over.)
> Without stopping to think, Father attacked the intruder.

(d) After an introductory element:

> That being the case, we decided not to go.
> John having arrived, the party got under way.

(e) After a vocative noun of address:

> Geoffrey, do your lessons.
> Mary, come here.

(f) After a transitional adverb:

> The dinner was good; however, the service was poor.
> We were anxious to arrive; nevertheless, we did not break the speed limit.

(g) After the introduction to a direct quotation:

> The girl said, "If only I had known."
> Marjory exclaimed, "Ah, to think that I missed seeing him."

(h) In certain conventional ways:

> Jan. 24, 1930
> Beulah Baxter, Salt Lake City, Utah
> *Moby Dick,* by Herman Melville.

Commas *always* come inside of end quotation marks:

> "If only I had known," the girl said.
> He's a "dingbat," no doubt, but inspired.

ENCLOSING PUNCTUATION

Enclosing punctuation always comes in pairs—as it must to enclose words, sentence elements, and sentences.

Enclosing Commas. These are used to enclose non-restrictive adjective clauses. Look carefully at the following:

> Cars *which have bad brakes* are dangerous.

The clause is *restrictive,* and hence it is not set off with commas. The sentence means something like this: "Not all cars have bad brakes, but those that do are dangerous." But

> Cars, which have bad brakes, are dangerous

means something like this: "All cars are dangerous, and all cars have bad brakes."

> Non-restrictive: This symphony, which we play over and over again, reminds me of my youth.
> Restrictive: The symphony which we play over and over again reminds me of my youth.

Paired commas are also used to set off interpolations:

> We decided, nonetheless, to buy the stereo.
> The troup resolved, in spite of hell and high water, to complete the march.

Enclosing Dashes. These function much like paired commas, and their use is a stylistic matter, not structural. If the writer feels that the material to be set off needs emphasis or is related to the main sentence only loosely, he may use dashes:

> Mark Twain—now just at the beginning of his literary apprenticeship —was a reporter for the *Territorial Enterprise.*

When the interpolated material has internal comma punctuation of its own, dashes are used for clarity:

> The group—George, Bill, Jack, and Tom—decided on a theater party.

Parentheses. These enclose so-called parenthetical expressions, sentence elements that enter as afterthoughts or as loosely related clarification:

> Enclosing dashes (the function of which is identical with that of paired commas) are used for purposes of style and emphasis.

And the use of parentheses is normally a stylistic choice.

Brackets. Their primary use is to set off interpolated material in quotes. Suppose, for instance, that in a direct quote pronoun reference is unclear; it can be explained by the insertion of an "antecedent" in brackets.

> "They [the members of Scriberus Club] were all devoted satirists."

In research writing, brackets have an important use. Suppose the quotation that the writer is copying contains an error. The writer must copy the quote as it is, but he does not want the reader to think that the error is his; he needs a way to show that the error was in the original quoted material. He does this by inserting *sic* (thus) in brackets:

> "The Misisipi [*sic*] is the longest river in America."

Quotation Marks.   Their primary use, of course, is to set off direct —not indirect!—quotations:

> He said, "I will go."
> He said that he would go.

They are used with caution to set off slang expressions, unfamiliar words, etc.

> The professor was a "slob."
> The term for the smallest meaningful unit speech is "phoneme."

The titles of poems, short stories, symphonies, essays, paintings, etc. are put in quotation marks:

> Robert Frost's "Stopping by the Woods on a Snowy Evening"
> "Uncle Wiggily in Connecticut," by J. D. Salinger
> Beethoven's "Eroica"
> Picasso's "Still Life with Orange"

Titles of plays or movies may be put in quotation marks or italics:

> "Hamlet"
> "Never on Sunday"
> *The Crucible*
> *Othello*

Titles of books and major works are underlined in writing and typing, italicized in printing:

> *The Encyclopaedia Britannica*
> *The Return of the Native*

Only the actual name of a newspaper is underlined or italicized, not the city in which it is published:

> Los Angeles *Times*
> Missoula *Hellgate Herald*

Names of magazines are underlined or italicized:

> *The Atlantic Monthly*
> *Life*
> *College English*

OMISSION PUNCTUATION

This shows omissions in words, phrases, and sentences. The apostrophe is included because originally that mark indicated the omission of a letter in a word.

The Apostrophe.   It is used for six purposes:

(a)   To precede the *s* in certain plurals (but not all plurals):

> You had better watch your p's and q's.
> He threw five 7's in a row.

(b)   To precede the *s* in the plurals of words that normally do not have plurals:

> His mother gave him a hundred don't's a day.
> All of his if's, and and's, and but's made me suspicious.

(c)   To show the genitive of plural nouns:

> the three girls' hats
> I prepared both classes' tests.

(d)   To show the genitive of singular nouns ending in *s*:

> Keats' "Endymion"
> Sophocles' plays

But sometimes the genitive *s* is added to nouns already ending in *s*:

> Ross's book
> the boss's orders

(e)   To form the genitive of group names:

> Schwarz and Rycenga's volume
> Merrill, Lynch, Pierce, Fenner, and Smith's report

(f)   To indicate abbreviations of dates:

> the class of '68
> in the year '79

Triple and Quadruple Periods.   These show omissions in quotations. Triple periods show the omission of any number of words from the middle of a sentence.

> *Original sentence*
> Scholars have been able to reconstruct a good deal of the pre-history of English and some other languages, in spite of the inconvenient absence of written records, complete with reliable dates.
> *Sentence with omission*
> "Scholars have been able to reconstruct a good deal of the pre-history of English . . . complete with reliable dates."

Quadruple periods indicate that something has been left off the conclusion of the sentence and that, possibly, any amount of material has been left out before the quotation resumes; that is, quadruple periods mean that some number of words have been omitted from the sentence in which they occur, but they can also mean that a sentence, a page, or several pages have been omitted before the quote resumes:

"Scholars have been able to reconstruct a good deal of the pre-history of English. . . ."

CONCLUSION

The student who understands this system in all its regularity should have little trouble with his punctuation, and mastering punctuation is worth the little effort that the job takes.

A word of warning: the dash does not substitute for any and all marks of punctuation. It is effective when used properly, but becomes an affectation when improperly used.

Anyone interested in a more detailed presentation of the system of punctuation may consult Chapter 10 in Harold Whitehall's *Structural Essentials of English.*

Exercise. Punctuate the following. Be ready to explain and justify your punctuation.

1. In the last election Brown Scott and Smith won
2. He was absent during most of the semester however he did well on the final
3. Seventy six trombones led the big parade
4. The sooner the better
5. The concert being over we left for home
6. To quote the *Times* More than ten thousand demonstrators thronged the square however I'm certain that that figure must be exaggerated
7. These people participated Sally Smith Burbank Joe Jones Anaheim Marian Bailey Huntington Park Arthur Wills Long Beach and David Malone Fullerton
8. These odes we might call them poems of meditation pleased eighteenth century readers
9. Men never make passes at girls who wear glasses
10. This idea to which no one responded at first turned out to be in the long run the most productive result of the conference
11. The restaurant is good but it is expensive
12. At least one half of the crop was lost in the freeze that is why the price of oranges has gone up

13. Moby Dick by Herman Melville A Clockwork Orange by Anthony Burgess and Tom Jones by Henry Fielding these are my favorite novels

14. Dear Sir At 7 00 p m I expect to arrive

15. I graduated in the class of 52

Explain the function of every mark of punctuation in the following passage:

In regard to I. A. Richards, one could go on at some length, for his works are seminal; however, in order to present a brief discussion that is at all fair, one must mention his stress on the operation of words in context—to my mind, at least, one of his most important contributions. In *The Philosophy of Rhetoric,* he asks this question: "What happens when we try with a sentence to decide what single words in it mean?" His answer is a discussion of "The Interinanimation of Words." His point is that it is utterly futile—if not destructive—to consider words out of context; indeed, we should consider as much of the total context as possible. Much of the value of this point he demonstrates in a penetrating analysis of a passage from Bacon. He concludes his chapter by saying, "As the movement of my hand uses nearly the whole skeletal system of the muscles and is supported by them, so a phrase may take its power from an immense system of supporting uses of other words in other contexts."

VI ✍ The Word

In the beginning was the Word, and the Word was with God, and the Word was God." This renowned passage from the Gospel of John reflects something of the mystery of words and the reverence man has always paid to them. The present chapter will be less than mysterious and slightly irreverent, but it will present some basic considerations about those fundamental *semantic* units, words.

Insofar as words mean (and, as we shall see, many of them contain only vestigial meaning), they do so in two ways. They have inherent meanings, much in the same way that a coin has a certain value because of the metal from which it is made. But words also gain and give meaning in relationship with other words in structures. Hence, it is a mistake to think of "word" as an isolable organism that can be studied in the "laboratory" away from the "environment," particularly if one is genuinely interested in *semantics* or what words mean and why.

The English word-stock can be divided into two categories: *function words* and *structure words*. The function words are *nouns, verbs, adjectives,* and *adverbs.* The structure words are the other parts of speech: pronouns, prepositions, conjunctions, modals, and so on.

FUNCTION WORDS AND STRUCTURE WORDS

The function words belong to *open classes,* which means that each class can and does gain new members and can and does lose old members. Nouns, for instance. New nouns are constantly entering the vocabulary, and within fairly recent years our language has acquired such additions as *beatnik, hippy, sputnik, rock 'n' roll, honky, Vietnik* (from *Time* magazine); *nylon, orlon, dacron* (coined by DuPont); *Platformate* and *Boron* (coined by oil companies); and countless more. *Astronaut* is not listed in the second edition of *Webster's New Collegiate Dictionary* (1956). The other open classes gain new members also.

Structure words belong to closed classes. (Just how many classes there are is currently a matter of conjecture.) If we make up a nonsense sentence, only our nouns, verbs, adjectives and adverbs will be invented "words"; the structure words will be drawn from the standard English vocabulary:

The sniddle *of my* crusk *may* hickle *a* grob, *but it cannot* nask *that* freb.

We feel somehow that structure words contain less meaning than function words. Prepositions, for instance, may contain vague meanings that we could call "direction," "location," "agency," and so on: *to* the store, *by* the lake, *with* the stick. Pronouns contain a certain increment of meaning also: *it* is singular and neuter while *she* is singular and feminine. But pronouns gain their full signification only in context when one can relate them to a noun.

In short, when we think of meanings, we think usually of function words rather than structure words.

HOW WORDS MEAN AND THE LIMITATIONS OF THE DICTIONARY

A common erroneous assumption is that one can find the complete meaning of a word by consulting a good dictionary. For instance, here is the definition of "eating" that *The Random House Dictionary* gives:

> *n.* 1. the act of a person or thing that eats. 2. food with reference to the quality it reveals when eaten: *This fish is delicious eating.* —*adj.* 3. good or fit to eat, esp. raw (distinguished from *cooking*): *eating apples.* 4. used in eating: *eating utensils.*

Superficially, this entry seems full. After a bit of thought, however, we can discover that the entry, illuminating though it might be, neglects much semantic data that is crucial to understanding the word "eating." Compare the two phrases eating apples

and

calculating machines

for instance. Since "eating" and "calculating" are obviously forms of verbs
(or, to put it another way, are derived from verbs), we might begin to
ask about the relationships between the nouns "apples" and "machines"
and the verbs that are coupled with them. Compare these two sentences:

Machines calculate.
*Apples eat.

Most speakers of English would probably feel that "calculating machines"
and "Machines calculate" stand in very close relationship with one another, but that "*Apples eat" somehow is the reverse of "eating apples."
Perhaps "eating apples" is very near to something like this: "Someone eats
apples." Our intuitive sense of the meanings that arise from word relationships is usually reliable, but when it fails us, we cannot turn to the
dictionary, for in this area of meaning even the best dictionary is blank.
Is "drinking water" related most closely to *Water drinks, Someone drinks
water, or Water is for drinking? Somehow that wonderful computer on
our shoulders sorts out the possibilities and, most often, leads us to the
right conclusion.

Dictionaries, then, seldom help us with the sum total of meaning
when one word is structured with another word or when five words are
structured with five other words or when ten words are structured with
ten more words. . . . Words meet, merge, and transcend themselves.

Furthermore, it would not be unreasonable to ask for two kinds of
dictionaries, one of the familiar sort that really means "dictionary" to most
people, and one of quite a different and exotic variety. For the sake of
simplicity, we will call the common garden variety a "dictionary" and for
the exotic plant use the synonymous term "lexicon." The lexicon would
explain why we feel that the following constructions are either downright
ungrammatical or at least metaphorical:

*rocks hate helplessness
*the elephant flowed through the jungle
*we see liberty

All function words have inherent *features* that will inevitably influence
the words that occur with them in structures. For instance, *rocks* has
these features:

(1)	it is a noun	+N
(2)	it is plural	−singular
(3)	it is a common noun	+common
(4)	it is inanimate	−animate

We might summarize with a lexical entry like this:

rocks
+N
−sing
+common
−animate

The verb *hate* also has inherent features. Among these are

+V
−sing
+or −common
+animate

This lexical entry tells us that *hate* is indeed a verb (+V), that it is plural (−sing), that it can take either a proper noun or a common noun as its subject (+ or −common), and that it must take an animate subject (+animate). It is grammatically understandable, then, that "Rocks [−animate] hate [+animate]" seems strange to us.

The nature of metaphor is in large part just exactly this strangeness. "We see liberty" seems metaphorical to us because the verb "see" has as a feature its ability to take a concrete or definite noun as an object; when an abstract or indefinite noun appears as the object, a metaphor comes into being.

In summary, the nature of meanings is complex, and the dictionary carries one only so far. True proficiency in the use of the language comes about from experience and a sensitivity to the way words interact. But there is indeed a "subject matter" for the study of words, a body of knowledge that has theoretical interest, and that also has the virtue of applicability in the student's own writing.

The discussion which follows will deal with three main topics: The Nature of Words, Diction, and Figures of Speech.

The Nature of Words

In *Language in Thought and Action*, S. I. Hayakawa said, "From the warning cry of primitive man to the latest newsflash or scientific monograph, language is social." This means that the whole business of language is to bring about cooperation and understanding among human beings. When we study language, we do so on the basis of some fundamental assumptions: that cooperation is better than conflict, that peace is better than war, that understanding is better than misunderstanding, and that the proficient and esthetic use of language is inherently better than the awkward and unesthetic use of language.

Since words do their work within the complex fabric of both linguistic structures and social structures, it should be worthwhile to know something about words as words and words as conveyers of meanings in the language community. It is toward this understanding that the following pages will move.

DENOTATION AND CONNOTATION

As everyone knows, words do not have one meaning, and one meaning only. A typical dictionary definition lists several meanings for most words.

> *mad* (mad) *adj. mad•der, mad•dest* 1. Suffering from or manifesting severe mental disorder; insane; lunatic; psychotic. 2. *Chiefly U.S. Informal* Feeling or showing anger; angry. 3. Going beyond the bounds of reason, decorum, or safety; wildly foolish; rash: a *mad* project. 4. Subject to an overpowering emotion; violently moved; unhinged: *mad* with grief. 5. turbulent and confused; extremely disordered: a *mad* jumble. . . .
> —*Standard College Dictionary*

Denotation is sometimes defined as "the dictionary definition," the base meaning of the word. Connotation is the associations that a word carries with it. Thus, all of the following words have roughly the same denotation: mad, crazy, nuts, psychotic, dingaling, disturbed, mentally unbalanced. But put some of them into a sentence, and see how they shift the meaning of that sentence:

> psychotic
> Mrs. Jones is nuts
> mentally unbalanced.

There is no point in talking about denotation as the "real" meaning of the word. A word has real meaning only in an extremely complex sense. Standing alone, a word has a variety of associations that cling to it and help make up its meaning. In context, the word gains other meanings from the interaction of word upon word. I. A. Richards appropriately terms this effect the "interinanimation of words." For example:

> winter
> the winter season
> the cold winter season
> the cold glistening winter season
> the cold glistening winter, season of good cheer

Some words have *pejorative* or unfavorable connotations, regardless of their contexts: think of the word "toilet," which in earlier centuries concerned the process of grooming oneself (and, perhaps, applying toilet water). If we now read that "Belinda sat at her toilet," we recognize the denotative meaning, but the unhappy connotations that cluster about the word cannot be forgotten.

The good writer is always aware of the connotations of the words that he uses; he strives for exactly the right shade of meaning, and in doing this, he plays with words, trying this one here and that one there until he achieves the shade of meaning that he wants.

Exercise.

1. Fill in the blanks left in the following paragraph from "The Pit and the Pendulum," by Edgar Allen Poe. In your choice of words, think of connotation: "The Pit and the Pendulum" is one of Poe's tales of horror. Be prepared to justify each choice that you make. Then turn to the original passage, and compare your choices with Poe's.

> There was another interval of _____ insensibility; it was brief; for, upon again _____ into life, there had been no _____ descent in the pendulum. But it might have been long—for I knew there were demons who took note of my swoon, and who could have arrested the vibration at pleasure. Upon my recovery, too, I felt very—oh, _____ sick and weak, as if through inanition. Even amid the agonies of that period, the human nature _____ for food. With _____ effort I outstretched my left arm as far as my bonds permitted, and took possession of the _____ remnant which had been spared me by the rats. As I put a portion of it within my lips, there _____ to my mind a half formed thought of joy—of hope. Yet what business had I with hope? It was, as I say, a half formed thought—man has many such which are never completed. I felt that it was of joy—of hope; but I felt also that it had perished in its formation. In vain I _____ to perfect—to regain it. Long suffering had nearly _____ all my _____ powers of mind. I was an imbecile—an _____.

LEVELS OF USAGE

It is fair to say that everyone with any degree of skill speaks not just one English language, but several. That is, we continually adjust our language to fit the occasion. Of course, the uneducated have less versatility than the educated, but, to a certain extent, everyone commands several levels of usage. The best way to define levels of usage is to illustrate them. But it is important to remember that any categories of usage are merely illustrative; they are not fixed and final, nor are they even very accurate. In general, however, we can say that the levels of usage are

> *Choice written*: the language of learned writing and extremely highbrow publications.
>
> *Choice spoken*: the language of formal lectures (such as most of those that you hear in your classes) and formal conversations.
>
> *General written*: the language of magazines; the language of most educated written discourse.
>
> *General spoken*: the "informal" usage of educated people when they talk.
>
> *Vulgate*: the language of the uneducated.

In *Understanding Grammar*, Paul Roberts illustrates the levels vividly and concisely:

> Choice written: I shall not return.
> Choice spoken: I'll not return.
> General written: I will not return.
> General spoken: I'm not coming back.
> Vulgate: I ain't coming back.

However, be it noted, the difference between choice written and general written and between choice spoken and general spoken is disappearing. For this development, we can thank whatever gods there be.

> *Exercise.* Find examples of the five levels of usage. For the choice written and general written, you can search through publications. For the choice spoken, you can go to records of speeches (but remember that many speeches are, in fact, readings of choice written scripts). For the general spoken, you will need to rely on your memory or your tape recorder. Of course, you never habituate places in which vulgate is spoken, but perhaps you can use your imagination and compose a fictitious transcription of a vulgate conversation.
>
> Now make as accurate a description as you can of the specific features of the samples you have found.

SYNONYMS

Synonyms, as you know, are words that mean approximately the same. (*Antonyms* are words with opposite meanings.) But no two words mean exactly the same. One reason that there can never be exact synonyms is connotation; no two words ever have exactly the same connotation. Nonetheless, the rich stock of synonyms in English is one of its great advantages, enabling the writer to achieve fine shades of meaning in an extensive variety.

One reason for the large stock of synonyms is the tendency of English to borrow words from other languages: Anglo-Saxon *house,* Latin *domicile,* and Spanish *casa.* In the following pairs of adjectives, the first word is from the native stock, and the second is borrowed: hearty/cordial, deadly/mortal, bloody/sanguinary, motherly/maternal, lively/vivacious, watery/aqueous.

Exercise.

1. From which language or languages were the second items in the above series borrowed?

2. Which is more appropriate to everyday usage, hearty or cordial, deadly or mortal, etc.? Why?

Diction

Good diction consists of proper words *for the occasion.* The diction of an address to Phi Beta Kappa would not be good diction in a dorm bull session. The diction of the pool hall (not the billiards parlor!) is perfectly good diction in the pool hall. The diction of a learned treatise is not appropriate diction for an informal essay.

Exercise. Carefully read these two passages from different articles in the same publication (*Calendar,* Los Angeles *Times,* Dec. 17, 1967).

> LONDON—*"The Mousetrap—16th Mind-Boggling Year"—advertisement in the Daily Telegraph.*
>
> Made me sit up, that ad did. Where have I been these last 16 mind-boggling years that I haven't seen "The Mousetrap," a play by Agatha Christie that opened when Truman was president? So I went. Let me tell you about "The Mousetrap." But first . . .
>
> Have you heard that very funny American comedian who opens a parody radio news program with the words: "Russia and the United States have declared nuclear war. Washington is in flames. News of that and other things in a moment. But first . . ."
>
> Where was I? Oh, yes, "The Mousetrap." Well, scarcely had "The Mousetrap" got into its 16th mind-boggling year when BBC sent out a man with a tape recorder to interview people in Picadilly and so forth. "Have you seen 'The Mousetrap'?" "No." "You sir, have you . . ." "No, and I don't intend to." And so forth for five

minutes. "Two million people have seen 'The Mousetrap' but we couldn't find any of them," said the BBC.

> —John Crosby, "Nobody Knows
> How to Build a Better 'Mouse-
> trap'"

These two books [*The Early Shakespeare,* by A. C. Hamilton and *Tudor Historical Thought,* by F. J. Levy] are a timely reminder that the Huntington Library is considerably more than the collection of pretty gardens and prettier pictures known to tourists. As one of the world's great repositories of humanistic knowledge, it has also served, through its publications, as a disseminator of that knowledge in ways that have radically altered our understanding of Shakespeare and the world of Elizabeth I. Both of the present works will add to the Huntington reputation in this respect.

In "The Early Shakespeare," Prof. Hamilton argues that the plays from "Henry VI" through "Midsummer Night's Dream" can stand on their own not as beginner's work but as steps in Shakespeare's own conscious working out of artistic principles that governed his entire career.

> —James E. Phillips, "Library
> Scholarship Noted in Shake-
> speare's, Elizabeth's World"

1. Briefly characterize the audiences for which you think each of these pieces was intended.

2. Contrast the vocabulary of the two pieces, and explain why the choice of words in each seems to be appropriate to the audiences.

3. Briefly explain what you think the purpose of each essay was.

The foregoing exercise should have demonstrated something to you, namely, that you are tremendously sensitive to diction, even though you might never have analyzed the reasons for what you know intuitively. Now it should be interesting to make a detailed analysis of why we tend to sense when *proper words* are in proper places.

NATURALNESS AND APPROPRIATENESS

As the foregoing discussion implied, good diction is a relative matter. A word, a phrase, or a sentence appropriate to one situation is inappropriate for another. Slang, for instance, can be both vivid and playful, but it is not effective in certain speech and writing situations. To repeat an idea that has appeared in this book again and again: the writer must adjust his discourse to his intended audience and to his purpose, a process which demands that the essay (or whatever) be written for someone or some group. Achieving appropriateness presupposes that the writer knows, in general at least, who his readers are likely to be.

The main cause of unnaturalness in discourse is the use of "big" or unfamiliar words where short, familiar words would do. Samuel Johnson defined "network" as "Any thing reticulated or decussated, at equal distances, with interstices between the intersections." The diction of that statement is highly unnatural. Beginning writers often feel that big words decorate their prose and make for impressiveness, but that is seldom the case, for idolatric philogyny in relevancy to cerebral valetudinarianism is not a philistinic cogency in oppugnancy to meliorism.

Unnaturalness arises not only from the words used, but from the ordering of sentence elements. Fortunately, almost everyone has a high degree of "sentence sense," so that he can recognize unnaturalness even though he might not be able to explain it. The problem, then, is wrestling with the sentences that one writes until they sound natural.

It might be possible to speak of a "naturalness-appropriateness" ratio. The more appropriate one's diction is, the more natural it will sound.

For instance,

> In a funeral oration: "Our dearly beloved friend has kicked the bucket."
>
> My wife calls out, "Who's there?" If I reply, "It is I," she assumes that I'm attempting to be mildly humorous, for the situation calls for the less formal "It's me."

These examples of inappropriateness are also examples of unnaturalness.

A further question arises: Is unnatural language always inappropriate? To answer this question, we might think of the "unnatural" usage in prayers: "Our Father Who art in Heaven, hallowed be Thy name. . . ." This special language of ceremony is definitely not the currency of everyday speech, and yet it is singularly appropriate to its own occasion. For language can be ceremonial and function, analogically, like priestly vestments or other signs of office. Writing for a highly rarefied audience, the Elizabethan court, John Lyly used an artificial language that was both effective and appropriate:

> But how should she be persuaded of my loyalty, that yet had never one simple proof of my love? Will she not rather imagine me to be entangled with her beauty, than with her virtue. That my fancy being so lewdly changed at the first, will be as lightly changed at the last, that there is nothing which is permanent that is violent? Yes, yes, she must needs conjecture so, although it be nothing so, for by how much the more my affection cometh on the sudden, by so much the less will she think it certain. The rattling thunderbolt hath but his clap, the lightning but his

flash, and as they both come in a moment, so do they both end in a minute.

The rule of thumb concerning naturalness and appropriateness in diction might be the following: be true to yourself as a writer, but keep the audience and occasion in mind.

Exercise. Point out and eliminate the unnaturalness in the following sentences.

1. In the extended chronology of the terraqueous globe *homo sapiens* has proffered many rationalizations for slaughter in armed conflicts.

2. The conduct of the bellicosity was virtually guaranteed not to bring victory.

3. On the *pater familias* reposes the responsibility of bringing sustenance to the hearthside.

4. The class, to complete its required work, needed three extra sessions.

SLANG

Everyone knows what slang is, and it can be extremely vivid. However, nothing has so short a life as today's slang, for tomorrow it will be ossified and put on display in museums (such as the present discussion). College slang is an aspect of language that changes with every new crop of freshmen. As this is being written, at the University of Southern California bubble-gummer (a student who goes out with high school girls), Mickey Mouse course, ace (A), and gut course are current. By the time the book gets in print, those terms will undoubtedly be passé.

Exercise.

1. Make a list of the slang expressions that are current on your campus.

2. Analyze the effectiveness of the slang in the following passage:

FLASH°#! ZAP/°! POW#°! !

L.A. is only a couple of weeks away from a 24-hour FM-stereo Adult Rock station. This is the first announcement anywhere. Pasadena's Presbyterian Church outlet, KPPC, has been bought up by the owners of San Francisco's hippiest FM station, KMPX, and a new pop music arsenal is being installed. Last spring KMPX escaped from its foreign language scheduling with a midnight-six a.m. Adult Rock shift.

The night rock was held down by Larry Miller, probably the most refreshing deejay on the West Coast. Miller is the Charley Brown of D.J.'s, he gulps and bubbles, and almost wags his tail with gratitude when a new sponsor kicks in.

—Nat Freedland, Los Angeles
Free Press, November 10, 1967

COLLOQUIALISM

A colloquialism is a word or phrase that would be more likely to appear in informal spoken English than in formal or general written English. "He was a goner" would be classed as colloquial, as would, probably, *hi-fi, Coke, buck* (meaning dollar). At one end of the scale colloquialisms merge imperceptibly with slang. Is *dough,* meaning money, colloquial or slangy? Many colloquialisms are also extremely trite: to burn the midnight oil, to keep one's nose to the grindstone, to have a bull session.

In a passage characterized by formal diction, the colloquialism *stands out like a sore thumb*. Even in general usage, the *frosh* who intersperses his serious prose with colloquialisms is likely to annoy his reader.

Exercise. Make a list of the colloquialisms that you commonly use. Try to distinguish the fine line between slang and colloquialism.

EUPHEMISMS

These are "softened" expressions used to avoid the unpleasant connotations of the words or phrases that they replace. Thus, *die* becomes *pass away; mortuary* becomes *funeral home;* and *cemetery* becomes *memorial park.* Euphemisms abound wherever the subject is unpleasant or indelicate. *Toilet* becomes *rest room* and then *powder room. Cancer* becomes *lingering disease.* Many euphemisms are simply too coy to have any effect but stiltedness: "Could you direct me to *the little boy's room?"*

Choosing the right euphemism at the right time involves the same sensitivity to language that other matters of diction do. And the right euphemism depends on time and place.

Exercise. Name at least one euphemism for each of the following words and phrases: syphilis, prison, underwear, lie (the noun), stink, garbage, vermin, gambling game, stripteaser, bar, soup, mush, drunk, dandruff, fat, failure, bad breath.

IDIOMS

The word "idiom" has two meanings. It can signify those expressions that typify the language spoken (as when we say, "Even though he comes from Italy, he speaks perfectly good idiomatic English"), or it can signify phrases that have come to be accepted in the language, but that are often a bit slangy. Into the first category fall such locutions as "He went to bed"; there is no reason why we shouldn't say, "He went to the bed," except that "He went to bed" is idiomatic, the way the language is. Into the second category fall such locutions as "act one's age," "fall into disfavor," "take after one's parents," "make a match," and so on.

> *Exercise.* You might like to speculate about the nature of idioms. For instance, we might say that "Mary approved of Joe" is perfectly idiomatic English, and so is "Mary went to New York." But "*Mary approved to Joe" and "*Mary went of New York" are not idiomatic English. In what respect are idioms grammatical—that is, in what ways do idioms depend on grammar? Is the idiom "make a match" a matter of grammar or not? Is the idiom "go to bed" a matter of grammar or not?

NEOLOGISMS

Interesting facets of the English vocabulary are the neologisms or newly coined words that enter it and frequently remain with it. As we have seen, there are four open classes among the parts of speech: nouns, verbs, adjectives, and adverbs (including interjections). These classes are constantly gaining and losing members. Some of the neologisms that we have already encountered are *nylon, orlon,* and *dacron.* Many trade names are neologisms that have become part of the language: Frigidaire, Bandaid, Coke. The names of the newly discovered elements are also neologisms: Einsteinium, Lawrencium.

COUNTER WORDS

Counter words are general terms of approval or disapproval that usually also have other, more precise applications: The meal was *fair* / His complexion was *fair.* The so-called *intensifiers* are often counter words: It was *very* good / The girl was *quite* pretty / The movie was *pretty* good. These intensifiers, through overuse, have lost their ability to intensify, so that "He was interested" is a stronger statement than "He was very interested." In general, overuse deprives words of their force.

FOREIGN WORDS

The English word stock comes to a great extent from borrowing, so that many common words in the English language are of foreign origin, and this process of borrowing goes on continually. Some words borrowed since the Second World War are *blitzkrieg, kamikaze, Volkswagen, apartheid, flak* (from *Flugzeugabwehrkanone*), *banzai, macht nichts* (usually pronounced *mock nix*), and *Nazi* (from *Nationalsozialist*). English has borrowed and continues to borrow from virtually all other languages. From the French: *chauffeur, cuisine, hors d'oeuvres, garage.* From the Italian: *spaghetti, ciao* (pronounced *chow*), *salami, macaroni, lasagna.* From the Japanese: *kimono, harikari, saki.* From the Spanish: *rodeo, ranch, tamale, plaza.* And so on. A study[1] of the origin of the 1,000 most frequently used words in English vividly shows the heterogeneous nature of our vocabulary:

Of Old English origin	61.7%
French	30.9
Latin	2.9
Scandinavian	1.7
Mixed	1.3
Uncertain	1.3
Low German and Dutch	0.3

Some words, however, become naturalized, while others retain their foreign aura. We scarcely sense that *garage* or *egg* (from the Scandinavian) is not a native English word, but *femme de chambre* or *weltanschauung* or *antepasto*, though used with some frequency, sound a bit exotic.

The writer striving for naturalness and ease will use foreign words only with the greatest care, and never for ostentation. Some foreign words convey meanings that are hard to arrive at with native words. For instance, the German *Gestalt* is extremely useful in some contexts; it means, according to the *Standard College Dictionary*, "A functional configuration or synthesis of separate elements of emotion, experience, etc., that constitutes more than the mechanical sum of the parts."

Foreign words and phrases that have not yet been "naturalized" are generally printed in italics and underlined in typing and handwriting. Your dictionary will guide you in your italicization. (*Webster's Collegiate* puts parallel lines in front of words to be italicized, thus || femme de chambre.)

---

[1]Edward L. Thorndike, *The Teacher's Word-Books*, cited in Stuart Robertson and Frederic G. Cassidy, *The Development of Modern English* (Englewood Cliffs, N.J.: Prentice-Hall, Inc., 1954), p. 155.

Exercise. In a good dictionary, look up the derivations (the etymologies) of the italicized words in the following passage:

All *assemblies* of *gaiety* are brought together by *motives* of the same kind. The *Theatre* is not *filled* with those that *know* or *regard* the *skill* of the *Actor*, nor the Ball-*room* by those who dance, or attend to the dancers. To all places of general *resort*, where the standard of *pleasure* is *erected*, we *run* with *equal* eagerness, for very different reasons.

—Samuel Johnson

OBSOLETE AND ARCHAIC WORDS

The open classes of words are in a state of flux. New words enter the vocabulary. Others move toward the fringes of usefulness, then beyond usefulness, and finally, in effect, out of the lexicon. An old-fashioned word, on the fringes of use and usefulness, is called archaic; a word that remains in the lexicon, but that is never used in modern language is obsolete. An example of a word that has completely disappeared from the modern lexicon is Old English *gied*, meaning "song." An example of an obsolete word is *mistress* in the sense of *Mrs*. An archaic word that still lingers on the fringes of the lexicon is *forsooth*.

Of course, the writer must avoid the use of archaisms and obsolete words, except for special effects such as humor.

Exercise. The following is a passage from John Milton's "Of Education" (1644). In it, find words that (1) have become obsolete, at least in the sense in which Milton uses them; (2) words that have become archaic; (3) words that have disappeared from the lexicon.

. . . I shall detain you no longer in the demonstration of what we should not do, but straight conduct ye to a hillside, where I will point ye out the right path of a virtuous and noble education; laborious indeed at the first ascent, but else so smooth, so green, so full of goodly prospect and melodious sounds on every side, that the harp of Orpheus was not more charming. I doubt not but ye shall have more ado to drive our dullest and laziest youth, our stocks and stubs [ungifted students], from the infinite desire of such a happy nurture, than we have now to haul and drag our choicest and hopefulest wits to that asinine feast of sow-thistles and brambles which is commonly set before them, as all the food and entertainment of their tenderest and most docible age.

MALAPROPISMS

The word *malapropism* comes from the character Mrs. Malaprop in Sheridan's play *The Rivals*. Mrs. Malaprop is one of many figures in literature whose humor arises from using proper words in *improper places*. Malapropisms are death in prose; they destroy the reader's confidence in the writer and make for laughs in the wrong places.

> *Exercise.* The following is one of Mrs. Malaprop's speeches. Find the malapropisms, and substitute the right words for them.

> I would by no means wish a daughter of mine to be a progeny of learning; I don't think so much learning becomes a young woman; for instance, I would never let her meddle with Greek, or Hebrew, or algebra, or simony, or fluxions, or paradoxes, or such inflammatory branches of learning—neither would it be necessary for her to handle any of your mathematical, astronomical, diabolical instruments.—But, Sir Anthony, I would send her at nine years old, to a boarding-school, in order to learn a little ingenuity and artifice. Then, sir, she should have a supercilious knowledge in accounts; —and as she grew up, I would have her instructed in geometry, that she might know something of the contagious countries;—but above all, Sir Anthony, she should be mistress of orthodoxy, that she might not misspell, and mispronounce words so shamefully as girls usually do; and likewise that she might reprehend the true meaning of what she is saying. This, Sir Anthony, is what I would have a woman know;—and I don't think there is a superstitious article in it.

JARGON

One meaning of "jargon" is, according to the *Standard College Dictionary,* "a colorless, yellowish, leaf-green, or smoky variety of zircon. . . ." In language, jargon is a colorless, yellowish, leaf-green, or smoky variety of language used by the in-groups of the professions. In jargon, brothers and sisters become "siblings," friendships become "interpersonal relationships," and holding hands becomes "interdigitation." In jargon, flat feet become *pes planus,* and the maternity ward is "OB." Elsewhere, I have said,

> Commentator after commentator tells us that we are in the age of jargon just as surely as we are in the atomic age. The danger of our jargonism is not that it prevents communication. In fact, I suspect that the learned jargons serve the . . . purpose of catching the listener's ear. The sociologist responds to his own cherished language when he hears it, as do the linguist, the critic, the physicist, and the educationist to theirs. Jargon does, however, tend to isolate scholars. . . .[2]

Jargon can also be a smokescreen behind which the person with little to say can hide.

---

[2]*Rhetoric: a Synthesis* (New York: Holt, Rinehart and Winston, Inc., 1968), p. 85.

Exercise. Just for the fun of it, you might like to do a parody of several jargons. Take a well-known, brief story ("The Story of the Three Bears," for instance), and translate it into various jargons. You can get samples of jargons from learned journals in the various disciplines.

TRITENESS

Triteness is the use of shopworn (or worn out) language and ideas. The following are trite expressions: fit as a fiddle, fat and sassy, pretty as a picture, dog-tired, it takes a heap o' livin' to make a house a home, sharp as a razor (or a tack). Some triteness comes from individual words in expressions: a *perfectly wonderful* dinner, an *amazingly good* performance. And words have an odd way of leaping into prominence so that they are used, re-used, and overused. At the present time, it seems that everyone has *charisma,* and, furthermore, almost everyone in the business of education is working on a *heuristic* model. Sometimes people get so caught up in trite ideas that they can never escape into clear, original thinking: all mothers are kind, the dog is man's best friend, children are curious, and so on. "To be or not to be" was fresh and original when Shakespeare wrote it; now it is trite.

GOBBLEDYGOOK

In an article in *Psychology Today* (Nov. 1968), Brendan Maher quotes this passage, written by a schizophrenic:

> The subterfuge and the mistaken planned substitutions for that demanded American action can produce nothing but the general results of negative contention and the impractical results of careless applications, the natural results of misplacement, of mistaken purpose and unrighteous position, the impractical serviceabilities of unnecessary contradictions. For answers to this dilemma, consult Webster.

This is a perfect example of gobbledygook, language characterized by circumlocution, evasion, wordiness, pseudo-scientific vocabulary, and general fuzziness. ("Gobbledygook" and "governmentese" are nearly synonymous.) The writer who wants to use language as a smokescreen becomes slightly schizoid and lapses into gobbledygook. George Orwell gives a striking example in his essay "Politics and the English Language." He quotes the well-known passage from *Ecclesiastes*:

> I returned and saw under the sun, that the race is not to the swift, nor the battle to the strong, neither yet bread to the wise, nor yet riches to men of understanding, nor yet favour to men of skill; but time and chance happeneth to them all.

Then Orwell translates the lovely, vivid passage into gobbledygook:

> Objective consideration of contemporary phenomena compels the conclusion that success or failure in competitive activities exhibits no tendency to be commensurate with innate capacity, but that a considerable element of the unpredictable must invariably be taken into account.

Notice that the original passage is direct and vivid; it is concrete; it uses examples to establish meaning. The haziness of the rewrite comes not merely from its penumbra of words, but also from its failure to be concrete.

Exercise. Translate the following gobbledygook into English.

1. Due to the fact that the generation of current has become increasingly expensive, and due to the fact that the cost of generating such current is passed on to the consumer, employees are respectfully requested to terminate illumination when it is not needed.

2. It is injudicious to enumerate one's expectations when they are yet in the embryonic stage of development.

3. Because unforeseen contingencies may well alter current estimates of future necessities, it is highly advisable to take precautionary measures before the unanticipated events arrive.

4. And here is a paragraph from, no less, *The National Interest and the Continuing Education of Teachers,* published by the National Council of Teachers of English:

> Today a preponderance of federal funds expended on higher education goes to support scientific and technological training. The nation must of course be concerned with its technological growth, with the health and safety of its people. In technology, our nation can afford to be second to none. Obviously we must seek to improve the quality of our mathematical and scientific education. Disease strikes us all, constantly reminding us of the need for biological and medical education and research.
>
> —Francis Keppel

How do you react to the locution "Today a preponderance of federal funds expended on higher education"? Does it have any advantages over "Today most of the money spent on higher education"? In your translation, think about boiling ideas down and avoiding repetitiveness.

JOURNALESE

Some diction is so cute or so strained that it soon bores any reader. Sports columns are notorious for their endless repetition of catch-phrases and clichés. The characteristic of journalese is its lack of naturalness, its straining to be clever. The following, from *Variety*, is an extreme example:

> THE MADISON AVE. tv turf fraternities—with their eyes on the Nielson totes and their ears bent to the networks' touts—have already started (much earlier than in previous years) to shell out what is expected to be a record budget for 1964-65. And with the rustle of the advertisers' long green, there's an excitement and electricity similar to that which builds up in front of the pari-mutuel windows before the first race of the "Big A."

Here is another example:

> *Kings Finally Score,*
> *But Still Lose, 5-2*
>
> Like amnesia victims, the Kings suddenly remembered what hockey was all about during the second period of Saturday night's clash of National Hockey League's division leaders at Long Beach Arena.
>
> Unfortunately, Boston held a 3-0 lead at the time and the Eastern pacesetters skated off with a 5-2 victory before 6,510 fans. The Kings, in falling out of first place in the West, also fell back into their lethargy in the final period to allow Boston the win.
>
> The Kings cut that early Bruin Bulge to 3-2 by the end of the fast, rough second period as they snapped a string of seven scoreless periods. But two goals by Derek Stanfield within two minutes in the third period assured the brawling Bruins the win and pushed their Eastern lead to two points over Chicago.
>
> —Los Angeles *Times*, December 17, 1967

Exercise. Briefly answer the following questions:

1. What effect do "shell out" and "long green" in the first selection have?

2. Does the first example sound artificial? If so, explain why.

3. If you follow the sports columns, point out the aspects of the second selection that would typify it as journalese. (Look up the meaning of alliteration if you don't already know it.) Are there any words that occur again and again in sports reports?

4. Examine the society columns of your local newspaper. Are they characterized by any kind of journalese?

FIGURES OF SPEECH

One of the characteristics of language is that it offers many alternatives in the expression of ideas; it has infinite variety, and hence the capability of great subtlety and freshness. A figure of speech, as the *Standard College Dictionary* says, "intentionally deviates from or abandons altogether the normal, literal meanings of words so as to create a more vivid or fanciful effect. . . ." Thus, I can say, "He is not very brave," or I can use a metaphor and say, "He's afraid of his own shadow." Other figures of speech are simile, irony, overstatement, understatement. And the list goes on and on.

Some figures of speech rely entirely on the thought and the way they express it; that is, these figures of speech do not employ unusual constructions or methods of figurativeness that are structurally identifiable. Simile can be recognized because it employs *like* or *as*: She was *like* a rose in bloom. But metaphor does not employ any structural devices: She was a rose.

So revelatory of the ways of language are figures of speech that the following sections will deal with them in detail. It is not important to memorize the tongue-twisting names of the figures of speech; the important thing is to concentrate on the principles of language that they illustrate. But everyone ought to be able to name, illustrate, and recognize metaphor, simile, and irony.

> *Exercise.* All exercises follow the discussion of the figures of speech.

Metaphor. The metaphor is at the very heart of language. In fact, it is possible to argue that all language is metaphorical. If we turn to a construct, we can see the rationale of the above statement. All language situations involve three elements: REFERENT SYMBOL MEANING. The referent is whatever the symbol refers to. The meaning is whatever the symbol conveys. The *referent* is now standing in a pasture in Montana chewing its cud. The *symbol* is C O W. The meaning is a complex of associations, both connotative and denotative, that the symbol C O W causes in the mind of the person who sees it. A language symbol, then, conveys a complex of meanings that adhere to cows in general, the cow in the Montana pasture, and one's experience with cows. The symbol is not the cow, but an intermediary device, for the conveyance of meaning.

The metaphor is much the same. I. A. Richards points out that metaphor has *vehicle* and *tenor*. The vehicle is the locution itself; the tenor is the complex of meaning conveyed. So that we can speak of "Sue is a cow" as both vehicle and tenor. The vehicle has a literal and structural meaning. But the literal meaning is of no value; obviously, the locution does not mean that "Sue is standing in a Montana pasture chewing her cud"—or we should hope that it doesn't. The metaphor brings about a comparison and a transference of meanings, as in "Life is but a walking shadow, a poor player who struts and frets his hour upon the stage, and is heard no more."

The basic quality of metaphor is best illustrated by the so-called *dead metaphors,* locutions in which the tenor has been lost: the *face* of the clock, the *leg* of the table, the *arm* of the chair, the *branch* of the service. These metaphors have become so much a part of the language that we do not think of them as metaphorical at all. The metaphors that bring language and ideas into a vivid new life are those that are fresh, original, and appropriate. One can find them by the thousands—or the hundreds of thousands—in any collection of poetry or prose:

> The bell-beat of their wings. . . .
> —William Butler Yeats

> . . . the last fingers of leaf / Clutch and sink into the wet bank.
> —T. S. Eliot

> The glassy lapses of uncloven time.
> —Richard Eberhart

> O unmannerable heart, / monk-dancer, be still, / be leashless, apart. . . .
> —R. P. Blackmur

> Love at the lips was touch / As sweet as I could bear. . . .
> —Robert Frost

> what if a much of a which of a wind / gives the truth to summer's lie. . . .
> —E. E. Cummings

> Her fist of a face died clenched on a round pain. . . .
> —Dylan Thomas

This list was gathered at random, and in a very short time with virtually no selectivity, from an anthology of poetry.

But what about prose? Is it unmetaphorical? Look at almost any passage of prose, and see what you find—the following, for instance:

> Jazz rhythms create what can only be called *momentum.* When the rhythms of one *voice* (say the trumpet, off on a rhythmic and melodic *excursion*) *lags behind* the underlying beat, its four-beat measure carries over beyond the end of the underlying beat's measure into the succeeding one, which has already begun. Conversely, when the trumpet *anticipates* the beat, it starts a new measure before the steady underlying beat has ended one. And the result is an exhilarating *forward motion* which the jazz trumpeter Wingy Manone once described as "feeling an increase in tempo though you're still playing the same tempo." Hence the importance in jazz of timing, and hence the delight and amusement of the so-called "break," in which the basic 4/4 beat ceases and a soloist goes off on a *flight* of rhythmic and melodic *fancy* which nevertheless comes back surprisingly and unerringly *to encounter* the beat precisely where it would have been if it had kept going. [Italics mine.]
> —John A. Kouwenhoven

Is this prose metaphorical, or is it not? In order to answer that question, look carefully at the italicized passages. And the following sentence in the same essay just caught my eye: " 'There now; that ties off all loose ends; I'm going to stop now; done; finished; concluded; signed, sealed, and delivered.' "

The same conclusion holds true for virtually all prose. Prose is metaphorical.

Sometimes unfortunately so.

The person who told me, "You threw a wrench into the monkey-works" had garbled her metaphor terribly, as did the student who talked about making a cow's purse out of a pig's ear. Somewhere I encountered this one (concerning *The Scarlet Letter*): Hester wore a scarlet A, while Dimmesdale put on a false front.

In other words, to serve their purpose, metaphors must be appropriate. *Mixed metaphors* are ludicrous: The *Iron Curtain* is a *wall* between the communist world and the free states. He needed a great deal of *backbone to stand up to* his professor. She was so kind that every time she opened her mouth, you could see her heart. The flower of love grew in her breast.

Simile.   Similes are like metaphors, except that the simile uses *like* or *as* to identify the relationship between tenor and vehicle. She was *like* a rose. He was *as* brave *as* a lion. The effect of the simile is not as potent as that of the metaphor. A good metaphor engages the reader in a strange and wonderful way; a good simile does not make him participate as much as does the metaphor, and hence the effect is less.

Irony.   On its least subtle level, irony is saying one thing and meaning another: He's really a genius (of the student who flunked Basket Weaving 101); That's a terrible tragedy (of a man who misses the monthly PTA meeting); She's really a doll (of the least desirable girl on campus).

The reason for irony's effect is much like that of humor. Humor must always engage the reader's participation; if it does not, the effect vanishes. That is, if you must explain a joke to the hearer, he does not participate, does not gain the sudden flash of insight and cognizance, and hence does not laugh. The following stunner, for example: Q. Why wouldn't the moron yell through the screen door? A. He was afraid of straining his voice. The humor—such as it is—of this joke lies in the pun on the word *straining*. If the hearer does not get the pun and the relationship must be explained, there is no humor. In irony, one ostensibly says one thing, but actually means another. The hearer or reader must perceive this relationship himself or there is no ironic effect.

In fact, metaphor works in somewhat the same way. The relationship between tenor and vehicle must be perceived. When it is, that perception brings about a kind of shock of recognition that is both powerful and highly satisfying.

Probably the most frequently quoted and famous piece of irony in the English language is Jonathan Swift's "A Modest Proposal." In this piece, Swift ironically argues that the children of Ireland should be used for food, bred and slaughtered like cattle. Such a course, Swift ironically says, would alleviate Ireland's problems of starvation and overpopulation.

> I am assured by our merchants that a boy or a girl before twelve years old is no salable commodity; and even when they come to this age they will not yield above three pounds, or three pounds and half a crown at most on the Exchange; which cannot turn to account either to the parents or the kingdom, the charge of nutriment and rags having been at least four times that value.
>
> I shall now therefore humbly propose my own thoughts, which I hope will not be liable to the least objection.
>
> I have been assured by a very knowing American of my acquaintance in London, that a young healthy child well nursed is at a year old a most delicious, nourishing, and wholesome food, whether stewed, baked, or broiled; and I make no doubt that it will equally serve in a fricassee or a ragout.

Other Figures of Speech. The following list (with examples) is illustrative of some of the figurative possibilities of language.

Alliteration. Repetition of the initial sound or letter of successive words: a *l*ovely *l*ake *l*ying in the valley.

Anadiplosis. Repetition of an important word contained in one clause in a succeeding clause: Fight to be *free*, but be *free* of fear.

Anaphora. Beginning a series of clauses with the same word or sound: The protest was futile, the protest was ill advised, and the protest was soon dissolved.

Antithesis. Vividly contrasting ideas: Man proposes, but God disposes; Art is long, but life is short.

Antonomasia. Using an epithet, usually with ironic intent: The blowhard; The sorehead; A Hitler.

Apophasis. Protesting that one will not mention a subject, and in the act of protesting, introducing the subject anyway: I won't even speak of the time that he deserted his wife and children; Let's not mention the fact that he is a convicted felon.

Aporia. Pretending to hesitate between choosing one of two alternatives: Whether he is overly prudent or merely penurious is hard to say; Should we call him unreliable or just plain untrustworthy?

Asyndeton. Leaving out "particles," *i.e.*, conjunctions and articles: The river roared down a canyon, it eddied into a calm pool, the salmon jumped, the ruffed grouse drummed its startling tattoo.

Auxesis. Exaggeration through the use of a weighted term for the accurate one: She was an angel out of the blue; He was an absolute Beelzebub; The teacher was a Job in his patience.

Chiasmus. Reversing the order of terms in adjacent clauses: Ask not what your country can do for you; ask what you can do for your country. Let learning bring light, and let light bring learning.

Climax. A form of "progressive" repetition of words or sounds: Work brings hope, and hope brings joy, and joy brings contentedness.

Comparison. The almost exact matching of clauses: If you love learning, you will be rewarded by knowledge, but if you love riches, you will be stricken by pride.

Dilemma. Presenting two sides of a question, each of which makes the other impossible: If Smith tries hard enough, he may succeed, but if he succeeds, then he won't have to try so hard.

Dissimile. Pointing out the nature of something by showing how dissimilar it is to other things: You can't take your wealth with you, but grace goes on forever.

Epistrophe. Emphasizing a point by ending several sentences in the same way: The girls put on eye makeup. They put on lip makeup. They put on face makeup. They put on every imaginable kind of makeup. They are completely made up.

Hirmos. Emphasizing by including a long series of appositives: The audience—men and women, boys and girls, rich and poor, young and old —applauded furiously.

Hyperbaton. Transposing the normal order of words: That the public will surely respond to; The Beatles teenagers like better than any other group.

Hyperbole. Overstating for the sake of emphasis: Junior, if you do that, I'll murder you; The jet roared away as fast as lightning.

Hypothesis. Using an impossible supposition: If he were the president of the United States, he would want still greater honors.

Litotes. Understating for the sake of emphasis: Yes, Einstein was a fairly bright man.

Meiosis. Depreciating for effect (making the big seem small and the important unimportant): The wound was nothing, a mere scratch.

Metonymy. Metaphorically substituting a related thought or item for the idea or thing itself: The crown decrees amnesty for all; The chair recognizes the speaker.

Oxymoron. Using contradiction or inconsistency for effect: a holy devil, an idiot savant, a hopeless aspiration.

Paradiorthosis. Using a familiar quotation, but applying a new twist to it so that it is in fact a misquotation: Life is but a walking flashlight; I must suffer the slings and harrows of fortune outrageously.

Paroemia. Applying a proverb in a new way: Your criticism of the wine is nothing but sour grapes; A bird in the hand is worth two in the bush, so don't forget to buy the chicken when you go to the store.

Rhetorical question. Posing a question that is not answered, but to which the audience knows the answer: Shall traitors run free in our streets? Shall law and order completely break down? Shall we degenerate into a state of anarchy?

Synecdoche. Using the part for the whole, the whole for the part, the genus for the species, the species for the genus, etc.: All hands on deck; The armada was fleet of a hundred sails; The skirts object to manly amusements.

Synonym. Piling up synonyms for emphasis: A lovely, beautiful, gorgeous, stunning spring day.

Zeugma. Using a word to govern two or more other words, with only one of which it makes *literal* sense: There great Anna did sometimes counsel take and sometimes tea; They brought gifts and adulation; The armies fought battles and malingering.

Exercise. Identify and explain the figures of speech in the following.

1. I will burn my candle at both ends.
2. Learn to be good, and be good to learn.
3. The man is a holy terror.
4. The question is this: Is he an out and out liar, or is he merely given to exaggeration.
5. The enemy was confronted by a troop of one hundred rifles.
6. Considerate, my neighbor is not; intrusive, he certainly is.
7. The crowd—rich and poor, young and old, men and women, lame and halt, hale and hearty—surged forward.
8. There is enough to condemn the accused without my mentioning that he deserted a family of six.
9. Work may be bitter, but accomplishment is sweet.
10. The president of the college is a little Napoleon.
11. My love is like a red, red rose.
12. Shall we relinquish our rights as American citizens?

VII ✐ Thinking Straight

The following are two of the various procedures for arriving at conclusions in formal logic:

    1. All Republicans are conservatives.
      Buckley is a Republican.
      ∴ Buckley is a conservative.
    2. All residents of Orange County are Republicans.
      All Republicans are conservatives.
      All conservatives are capitalists.
      All capitalists are millionaires.
      All residents of Orange County are millionaires.

Exercise.

1. As nearly as you can, describe the process whereby the conclusions from the first example (a syllogism) and from the second example (a sorites) are derived.

2. Given the form in which the arguments are presented, are any other conclusions possible?

3. Are the conclusions necessarily true? That is, in actuality might Buckley be a radical, and might some residents of Orange County be less affluent than millionaires?

There is a great difference between a *valid* conclusion and a *true* conclusion. A conclusion can be valid and still be untrue. For example,

> All men are elephants.
> Joe is a man.
> . ˙ . Joe is an elephant.

In the present chapter, we will be concerned not so much with truth as with validity in arguments. And we will take the negative approach to validity, in that we will illustrate logical pitfalls and kinds of arguments to be avoided.

Logic and rhetoric have always been sister arts. Logic is concerned with validity in thought; rhetoric is concerned with effectiveness in expression. Therefore, one might say that they are two sides to the same coin. The great part of this book has been devoted to effectiveness in expression—to rhetoric. But now, briefly, we must turn to the consideration of validity in thought.

No sane man would purposely try to be illogical, and no moral man would try to convince an audience of an untruth or of a point that he felt to be untrue. However, the writer may well attempt to advance a point that he is convinced is true and in so doing use either *valid* or *invalid* arguments. Logic is not so much concerned with the truth of premises as it is with the validity of arguments, and this is precisely why some knowledge of logic is valuable for the writer: with this knowledge he can avoid arguments that are patently invalid. A knowledge of logic does not necessarily convert a sloppy thinker into a cogent thinker. Nonetheless, some understanding of the ways whereby theses can be demonstrated must inevitably be of great use to anyone who is involved in expository writing.

DEDUCTION AND INDUCTION

Anyone familiar with the scientific method knows that it is generally called inductive. The method of the syllogism and sorites above is deductive. But "inductive" and "deductive" are only loose descriptions of methods whereby logical problems are solved. In fact, the two might, in reality, not be so very different. In an idealized model, the scientist tests members A_1, A_2, A_3, A_4 of Class X and finds that all of the members of the Class behave in the same way under identical controlled conditions. On the basis of his testing of the members of the Class, then, he arrives at a conclusion, Y. Induction, thus, moves from individual data to a general conclusion.

Deduction starts on the basis of a general theory or widely accepted truth and applies it to individual instances:

All professors are wise.
No professors are wise.
Some professors are wise.
Some professors are not wise.

From each of these *categorical propositions,* a chain of deductive logic can be developed:

All professors are wise.
Smith is a professor.
. ˙ . Smith is wise.
No professors are wise.
Smith is a professor.
. ˙ . Smith is not wise.
Some professors are wise.
All wise professors are in the English Department.
. ˙ . Some professors in the English Department are wise.
Some professors are not wise.
All unwise professors are in the English Department.
. ˙ . Some professors in the English Department are not wise.

Exercise. On the basis of the following categorical propositions, construct valid syllogisms.

1. Some truths are self-evident.
2. Mary is divine.
3. No politician is honest.
4. Some soldiers are not heroic.

At first glance, the processes of induction and deduction seem radically different, induction moving from the specific instances to the general conclusion, deduction moving from the general statement to a specific instance and to a conclusion. But, in fact, the difference between the two methods of reasoning is only apparent, not real—if, indeed, it exists at all. And this brings us to the point about induction and deduction in writing (for this book is not an introduction to formal logic). When the scientist begins his "inductive" research, he does not do so blindly, at random, with no firm intent; rather he works on the basis of a hypothesis, a roundly formed general theory (or hunch), the validity of which he sets out to prove or disprove. So we can say that his method is inductive-deductive or vice versa. On the other hand, the deductive argument, except in the artificial form of the syllogism, seldom proceeds directly from a categorical proposition. In an essay, for instance, the thesis or topic is established by evidence before the development of the argument begins, or, conversely, the development of the argument is the substantiation of the general thesis. An outline of a typical essay might look something like this:

Thesis	Professional schools should not be part of the university. or Universities should educate, not train.
First qualification of thesis	I. Currently, universities attempt both to train and to educate.
Support	A. Training takes place largely in the professional schools.
Support	B. Education prevails in the liberal arts and pure sciences.
Second qualification of thesis	II. The main purposes of learning are twofold.
Support	A. Learning humanizes.
Support	B. Learning provides techniques for further learning.
Support	C. Etc.
Third qualification of thesis	III. The professional schools must concentrate on narrow, particular skills.
Support	A. ....
Support	B. ....
Support	C. ....
Conclusion	IV. Since the professional schools train, but do not educate, they should not be part of the university.
Explanation	A. ....
Explanation	B. ....

The major framework of this outline could be expressed neatly in a syllogism

> Education is the purpose of the university.
> Training is not education.
> $\therefore$ Training is not the purpose of the university.

or a sorites

> The purpose of a university is education.
> Education is learning to be human and to think.
> Learning to be human and to think are the provinces of the liberal arts and pure sciences.
> $\therefore$ The provinces of the liberal arts and pure sciences are the purposes of the university.

What clearly emerges is that the general structure of an essay has an over-all deductive movement, but the individual parts are developed in an inductive way through the use of particular data, examples, etc. And the more we think about induction and deduction, the more we realize that they are not separate and distinct genres in the anthology of thought processes—in fact, that is a conclusion that modern logic demonstrates again and again.

Exercise. In your own words, summarize the points about logic that have been made so far.

Three kinds of proof. Presumably the end of writing is (a) to inform and (b) to bring about conviction in the reader. In the scale of reader reactions

> Ah, so!
> Perhaps!
> Hogwash!

the first is the desideratum.

If the human animal were completely rational, and if the human situation were completely clear and unambiguous, the facts and nothing but the facts would suffice to convince the reader. But the human situation is endlessly complex, and a horse is not just a horse:

"Girl number twenty," said Mr. Gradgrind, squarely pointing with his square forefinger, "I don't know that girl. Who is that girl?"

"Sissy Jupe, sir," explained number twenty, blushing, standing up, and curtseying.

"Sissy is not a name," said Mr. Gradgrind. "Don't call yourself Sissy. Call yourself Cecilia."

"It's father as calls me Sissy, sir," returned the young girl in a trembling voice, and with another curtsey.

"Then he has no business to do it," said Mr. Gradgrind. "Tell him he musn't. Cecilia Jupe. Let me see. What is your father?"

"He belongs to the horse-riding [circus], if you please, sir."

Mr. Gradgrind frowned, and waved off the objectionable calling with his hand.

"We don't know anything about that, here. You musn't tell us about that, here. Your father breaks horses, don't he?"

"If you please, sir, when they can get any to break, they do break horses in the ring, sir."

"You mustn't tell us about the ring, here. Very well, then. Describe your father as a horsebreaker. He doctors sick horses, I dare say?"

"Oh yes, sir."

"Very well, then. He is a veterinary surgeon, a farrier, and horsebreaker. Give me your definition of a horse."

(Sissy Jupe thrown into the greatest alarm by this demand.)

"Girl number twenty unable to define horse!" said Mr. Gradgrind, for the general behoof of all the little pitchers. "Girl number twenty possessed of no facts, in reference to one of the commonest of animals. Some boy's definition of a horse. Bitzer, yours."

"Quadruped. Gramnivorous. Forty teeth, namely twenty-four grind-ers, four eye-teeth, and twelve incisive. Sheds coat in the spring; in marshy countries, sheds hoofs, too. Hoofs hard, but requiring to be shod with iron. Age known by marks in mouth." Thus (and much more) Bitzer.

"Now girl number twenty," said Mr. Gradgrind. "You know what a horse is."

—Charles Dickens, *Hard Times*

Exercise. In your own words, briefly explain the point about "the facts and nothing but the facts" that the above passage illustrates.

The first kind of proof that the author must be concerned with is the *logical*. No argument should be irrational. The bulk of the present chapter will be concerned with logical proof.

The next kind of proof with which the author must concern himself is called *ethical*. This means, simply, that the reader must trust the au-thor—must feel that he is serious, honest, and well-informed. (Which, after all, is one reason that grammar, punctuation, and spelling are im-portant. The reader is likely to say to himself, "If this person can't even handle the English language, how can he presume to know anything about such a complex subject as. . . .") It is difficult to illustrate exactly what is meant by ethical proof, for that kind of proof arises from in-tangibles. But there are some general points of advice that help: (a) Know your subject; the reader will distrust you if you appear to be floundering about in unfamiliar territory. (b) Don't be flippant about serious subjects. This does not mean that any writer should be grim or lugubrious, but it does mean that every writer must convey the correct attitude toward his material.

The third general kind of proof is traditionally called *emotional*. It is based on the sound assumption that audiences vary and that discourse should be adjusted to its intended audience.

Exercise. In what ways are the following brief passages illustra-tive of attempts at establishing emotional proofs?

1. *Audience: third-grade children.* Today, we're going to learn a new game. It is called "The Multiplication-Table Game." Here are the rules. . . .

2. *Audience: a convention of the county medical society*: Ladies and gentlemen, on this occasion it is a pleasure for a layman such as myself to express his thanks to the dedicated physicians and researchers who have brought unbelievable progress to the science of medicine and who have so unstintingly dedicated them-selves to the alleviation of human suffering. But, like all other professions, that of medicine has its problems, and we must now

THINKING STRAIGHT • 213

ask ourselves this searching question: Have doctors' fees become excessive?

3. *Audience: college seniors in a history of the language course.* This book attempts to present the historical background necessary for an understanding of the English language as it is spoken and written today. The author has endeavored to introduce the general reader and the student who is beginning the systematic study of English to a selected portion of the mass of facts and doctrine that linguistic scholarship, of the last half-century particularly, has made available.

> —Stuart Robertson and Frederic G. Cassidy, *The Development of Modern English*

4. *Audience: sixth-grade arithmetic class.* When things fit together and work well, we say there is a "system." A *numeration system* is a certain kind of system. To learn about it, you will explore. You will do some problems. You will answer some questions. You will think about the ideas. This way you will find out what we mean by a numeration system.

> —Mervin L. Keedy and others, *Exploring Modern Mathematics*

In other words, the writer should keep the audience in mind; he should not "mumble to himself." He should bring to writing all the consideration, personality, and vigor that he uses when he is interested in a conversation with someone.

EVALUATING THE EVIDENCE

Rules of law classify evidence as circumstantial, inadmissable, and so on. In all arguments, the evidence is of varying degrees of validity: some highly reliable, some doubtful, some worse than doubtful and useless.

Exercise. Explain why the evidence for the following is doubtful or useless.

1. Fords have the best designed engines of any cars on the road this year. The head salesman at the Ralph Williams Ford agency told me so.

2. Cigarette smoking has no effect on the health. I found this out from an official of the Tobacco Institute of America.

3. Wheaties are America's most nutritious breakfast food. Wilt Chamberlain endorsed them.

4. By the year 1970, the implantation of artificial hearts will be routine. A friend of mine heard this from a friend of his who knows a doctor who heard it at the national AMA convention.

5. Shakespeare is the greatest poet of all times. That is a *fact* established by the consensus of critics.

In evaluating evidence, then, one must observe three cautions. First, what is the source? If the source is biased or is likely to be uninformed, the evidence comes into question. Second, is the evidence firsthand, secondhand, or at a farther remove from the source? To put the question another way, is the evidence "hearsay"? Third, is the established "fact" really a fact? All of the critics in the world can never establish it as a *fact* that Shakespeare is the world's greatest poet. That kind of conclusion always remains an opinion.

> *Exercise.* Explain why some conclusions must always remain opinions and can never be facts. (Think about this: What is a "fact"?)

Patently unreliable evidence destroys both logical and emotional proof.

EXAMPLES

The chapter on the paragraph demonstrated that examples constitute one of the primary methods for developing discourse. The very importance of examples raises a question: Do they *prove*? The answer must be a qualified "No." The most common function of examples is illustrative: they make the subject clear, immediate, and concrete. The example of de Sade does not prove that man is basically sadistic; the example of Schweitzer does not prove that man is basically altruistic. But de Sade illustrates man's sadism, and Schweitzer illustrates his altruism. There is a large difference between a number of individual cases used to prove a theory and one or two isolated instances used to illustrate that theory. In order to argue inductively, one needs a great deal of evidence.

As an *example* to *illustrate* the point of this discussion, we might look at a paragraph from Milton's resounding defense of freedom of the press, "Areopagitica." You will note that Milton uses Spencer as an example not to carry the burden of proof for the paragraph, but to show that the most revered poets in the language represent vice in order to inculcate virtue:

> I cannot praise a fugitive and cloistered virtue, unexercised and unbreathed, that never sallies out and sees her adversary, but slinks out of the race, where that immortal garland is to be run for, not without dust and heat. Assuredly we bring not innocence into the world, we bring

impurity much rather; that which purifies us is trial, and trial is by what is contrary. That virtue therefore which is but a youngling in the contemplation of evil, and knows not the utmost that vice promises to her followers, and rejects it, is but a blank virtue, not a pure; her whiteness is but an excremental whiteness. *Which was the reason why our sage and serious poet Spencer, whom I dare be known to think a better teacher than Scotus or Aquinas, describing true temperance under the person of Guion, brings him in with his palmer through the cave of Mammon, and the bower of earthly bliss, that he might see and know, and yet abstain.* Since therefore the knowledge and survey of vice is in this world so necessary to the constituting of human virtue, and the scanning of error to the confirmation of truth, how can we more safely, and with less danger, scout into the regions of sin and falsity than by reading all manner of tractates and hearing all manner of reason? And this is the benefit which may be had of books promiscuously read. [Italics mine.]

Milton's conclusion, at first glance, appears to derive from the example, but closer analysis reveals that the conclusion is the result of the logic of the paragraph and that the example serves primarily to illustrate.

Aristotle's advice about the example is completely valid. In the *Rhetoric*, he says,

When they follow the Enthymemes [propositions or topics], Examples function like witnesses—and there is always a tendency to believe a witness. Accordingly, when the speaker puts the Examples before, he must use a good many of them; if he puts them after, one may suffice— on the principle that a single witness, if you have a good one, will serve the purpose.

—Translated by Lane Cooper

Aristotle is saying something like this: When the main point has been established or implied, the example substantiates. But if the main point must arise *from* the examples, a great deal of "statistical" evidence is needed. Another way of looking at the matter is to view the example on the one hand as a typical instance of something and, on the other, as a bit of data among other bits. One bit of data might clarify; many bits of data are needed to substantiate.

PROBABILITY

One should not confuse probability with certainty. The following syllogism must prove a certainty if one accepts the premises:

All authors are creative.
Jones is an author.
Jones is creative.

But the following sequence is of quite another order:

> Most loan sharks are greedy.
> Smith is a loan shark.
> . ˙ . Smith is probably greedy.

Exercise. If the words *most* and *probably* are removed from the second sequence, then it becomes of the same order as the first sequence. Can you explain why?

The point here is simple. Do not confuse probability with certainty.

ANALOGY

Analogy is a striking similarity of some aspect of two things that are basically dissimilar.

> The academic world resembles business. Both are based on competition, and both have their winners and their losers, their "millionaires" and their "bankrupts."

The above example, actually not a very good analogy, illustrates the dangers of arguing analogically. The perceptive reader will immediately begin to ask questions: Granted that both the business world and the academic world are competitive, but is the competition of the same order? Do the business and academic worlds have the same goals? Can we judge the academic world on the basis of the commercial success of its product? The analogy serves its purpose best as illustrative clarification. The writer chooses something with which the reader is likely to be familiar in order to clarify the unfamiliar:

> In a sense, the system of English grammar and mathematics are analogous. Take addition, for example. With the limited number of rules that allow us to perform addition, we can solve an infinite number of problems, or, to put it another way, the system of addition will "generate" an unlimited number of sums. In a like manner, the rules of English grammar are finite in number, but allow us to generate an unlimited number of sentences.

Exercise.

1. Write a paragraph in which you argue a point on the basis of analogy.

2. Write a paragraph in which you clarify a point on the basis of analogy.

3. Exchange paragraphs with another member of the class, and do a critique of the use of analogy in the paragraphs.

FALLACIES

Formal fallacies have to do with errors in systematic, formal logic, such as errors in the composition of the syllogism. With these we will not concern ourselves, but rather with *informal fallacies*, the kind that are likely to mar the thought of essays and discussions, the kind that lead readers of advertisements astray, the kind that frequently impel men to act on the basis of really irrational impulse—and, finally, the kind that demagogues purposely use to get results. The informal fallacies are the kind of which we must be aware in our daily intellectual concourse.

The appeal to force or argumentum ad baculum. This is, of course, one way of categorizing the old "might makes right" argument. Recently in an interview, Congressman Adam Clayton Powell stated that he did not know whether militant Black Power advocates are right or wrong, but if they win, he concluded, then we may assume that they are right. *Argumentum ad baculum* is almost always a potent factor in political campaigns. Candidate X has the power to win; therefore, we must support him (a pragmatic stance), and he must be right in his views (an appeal to force).

Argument against the man (argumentum ad hominem). This is one common way of ignoring the real issues. Arguing that Rockefeller would not make a good president because he divorced his first wife is patently *argumentum ad hominem*. But note a subtle difference: arguing that because Rockefeller divorced his first wife and hence would set a bad example for the young people of America and hence would not be a good president might be a silly argument, but it is not *argumentum ad hominem*. This kind of argument comes in two categories, the *abusive* and the *circumstantial*. The abusive is an attempt to discredit the man's argument by attacking him personally: Jones beats his wife, so we shouldn't listen to his opinions about the national debt. The circumstantial attempts to make a correlation between what a person is and does and what he should believe: Jones, you're a businessman, so you must be in favor of new depreciation allowances in the tax structure.

Argument from ignorance. The "*argumentum ad ignorantium*" goes something like this: There are no such things as ghosts because I have never seen one *or* Since I have never met an honest man, there must be no such thing. In other words, it is invalid to argue that because *I* personally don't know of something, that thing must not exist. Even scientists are prone to commit this fallacy: There is no God because there is no scientific evidence that he exists.

Appeal to pity or argumentum ad misericordium is often insidious, for it shifts the focus from the issue to the emotional aura surrounding the issue. For instance: a citizen inquires about the proportion of funds used for administration and salaries in a local charity, and he is countered with, "Don't you want to help the underprivileged children in this city?" That simply is not the issue.

Bandwagon appeal or the "argument to the gallery" or the *argumentum ad populum* is a favorite device of modern advertising. It is a way of avoiding the issue of quality—or any other issue for that matter. "Today, more people smoke Carcinogens than any other filter cigarette." "Ford is Southern California's most popular car." "Everyone's doing it, so why don't you?" In elections since the TV age, there has possibly been an *argumentum ad populum* influence. Before Western polls have closed, the Eastern polls have already shown definite trends on the basis of which winners can reliably be predicted. The feeling is that these early predictions might have a bandwagon appeal for Western voters and influence their choice of national candidates.

Appeal to authority or argumentum ad verecundiam can be a perfectly valid device in argument. It becomes fallacious only when the "authority" is not necessarily an authority in the field under question. There is no reason why an eminent nuclear physicist should know any more about foreign policy than the butcher, the baker, or the candlestickmaker. There is no reason why an M.D. should be viewed as an authority on politics. And so on. A recent letter to the *Journal* of the American Medical Association illustrates this point:

> Sir:
>
> "Listen! My son the doctor has an opinion."
>
> Certainly the best trained and probably the least educated professional people in America today are the members of the healing arts, the sundry -ologists who have such success in curing everything from corns to cancer.
>
> One glaring instance of the physician's lack of genuine intellectual perspective is his tendency to validate his pronouncements in public forums by appending his M.D. or D.O. to his signature, as if a knowledge of medicine confers general omnisciency, a superhuman competency in matters political, economic, sociological, moral, and metaphysical.
>
> Indeed, my physician friends—who, by the way, always include their academic alphabets on the return addresses of their personal letters—keep protesting to me that the press of their duties coupled with the explosion in medical knowledge makes it impossible for them to be informed citizens. In other words, the good physician incapacitates himself as a useful community leader. That, I suppose, is the nature of the game.

Why, then, does the physician, unlike other doctors (for there are others), insist on whiting the sepulchre with that pompous non sequitur: M.D.?

Be wary of the English teacher who pontificates about psychiatry; be wary of the chemist who pontificates about taxes; be wary of the M.D. who takes over the school board. On the other hand, an informed citizen has the right and duty to speak out; but neither he nor his audience should assume that his competence in one field gives him special competence in another.

Accident. This fallacy consists in misapplication of a general rule. It is, perhaps, a general rule that women barbers are few and far between, but that does not mean that Joan is not a barber; in fact, she is a barber. The fallacy of accident can be downright invidious when it is coupled with the general preconceptions that muddy the thinking of so many people: Ivan is a communist, so he advocates the violent overthrow of the United States government; William is an English teacher, so he loves poetry; Alice is a mother, so she is kind and loving. In "Informal Fallacies," from *Introduction to Logic,* Irving M. Copi cites the following ludicrous instance of the fallacy of accident: "What you bought yesterday, you eat today; you bought raw meat yesterday; therefore, you eat raw meat today."

Converse accident. Converse accident is hasty generalization—the bane of science. From only exceptional cases, one generalizes about that class of things or circumstances in general. For instance, the teacher reads the first three essays in a stack of thirty, they are brilliant, and he immediately concludes that all the members of the class are brilliant writers. Or a procedure works in two or three instances, and the engineer concludes that it will work in all or most instances.

False cause. This fallacy consists in the establishment of an improper cause-effect relationship. Its most common variety is *post hoc ergo propter hoc,* "After this; therefore because of this." As the name implies, it is attributing cause and effect to what is only a chronological relationship: I ate at the Fleur de Lis last night; this morning I am ill; therefore the food at the Fleur de Lis made me ill. But there are countless other varieties of false cause: The communists want to conquer the world because they are not Christians; After the rain dance, the heavens opened up, and a veritable deluge ensued. In actual practice, establishing cause and effect relationships is usually a complicated affair. False cause usually arises from oversimplification. The writer should be as critical of his own thought processes as he is of those of others.

Complex question. "Have you stopped beating your wife?" is the most famous example of the complex question. Whether the subject answers "yes" or "no," he incriminates himself. Dryden used a subtle variation of the complex question when he said, "But Shadwell never deviates into sense." If Shadwell replies, "Yes I do," he is admitting that when he makes sense, he does so inadvertently, and he can't say, "No, I don't." The problem with the complex question lies in the fact that it is many sided, but demands a simple "yes or no" answer.

Begging the question or petitio principii involves using the premise to be proved as one of the proofs. The fallacy is more easily illustrated than defined. Copi cites this example from Richard Whately's *Elements of Logic* (1826):

> To allow every man unbounded freedom of speech must always be, on the whole, advantageous to the state; for it is highly conducive to the interests of the community that each individual should enjoy a liberty, perfectly unlimited, of expressing his sentiments.

This is saying, "Freedom of speech is good for the state because freedom of speech is good for the state."

The irrelevant conclusion (begging the question or ignoratio elenchi). This fallacy shifts the argument away from the point intended to be established toward another point. In a faculty meeting, one professor advocated establishing a course in the history of the language. A second eagerly took the argument up and said that a knowledge of the history of the language would do everyone a great deal of good. But the argument of the second professor moved away from the specific point: should such and such a department establish such and such a course under such and such conditions at such and such a time? The legislator who argues in favor of a specific bill on the basis only of general humanitarian grounds is committing *ignoratio elenchi*.

Equivocation. This fallacy comes about because words and their synonyms have varieties of denotative and connotative meanings. In the equivocal argument, these meanings slide from one end of the scale to another. Copi cites an example of equivocation in a syllogism:

> Some dogs have fuzzy ears.
> My dog has fuzzy ears.
> Therefore my dog is some dog!

Another example that Copi cites is this one: "The end of a thing is its perfection; death is the end of life; hence, death is the perfection of life." The problem here is that the first *end* means "purpose," and the second *end* means "termination."

Amphiboly. This is a fallacy based on ambiguous construction—the propensity for a statement to be interpreted in two different ways. The steamship *Queen Mary* gained her name through an amphibolous mix-up. Cunard officials wanted to name her the *Queen Victoria,* and they asked permission of King Edward if they might use the name of the greatest lady in British history. He gladly gave the company permission to name the ship after Mary, his wife. Or again, Croesus consulted the oracle before he went to war with Persia. The oracle said, "If Croesus went to war with Cyrus, he would destroy a mighty kingdom." Croesus, reassured, went to war. What was the result of the amphibolous statement of the oracle? And our old friend the dangling modifier is often amphibolous: Wrapped in a hunk of brown paper, she carried a huge sausage.

Composition. The fallacy of composition comes about when one reasons that the characteristics of the parts will be typical of the characteristics of the whole or that the characteristics of the whole will be typical of the parts. This fallacy appears in such reasoning as this: The whole group of Harvard graduates can be described as above average in intellect; Joe is a graduate of Harvard; therefore, Joe is brilliant. Or, conversely: I knew every member of the mob; each one was a harmless creature; I can't understand why they lynched that poor fellow. Sometimes reasoning from the whole to its parts is called the fallacy of *division,* the reverse of composition. An amusing example is cited by Copi:

> American Indians are disappearing.
> That man is an American Indian.
> Therefore that man is disappearing.

But in the example, the fallacy of equivocation plays as big a part as does the fallacy of division.

Non sequitur. This is a useful catch-all term meaning "it does not follow." "Your conclusions do not follow from your premises." "*This* has nothing to do with *that.*"

POSTSCRIPT ON LOGIC IN WRITING

Logic is an endlessly fascinating discipline. In its two varieties—traditional and symbolic—it underlies the study of relationships and hence is the basis for both mathematics and the new kind of grammar. But just as one need not be a grammarian to use the language with accuracy, grace, and power, so one need not be a logician to think clearly. It is safe to say that illogicality in student writing comes about not because the writers lack a knowledge of logic, but because they do not flex their intellectual muscles when they write. They do not try to think rigorously, and they do not test themselves at every step, as they should know the reader will test them.

We can say, then, that logically convincing writing comes about through conscientious application of the individual intelligence to what is being said. Even the fallacies outlined in this book are nothing more than fairly obvious results of sloppy brainwork.

Any student who is interested in formal logic as a discipline can easily get an introduction to that subject. But the best practice for producing logically valid and convincing discourse is that old laboratory, the student's writing desk.

Exercise. Name and explain the fallacies in the following.

1. Everyone is enjoying the leisurely living of Orange County. Why don't you join the happy throngs who have found their home of homes at Franciscan Fountains in the heart of Orange County.

2. I tried my new method of teaching grammar on five students, and it was tremendously successful. I suggest that it be adopted for the whole district.

3. Now, then, Mr. Jones, I want to ask you: "Have you stopped cheating on exams?"

4. Teachers simply do not make enough money; hence, we leave the education of our children in the hands of a bunch of impoverished pedants.

5. All the parts of the engine are light; therefore, the engine will be light.

6. We must be right, because we're winning the war.

7. Opera is an absolutely silly art form. I've never seen an opera, and I never intend to.

8. Since Smith is completely immoral, I don't see how he could possibly handle our plumbing work.

8. Support Community Charities. Think of the little children who need your help.

9. The war in Viet Nam is immoral. Dr. Spock says so.

10. Fords are better cars than Cadillacs because people who know about cars drive them. This proposition is obvious because naturally people who understand cars would drive Fords.

11. A jury convicts a man of the ax slaying of three little children because such a crime cannot go unpunished.

12. "If you invest in Spectacular Chemicals," said the stockbroker, "money will be made."

13. Analyze the logic of the familiar Shell gasoline commercial. It claims that cars using Shell with Platformate get better mileage than cars using Shell without Platformate. It then recommends that everyone use Shell with Platformate. What factor does it purposely overlook?

VIII ✐ The Long Paper

Every scholar—neophyte and master—has two primary obligations: to search out knowledge and to disseminate that knowledge. For this reason, universities stress publications by the faculty, for the professor is not only a teacher, but also a scholar who has the obligation to make his findings available to others. At its very best, scholarship is an adventure second to none; it is a mental excursion into the unknown, where both illumination and surprise lie in wait. Scholarship is not a dry-as-dust grubbing around in the desert of pedantry, but a safari to exotic lands where strange adventures await the explorer.

Every student is a neophyte scholar, and he should, very early in his career, begin to organize his trips into the unknown. This does not mean that the ordinary or even the exceptional student is likely to make a significant original contribution to the world of knowledge. But as the well-explored continent of Europe is a unique experience for the first-time visitor, so any area of scholarship can open new and exciting vistas for the young traveller.

The long paper that seems to be an inseparable part of freshman English courses is sometimes called "the library paper," sometimes "the research paper." In any case, it is usually the student's first excursion into the world of independent research and reporting on the results of that research. It is a wonderful opportunity for the student to show his independence, to cut the apron strings of close supervision and oppressively structured assignments. At its best, the research paper is an adventure in free inquiry.

The following discussion will briefly outline the process of library research and research writing.

GETTING UNDER WAY

Your instructor will undoubtedly help guide you toward a workable topic. As in any writing situation, your topic must be narrow enough that you can handle it adequately in the space and time requirements imposed on you.

> *Exercise.* From the following list of possible research paper topics, choose the ones that you think might be handled in a relatively brief (say, 2000-word) paper, and explain your choice.
> 1. War
> 2. The War of the Spanish Succession
> 3. English Ministries During the War of the Spanish Succession
> 4. Cancer
> 5. Causes of Cancer
> 6. The Relationship Between Smoking and Lung Cancer
> 7. Earthquakes
> 8. Earthquakes in America
> 9. Earthquakes along the San Andreas Fault
> 10. Outer Space
> 11. Exploring Outer Space
> 12. America's First Expedition to the Moon
> 13. English Literature
> 14. Shakespeare
> 15. The Problem of Indecision in *Hamlet*

Once you have chosen a workable topic, you are ready to get under way with your investigation.

PRELIMINARY INVESTIGATION

Presumably, your topic will take you into unfamiliar territory, and you risk wandering about, without reaching any significant goal. Somehow you need a map, a sketch of the terrain, an idea of where you might arrive. To achieve this, you need a general idea of the problem that you are entering.

There are many ways to get a general survey of the field. One of the most common is consulting a good general encyclopedia. A reliable encyclopedia will inform the inquirer about the general outlines of almost any subject and hence constitutes a good point of departure. The encyclopedia also provides surveys of standard works on subjects and therefore guides researchers to more specialized sources. The standard general encyclopedias are

> *The Encyclopaedia Britannica.* 24 vols. Chicago: Encyclopaedia Britannica, Inc., 1961. *The Encyclopaedia Britannica* is one of the two major works in the field. Traditionally, it is noted for the excellence of its articles in the humanities.
>
> *The Encyclopedia Americana.* 30 vols. New York: Americana Corporation, 1961. The second major work in its field, *The Americana* has traditionally been valued for its articles in the sciences.
>
> *Chamber's Encyclopedia.* 15 vols. New ed. London: George Newnes, Ltd., 1950.
>
> *Collier's Encyclopedia.* 20 vols. New York: P. F. Collier & Son Corporation, 1961.
>
> *Columbia Encyclopedia.* 2nd ed. New York: Columbia University Press, 1950. Supplement, 1959.

Besides the general encyclopedias, there are standard books about subjects, the generally accepted surveys of fields of knowledge. In order to find these general sources, you may need to consult your instructor, but chances are, the lists of books included in general encyclopedias will lead you to them.

BIBLIOGRAPHY

Now you have a general idea of your subject and its problems. The next step is to find all of the sources of information that your ingenuity, your time, and your library resources can lead you to. You will need to do some spadework and compile a list of sources that might lead you to pertinent information. This list is called a *bibliography.*

The Bibliography Card. You will find that the most efficient method of compiling *all* of your information is on 3 × 5 or 4 × 6 cards. They can be shuffled; they can be thrown away if useless; they can be supplemented. Taking information sequentially on sheets of paper always leads to chaos, extra work, frustration, and sometimes neurosis. Get a stack of cards, and use them. You will compile your bibliography on cards.

A bibliography card for a book includes:

1. Author, last name first
2. Title of book
3. Place of publication
4. Publisher
5. Date of publication or copyright
6. Library call number, if any.

(1) Abrams, M. H.
    (2) _The Mirror and the Lamp: Romantic Theory and the Critical Tradition_. (3) New York: (4) Oxford University Press (5) 1963
    (6) 801
    A161m

A bibliography card for a magazine includes:

1. Author, last name first
2. Title of article
3. Name of journal
4. Volume number of journal
5. Date of journal
6. Page numbers of article.

(1) Myers, L. M.
    (2) "Generation and Deviation,"
    (3) College Composition and Communication, (4) XVIII
    (5) (December, 1967), (6) 214-220.

These are the basic forms for bibliography cards. For the form to use in special cases—such as encyclopedias, government documents, and newspapers—see "Final Bibliography."

Compiling the Bibliography. Your working bibliography is the list of sources that you will consult. It will be the result of your search for sources of information. And in this search, it is well to follow a standard, systematic procedure. Your first investigation into your subject has taken you to a general source, such as an encyclopedia. Now you will work from the general to the particular, finding as many possible sources of information as your time and your library will allow.

The first and most obvious bibliographic resource in any library is the card catalogue. Most freshmen receive an introduction to the use of the library and the card catalogue, and we will not here repeat that information—except to remind that the card catalogue has entries under *subject, author,* and *title,* a three-way system of indexing.

The researcher systematically makes a list of possible sources of information, and he usually starts with the card catalogue. But there are countless other useful resources—useful if the researcher knows what he is looking for and how to find it.

Unabridged Dictionaries.

> Craigie, Sir William A. and Hulbert, James R. (eds.) *A Dictionary of American English on Historical Principles.* 4 vols. 2nd ed. Chicago: University of Chicago Press, 1960. This valuable work shows the histories of meanings of words in the American lexicon.
>
> Murray, Sir James A. H. and others (eds.). *A New English Dictionary on Historical Principles.* 13 vols. Oxford: Oxford University Press, 1888–1933. Often called *The Oxford English Dictionary* or the *OED,* this work is the most valuable source for the history of words in English.
>
> *Webster's Third New International Dictionary.* Springfield, Mass.: G. & C. Merriam Company, 1961. This is *the* unabridged dictionary of the English language, the large tome that you will find in the reading room of your library, and the work that caused an international uproar because of its permissiveness in its view of language.

General Indexes. Naturally, in your research, you will want to consult periodicals as well as books. And newspapers will often be crucial. Fortunately, a number of indexes—arranged like the card catalogue according to author, title, and subject—list periodical articles, in effect providing indexes to almost all magazines published.

> *Book Review Digest.* New York: The H. W. Wilson Company, 1946–. This index comes out monthly except February and July. It provides an index to reviews of books and hence is a valuable source of opinion about the books that you choose to rely on in your research.

International Index. New York: The H. W. Wilson Company, 1913–. This index appears quarterly and cumulatively every year and every two years. It is a list of articles in the humanities and social sciences in scholarly journals.

New York Times Index. New York: The New York Times, 1913–. This is an author-title-subject index to articles in the New York *Times.*

Nineteenth Century Reader's Guide to Periodical Literature, 1890-1899. 2 vols. New York: The H. W. Wilson Company, 1944. This is an author-subject index to some fifty periodicals of the period covered.

Poole's Index to Periodical Literature, 1802-1881. 2 vols. Rev. ed. Boston: Houghton, Mifflin Company, 1891. An invaluable index to British and American periodicals of the period covered.

Reader's Guide to Periodical Literature. New York: The H. W. Wilson Company, 1900–. This invaluable series, issued semi-monthly with annual and five-year cumulative editions, indexes around 125 periodicals of general interest.

Biographical Sources. If your research involves the biographies of persons living or dead, you can consult a number of standard, reliable sources.

Biography Index: A Cumulative Index to Biographical Material in Books and Magazines. New York: The H. W. Wilson Company, 1947–.

Current Biography: Who's News and Why. New York: The H. W. Wilson Company, 1940–. This series does just what the name implies; it gives reliable and fairly extensive biographies of people in the news.

Who's Who. London: Adam and Charles Black, Ltd., 1849–. Biographical data concerning figures of the British Commonwealth.

Who's Who in America. Chicago: A. N. Marquis & Co., 1899–. Annual collection of biographies of living Americans.

Dictionary of American Biography. Published under the Auspices of the American Council for Learned Societies. 21 vols. New York: Charles Scribner's Sons, 1928-37. With supplements that bring the work up to 1940. The set contains highly reliable biographies of dead Americans.

Dictionary of National Biography. Ed. Leslie Stephen and Sidney Lee. 63 vols. London: Smith, Elder & Co., 1885-1900. With supplements at intervals of ten years. Highly reliable biographies of dead members of the British Commonwealth.

Specialized Sources. The following list gives a brief idea of some of the specialized reference sources available.

Fine Arts

Dictionary of Modern Ballet. New York: Tudor Publishing Company, 1959.

Apel, Willi. *Harvard Dictionary of Music.* Cambridge, Mass.: Harvard University Press, 1956.

Grove's Dictionary of Music and Musicians. 9 vols. 5th ed., edited by Eric Blom. London: Macmillan & Co., Ltd., 1954.

American Art Annual. Washington, D.C.: American Federation of Arts, 1898–.

Art Index. New York: The H. W. Wilson Company, 1933–. This is the standard index for periodical materials on the arts.

Literature

Cambridge Bibliography of English Literature. Ed. F. W. Bateson. 4 vols. Cambridge: Cambridge University Press; New York: The Macmillan Company, 1941.

Granger's Index to Poetry. Ed. Raymond J. Dixon. 4th ed., rev. and enl. New York: Columbia University Press, 1953.

Harvey, Sir Paul. *The Oxford Companion to Classical Literature.* Oxford: The Clarendon Press, 1940.

Hart, James D. *The Oxford Companion to American Literature.* 3rd rev. ed. New York: Oxford University Press, 1956.

Harvey, Sir Paul. *The Oxford Companion to English Literature.* 3rd ed. Oxford: The Clarendon Press, 1946.

Myth and Folklore

Frazer, Sir James G. *The Golden Bough: A Study in Magic and Religion.* 12 vols. 3rd ed. London: Macmillan & Company, Ltd., 1907-15.

Larousse Encyclopedia of Mythology. New York: Prometheus Press, 1959.

Philosophy and Psychology

Dictionary of Philosophy and Psychology. Ed. James M. Baldwin and others. 3 vols. New ed. New York: The Macmillan Company, 1925-33.

Encyclopedia of the Social Sciences. Ed. Edwin R. A. Seligman and Alvin Johnson. 15 vols. New York: The Macmillan Company, 1930-35.

Religion

The Catholic Encyclopedia: An International Work of Reference on the Constitution, Doctrine, Discipline, and History of the Catholic Church. 16 vols. New York: Catholic Encyclopedia Press, 1907-14. Supplements 1922 and 1954.

Hastings, James (ed.). *Encyclopaedia of Religion and Ethics.* 13 vols. New York: Charles Scribner's Sons, 1928.

The Jewish Encyclopedia: A Descriptive Record of the History, Religion, Literature, and Customs of the Jewish People from the Earliest Times to the Present Day. 12 vols. New York: Funk & Wagnall's Company, 1901-6.

Schaff, Philip. *The New Schaff-Herzog Encyclopedia of Religious Knowledge.* Ed. Samuel Jackson and others. 12 vols. New York and London: Funk & Wagnalls Company, Inc., 1908-12. Supplement: *Twen-*

tieth Century Encyclopedia of Religious Knowledge. Ed. Lefferts A. Loetscher. 2 vols. Grand Rapids, Mich.: Baker Book House, 1955.

Science, General

American Yearbook. Publisher varies. 1929–. A summary of work in the sciences.

Chambers's Dictionary of Scientists. Ed. A. V. Howard. New York: E. P. Dutton & Co., Inc., 1952.

Industrial Arts Index. New York: The H. W. Wilson Company, 1913-1957. After 1957, it divided into *Applied Science and Technology Index and Business Periodicals Index.* New York: H. W. Wilson Company, 1958.

Van Nostrand's Scientific Encyclopedia. 3rd ed. Princeton: D. Van Nostrand Company, Inc., 1958.

Science, Biological

Cattell, Jacques (ed.). *American Men of Science.* Vol. II: *The Biological Sciences.* 9th ed. New York: R. R. Bowker Company, 1956.

Stedman's Medical Dictionary. 19th ed. Baltimore: The Williams and Wilkins Company, 1957.

U. S. Department of Agriculture. *Yearbook of Agriculture.* Washington, D.C.: U. S. Government Printing Office, 1894–.

Science, Physical

Cattell, Jacques (ed.). *American Men of Science.* Vol. I: *The Physical Sciences.* 9th ed. New York: R. R. Bowker Company, 1956.

Chambers's Technical Dictionary. Ed. C. F. Tweney and L. E. C. Hughes. 3rd ed. rev., with supplement. New York: The Macmillan Company, 1958.

International Dictionary of Physics and Electronics. Ed. Walter C. Michels and others. 2nd ed. Princeton: D. Van Nostrand Company, Inc., 1961.

Van Nostrand Chemist's Dictionary. Princeton, N.J.: D. Van Nostrand Company, Inc., 1953.

Social Sciences, General

Cattell, Jacques (ed.). *American Men of Science.* Vol. III: *The Social and Behavioral Sciences.* 9th ed. New York: R. R. Bowker Company, 1956.

———. *Directory of American Scholars.* New York: R. R. Bowker Company, 1942, 1951, 1957.

Encyclopedia of the Social Sciences. Ed. Edwin R. A. Seligman and Alvin Johnson. 15 vols. New York: The Macmillan Company, 1930-35.

International Index. New York: The H. W. Wilson Company, 1913–.

Education

Education Index. New York: The H. W. Wilson Company, 1929–.

Monroe, Walter S. (ed.). *Encyclopedia of Educational Research.* Rev. ed. New York: The Macmillan Company, 1950.

U. S. Office of Education. *Education Directory*. Washington, D.C.:
   U. S. Government Printing Office, 1912—.
Who's Who in American Education. Nashville, Tenn.: Who's Who in
   American Education, Inc., 1928—.

History

   The Cambridge Ancient History. Ed. J. B. Bury and others. 12 vols.
      Cambridge: The University Press, 1923-39.
   The Cambridge Medieval History. Ed. Henry W. Gwatkin and others.
      8 vols. Cambridge: The University Press, 1911-36.
   The Cambridge Modern History. Ed. A. W. Ward and others. 13 vols.
      and atlas. Cambridge: The University Press, 1902-26.
   The New Cambridge Modern History. Ed. G. R. Potter. Cambridge: The
      University Press, 1957—. Work in progress.
   U. S. Library of Congress, Reference Division. *A Guide to the Study of
      the United States of America*. Washington, D.C.: U. S. Government
      Printing Office, 1960.

Research, Research Writing, and Bibliography

   Turabian, Kate L. *Student's Guide for Writing College Papers*. Chicago
      and London: The University of Chicago Press, 1963.

GATHERING MATERIALS

After you have compiled your working bibliography—a list of possible sources for information—the actual research work begins, for now
you must get into your sources and assemble information about your
subject. The actual research becomes an intriguing process of detective
work, logic, common sense, value judgment, with a portion of serendipity
thrown in for good measure. By now, you have defined your subject; you
know what its problems and limits are. You are ready to proceed.

The good researcher works systematically through those materials
that seem pertinent to him, but he keeps his eyes open for hints about
other sources: two or three sources on a given subject may repeatedly
mention another source, informing the alert researcher that he should
go to a source that keeps popping up in discussions of his subject. The
longer one works, the more clearly will the subject take shape. This is
one of the many rewards of research.

The key to successful and pleasant research is working accurately
and systematically. And accuracy and system depend on how you handle
your note taking. Once again, the 3 × 5 or 4 × 6 card is a crucial tool
in the process. As you read, you will want a way of recording your data
and of making that data readily available when you start to write. Since
cards can be arranged and rearranged, they are the most satisfactory for
note taking.

NOTE TAKING

Your notes will be of two kinds: (a) *direct quotes* and (b) *paraphrases*. Do not confuse or scramble the two. A direct quote is a word-for-word rendition of the source. A paraphrase is a statement of the ideas *completely in your own words*. Here is a quotation from *The Mirror and the Lamp*, by M. H. Abrams:

> For convenience we may name criticism that, like Sidney's, is ordered toward the audience, a 'pragmatic theory,' since it looks at the work of art chiefly as a means to an end, an instrument for getting something done, and tends to judge its value according to its success in achieving that aim.

Here is an *inadequate* paraphrase of that passage:

> Criticism that, like Sidney's, is ordered toward the audience we can call, for the sake of convenience, a 'pragmatic theory,' because it views the work of art primarily as a means to an end, a tool for getting something done, and usually judges its value according to its success in attaining that aim.

Exercise. Explain why the above "paraphrase" is not a paraphrase at all, but rather plagiarism.

In order to paraphrase, one must digest the idea and then state it completely in his own words.

It is axiomatic that one should quote only when necessary: (a) to preserve the source's exact meaning, as, for instance, when the interpretation of a passage is in question; (b) to preserve the unique flavor of a particularly well expressed idea. But no paper should be a stringing together of quotes; each paper should represent the synthesis of the author's thinking in his own words.

As to note cards: (1) they must be keyed to the bibliography card, for that is where complete footnote information is found; (2) they should also have a subject key; (3) they should indicate the exact page or pages of the source on which the information is found. With the following kind of note card, the problem of organizing to write is minimal. The subject heading allows the ordering of the cards according to the material that they deal with. The name of the author facilitates reference to the bibliography card for footnote information, and the page numbers supply the footnote information that the bibliography card does not.

Exercise. At this point, stop for a moment and mull over what has been said so far. In your own words, either written or spoken, can you give a running narrative of the process of research writing as it has been explained so far?

[name of author, referring to bibliog. card]	[subject key]

Abrams, M. H.

theories of criticism

[pg. nos.] 14-21   [notes]   A. Calls critical theories based on the effect a work is intended to produce "pragmatic theories." He cites Sidney as an example. During the Renaissance, pragmatic criticism, stemming from Horace, was ascendant.

WRITING THE PAPER

Writing the long paper should be a less arduous process than writing an ordinary essay. After all, you have investigated your subject, you have gathered copious material, you have reached a conclusion, your subject has incubated and is ready to be hatched. The principles of coherence, unity, and style that apply to any writing also apply to the long paper. Organization is not a tremendous problem, for you can group your note cards, and, anyway, you know your subject and its outlines. But there are some purely mechanical problems that you will need to be aware of.

FOOTNOTES

Everyone knows *what* a footnote is, but perhaps the *why* needs explanation. You have done your research. You have reached your conclusions. Now, the reader wants to follow the process whereby you came up with whatever you did. He wants to know the sources of the facts, data, and opinion on which you build your paper. Footnotes show the reader your sources. And there is another reason for footnoting: the reader may want to delve further into some idea that you introduce; the footnote shows him where to look.

Young researchers often view footnoting as a monstrous obstacle to be overcome. Actually the process is not so fearsome at all. If you will look at the following kinds of footnotes, most of your questions will be answered. If you encounter special problems, take them to your instructor.

Book with One Author

[1]M. H. Abrams, *The Mirror and the Lamp* (New York: Oxford University Press, 1953), pp. 14-21.

Book with Two Authors

[2]Harold C. Martin and Richard M. Ohmann, *The Logic and Rhetoric of Exposition* (New York: Holt, Rinehart and Winston, Inc., 1963), p. 17.

Book with More Than Two Authors

[3]Albert C. Baugh and others, *A Literary History of England* (New York: Appleton-Century-Crofts, Inc., 1948), pp. 1021-22.

No Author Given

[4]*Literary Masterpieces* (Joplin, Mo.: People's Press, 1918), p. 5.

Edited Collection

[5]Donald W. Lee (ed.), *English Language Reader* (New York: Dodd, Mead & Company, 1963), pp. 18-19.

Edition

[6]Bonamy Dobrée, *Modern Prose Style* (2nd ed.; Oxford: The Clarendon Press, 1963), p. 221.

Work of One Author Edited by Another

[7]Frank Norris, *McTeague,* ed. Carvel Collins (New York: Holt, Rinehart and Winston, 1963), p. 171.

Work by One Author in a Collection Edited by Another

[8]William James, "What Pragmatism Means," *The Relevance of Rhetoric,* ed. Edward V. Stackpoole and W. Ross Winterowd (Boston: Allyn and Bacon, Inc., 1966), p. 299.

Magazine Article

[9]L. M. Myers, "Generation and Deviation," *College Composition and Communication,* XVIII (December, 1967), 214-220.

Anonymous Magazine Article

[10]"L.B.J. and His Dollar," *Life,* LXIV (January 19, 1968), 4.

Encyclopedia Article
> [11]"Sitting Bull," *The Encyclopedia Americana*, XXV (1962), 48.

Newspaper Article
> [12]Aussie, Russian Stars to Compete in Times Games," Los Angeles *Times*, January 21, 1968, Sec. D1, p. 1.

The above list does not, by any means, represent all of the kinds of footnotes that every writer will need to use, nor does it show the only or necessarily the best footnote form. It does, however, cover most cases, and it represents a widely used and generally accepted method. If you encounter problems, consult *Student's Guide for Writing College Papers*, by Kate L. Turabian (Chicago: University of Chicago Press, 1963), or go to your instructor. The main criteria for footnotes are accuracy and consistency.

Ibid. The most frequently used scholarly abbreviation—and a handy device—is *ibid.* It means "in the same place" (Latin: *ibidem*). It works like this: If one footnote refers to the source directly preceding it, there is no use in repeating the whole citation. So one does this:

> [1]M. H. Abrams, *The Mirror and the Lamp* (New York: Oxford University Press, 1953), p. 100.
> [2]*Ibid.*, p. 102.

This means that the material cited by footnote number two is found in the same source as that cited in footnote number one, but on a different page. Note that *ibid.* is printed in italics; in handwriting or typing it is underlined.

Other Scholarly Abbreviations. In your research, you are likely to encounter the following abbreviations, some definitely archaic and out of fashion:

c., copyright

c. 1400, circa
> Used to indicate that a date is not certain, it means "about."

cf., compare

chap., chapter (plural chaps.)

e.g., *exempli gratia* (for example)

ed., edition

ed. Before a name, it means "edited by."

et al, et alii (and others)
> Used less frequently than its English equivalent.

i.e., *id est* (that is)

infra, below

loc. cit., in the place cited
Used infrequently, for it tells the reader nothing that *ibid.* doesn't.

MS, manuscript (plural MSS)

n.d., no date
Used in footnotes to indicate that a source is undated:
[1]Herrmann Traugott, *The Devil as a Force in History* (Salt Lake City: Deseret Press, n.d.), p. 5.

n.p., no place, no publisher
Used in footnotes where place of publication or publisher is lacking.

op. cit., opere citato (in the work cited)
Seldom used in modern footnotes, but frequently appearing in nineteenth-century and early twentieth-century works.

passim, here and there throughout the work cited
[1]M. H. Abrams, *The Mirror and the Lamp* (New York: Oxford University Press, 1953), *passim.*

sic, thus
Used in direct quotes, between brackets, to show that the material was copied just as it was in the source and that errors are those of the source, not of the copier: "The Misisipi [*sic*] is America's greatest river."

Second and Further References to a Source Once Cited. Once the full information on a source has been given in a footnote, there is no need to repeat all of the information. Thus, second and subsequent references merely cite the author's last name—or the title of an anonymous work. The following sample list of footnotes will illustrate:

[1]M. H. Abrams, *The Mirror and the Lamp* (New York: Oxford University Press, 1953), pp. 14-21.
[2]*Ibid.,* p. 80.
[3]"Aussie, Russian Stars to Compete in Times Games," Los Angeles *Times,* January 21, 1968, Sec. D1, p. 1.
[4]Abrams, p. 90.
[5]"Aussie, Russian Stars to Compete in Times Games."
[6]*Ibid.*

And so on.

When and What to Footnote. Remember the purpose of footnotes: they guide your reader to your sources of information, and they allow him to make a judgment about the validity of the material that you cite. Therefore, it is utterly useless to footnote anything that is easily checked or that is common knowledge. Suppose, for instance, that you are writing about the Elizabethan period and have forgotten Queen Elizabeth's dates, which then you must look up in the biographical section of your dictionary. Would you footnote these dates? No. For anyone can easily check on your accuracy. But you must footnote facts, opinions, and ideas which are not common knowledge and which you derive from your research. However, do not make the mistake of believing that the quality of your paper will be in direct proportion to the number of footnotes that you include. You must use your judgment and ask yourself about the usefulness of each footnote.

BIBLIOGRAPHY

The final element in your paper will probably be a bibliography, or list of works to which you refer in the paper. This list is actually a courtesy to the reader, giving him a handy way to check your sources. Bibliography form differs slightly from footnote form:

[book]
> Abrams, M. H. *The Mirror and the Lamp.* New York: Oxford University Press, 1953.

[magazine article]
> Chapman, Jewell A. "The Prose Portrait." *College Composition and Communication,* XVIII (December, 1967), 252-254.

[edited collection]
> Dean, Leonard F. and Kenneth G. Wilson (eds.). *Essays on Language and Usage.* New York: Oxford University Press, 1963.

[magazine article, no author given]
> "L.B.J. and His Dollar." *Life,* LXIV (January 19, 1968), 4.

[encyclopedia article]
> "Sitting Bull," *The Encyclopedia Americana,* XXV (1962), 48.

The important things to notice are (a) that the author's last name comes first and (b) that the bibliography is alphabetized.

EXAMPLES

Of course, the best way to learn about the nature of research papers is to read some carefully. They are to be found in the sections on the research paper of many handbooks. Turabian reproduces one in *Student's Guide for Writing College Papers.* The following example paper was written by a student; you can learn a great deal by analyzing it carefully.

Modern Writers on Style

by

Raymund Paredes

Submitted in partial fulfilment of the requirements for English 101, University of Southern California, Dec. 3, 1968.

There has been an interest in style, no doubt, since the second piece of literature appeared. We know Plato and Aristotle talked about style, and presumably some forgotten Egyptian, six thousand years ago, gathered his students around him to explain how a new tool—writing— could be used most effectively. Interest in style—once the concern of a few lonely writers, philosophers, and professors—has increased remarkably in this century, and with good reason. Although more than half the people in the world remain illiterate, the ability to write clearly and lucidly, the hallmarks of a good style, becomes increasingly more crucial. As more and more people learn to write, it is imperative that these people learn to write well.

Curiously, however, most people who write don't write well. Nowhere is this phenomenon more apparent than in the United States. Here, we have the highest literacy rate in the world and the highest level of education, yet the ability to write clearly remains to most of us a mysterious, gossamer process. We know the language, but we don't know how to use it effectively. Our styles, in other words, are poor.

Now, not everyone knows what style is, but everyone agrees that it's important. Great literature is almost invariably applauded for great style; conversely, bad literature is bad largely because of stylistic deficiencies. Obviously, a good style is one of the keys to good writing. In this day of mass culture and instantaneous communications, writers are pursued and interviewed, cornered and badgered in the hope that they might reveal some dark secrets about the elements of effective style. It seems as if the vast, unimaginative majority of the population hopes that there is some covert, but learnable formula—somewhat akin to a cookbook recipe—to writing well. Writers, like all craftsmen protective of their livelihood, respond with varying degrees of enthusiasm. Some arrogantly dismiss the term "style" altogether, claiming they have no conscious knowledge of what it is; some respond defensively, arguing that it is harmful for a writer to talk about his creative process; some delight in deceiving and misleading a guileless reporter with meaningless prattle; and some few are genuinely helpful with their own detached curiosity about how literature is created.

When talking about style—either to writers or critics—there is an inherent problem of definition. Some definitions are vague, elusive, and metaphysical:

> It is difficult to analyze the airy substance we call style. At its best, it seems to escape all definition. It is as evasive as life. It would be as hard to predict the dancing flight of a flock of finches or the subterranean movement of a single mole, as to explain a great writer's peculiar gift. The reason for this seems to me to lie in the fact that style is the ultimate expression of the author's unique spiritual consciousness. . . .

It has been suggested that style consists in saying what has to be said as exactly as possible. This, however, is another matter. True style has nothing to do with imparting information lucidly. It is not this. It is the scent of the herb, the mist over the blackberry hedge, the soul of the man.[1]

Llewelyn Powys' rhapsody is one extreme of definition and not much use to us here. The opposite pole is to define style as a series of linguistic choices from the whole realm of language alternatives, but this definition, from the point of view of modern writers, seems too narrow. When writers talk about style, they are talking about the total manner in which a writer confronts a literary situation. Style means not only the manner in which a writer manipulates the language, but the manner in which the writer chooses to handle the subject he is writing about. Style also means form, structure, technique. Style to the modern writer is an extension in prose of a man's personality. It's a bit trite at this point to say that "style is the man," but writers really do believe this. As Donald Hall says, "By a man's metaphors, you shall know him."[2]

Given this view, most writers believe that a particular style cannot be acquired or learned any more than a youngster can determine that he will one day become another Gandhi. Writers thus claim that honest writers develop a style of their own subconsciously, or if they are aware of style, it is because they are trying new techniques and trying to extend the boundaries of language. Francois Mauriac articulated nicely the feelings of many writers:

> My opinion hasn't changed. I believe that my younger fellow novelists are greatly preoccupied with technique. They seem to think a good novel ought to follow certain rules from outside. In fact, however, this preoccupation hampers them and embarrasses them in their creation. The great novelist doesn't depend on anyone but himself. Proust resembled none of his predecessors, and he did not have, he could not have, any successors. Balzac created the "Balzacian" novel; its style was suitable only for Balzac.
>
> There is a close tie between a novelist's originality in general and the personal quality of his style. A borrowed style is a bad style. American novelists from Faulkner to Hemingway invented a style to express what they wanted to say—and it is a style that can't be passed on to their followers.
>
> In all the time I have been writing novels I have very seldom asked myself about the technique I was using. When I begin to write I don't stop and wonder if I am interfering too directly in the story, or if

---

[1]Llewelyn Powys, "Letter to Warner Taylor," *The Creative Process*, ed. by Brewster Ghiselin, (New York: Mentor Books, 1952), p. 176.
[2]Donald Hall, ed., *The Modern Stylists*, (New York: The Free Press, 1968), p. 5.

I know too much about my characters, or whether or not I ought to judge them. I write with complete naiveté, spontaneously. I've never had any preconceived notion of what I could or could not do. . . . The crisis in French novel writing . . . will be solved as soon as our young writers succeed in getting rid of the naive idea that Joyce, Kafka, and Faulkner hold the Tables of the Law of fictional technique. . . . A novelist spontaneously works out the techniques that fit his own nature.[3]

Mauriac holds that he writes without thinking about technique or style, that he writes spontaneously. Other writers, time and again, agree. Katherine Ann Porter made these interesting remarks about style:

The first time someone said to me, "Why did you write 'Flowering Judas' in the historical present?" I thought for a moment and said, "Did I?" because I'd never noticed it. Because I didn't *plan* to write it any way. . . . I never think about form at all.

I've been called a stylist till I really could tear my hair out. And I simply don't believe in style. Oh, the style is you. Oh, you could cultivate a style, I suppose, if you like. But I should say it remains a cultivated style. It remains artificial and imposed, and I don't think it deceives anyone. A cultivated style would be like a mask. Everyone knows it's a mask. . . .

Style is the man. Aristotle said it first, as far as I know, and everybody has said it since, because it is one of those unarguable truths. You do not create a style. You work and develop yourself; your style is an emanation from your own being.[4]

Mauriac, Porter and many other writers agree on a crucial point: style is not learned; it seems to rise spontaneously out of a desire to say or write something. This is not to say style cannot be developed—no doubt it can. But style, writers argue, develops unwittingly and unconsciously. Faulkner puts it this way:

There is no mechanical way to get the writing done, no short cut. The young writer would be a fool to follow a theory. Teach yourself by your own mistakes; people learn only by error. The good artist believes that nobody is good enough to give him advice. He has supreme vanity. No matter how much he admires the old writer, he wants to beat him. . . . Sometimes technique charges in and takes command of the dream before the writer himself can get his hands on it. That is tour de force and the finished work is simply a matter of fitting bricks neatly together since the writer knows probably every single word right to the end before he puts the first one down. This happened with *As I Lay Dying*. It was not easy. No honest work is.[5]

---

[3]Malcolm Cowley, ed., *Writers at Work: The Paris Review Interviews* (New York: The Viking Press, 1958), pp. 40-41.
[4]Van Wyck, Brooks, ed., *Writers at Work: Second Series* (New York: The Viking Press, 1963), pp. 154, 156.
[5]Cowley, p. 129.

Faulkner explains here that style develops naturally as a writer learns to write better. A style develops, as Nelson Algren says, as a writer learns to capture reality more closely. A truer style comes with a truer sense of reality. Faulkner makes clear that style can handle itself, sometimes without the writer "getting his hands on it." This introduces a point other writers make. Sometimes a story or book "writes itself." The idea is comprehensive in the writer's mind; he is only an agent of the idea; it, in effect, has a style and a life of its own. The writer merely gets it down on paper.

If writers are not very conscious of style, per se, they are certainly aware of stylistic deficiencies. Writers may not be aware of how they are writing, but they are alert to errors of tone, the use of an inappropriate or unnecessary word. Writers rewrite because something "doesn't sound right" or "look right." They are, as Truman Capote says, "obsessed with detail." Georges Simenon, a fantastically prolific author, rewrites by "cutting out words which are there just to make an effect, every sentence which is there just for the sentence."[6] F. Scott Fitzgerald in his "Notes" to The Last Tycoon fortified the writers' claim that literature "is not written by formula, by exhorting himself." "Rewrite from mood. . . . Don't look. Rewrite from mood."[7] William Styron's manuscripts are heavily rewritten, because, as he says, he "seems to have a neurotic need to perfect every paragraph—each sentence, even."[8] Yet, he too rejects any conscious preoccupation with style. Mature writers seem to comprehend problems of style intuitively—often not being quite able to articulate them—but they rewrite methodically with an earnest and clear understanding of stylistic weaknesses. They may not know how they write a book, but they certainly understand when they're writing it wrong.

Writers list only two ingredients of effective style: clarity and honesty. Now, some writers may disagree on the need for one or the other, but beyond these two qualities, writers are mute about necessary characteristics; a style is good if it works. Aristotle listed both clarity and honesty as indispensable to rhetoric; Stendahl advised simply: "I see but one rule: to be clear. If I am not clear, all my world crumbles to nothing."[9] Hemingway stated his position more strongly:

> . . . No matter how good a phrase or a simile he may have, if he puts
> it in where it is not absolutely necessary and irreplaceable, he is spoil-

---

[6]Ibid., p. 146.
[7]John Kuehl, Write and Rewrite (New York: Meredith Press, 1967), p. 163.
[8]Cowley, p. 271.
[9]Walter Allen, ed., Writers on Writing (Boston: The Writer, Inc., 1948), p. 205.

ing his work for egotism. Prose is architecture, not interior decoration, and the Baroque is over.[10]

H. G. Wells advised us to write as we walk: in a straight line. Faulkner, on the other hand, was no stickler for clarity; his passion was honesty. If his prose was difficult and complex, it was because the reality he tried to capture honestly was also so. By now it becomes clear that there is no right way or any single way to achieve an effective style. Clarity and honesty, many writers agree, are fundamental, but not essential. Faulkner, to take a recent example, demonstrated that writers can occasionally transcend the requirement for stylistic clarity. As for honesty, we give ourselves too much credit as perceptive critics if we maintain that all literature we admire was honestly and sincerely conceived. Literature is full of charlatans, and no doubt some remain uncovered. Perhaps it should be said that style need only appear to be honest.

The inescapable fact remains that writers simply aren't much help to students trying to improve their writing style. Truman Capote articulates the position of most writers when asked about style:

> What is style? And "what" as the Zen Koan asks, "is the sound of one hand clapping?" No one really knows yet, either you know or you don't.[11]

When we ask writers about style, we may as well ask Mickey Mantle how he hits a hard, high inside pitch out of Yankee Stadium. Mantle is no coach, and most writers are simply not teachers. The greatly gifted seldom understand their own talents. It is the less talented who study techniques and methods carefully to derive the most from their own limited capabilities that can articulate best what their crafts are about. Writers can tell us that experience, observation, and imagination are the three qualities a writer must have, but how these are harnessed into the creative process is for someone else to explain.

One last point. A recent story goes that a tourist was wandering about in New York, quite lost. He walked up to an obviously knowledgeable young man and asked, "How do I get to Carnegie Hall?" The young man, puffing casually on a cigarette, answered without pausing, "Practice, man, practice." The key lesson to be learned from accomplished writers is the same as the young man's reply. Writers to a man believe that writing and, hence style, are improvable. Many notable novelists went through a long, hard apprenticeship writing about anything—but

---

[10]Hall, p. 59.
[11]*Ibid.*, p. 124.

writing. Writers are notoriously self-made men. For many, learning to write is a lonely, tedious process, but a necessary one. Perhaps writers are subtly telling us that the key to a good style is practice in writing—that its ingredients are self-evident after hard work. Certainly, the point might be, that there are, under any conditions, only a few Balzacs and Faulkners, but a lucid and trenchant style may be within the reach of many.

Bibliography

Allen, Walter. *Writers on Writing*. Boston: The Writer, Inc., 1948.

Bader, A. L. ed. *To the Young Writer*. Ann Arbor: University of Michigan Press, 1965.

Brooks, Van Wyck, ed. *Writers at Work: Second Series*. New York: The Viking Press, 1963.

Cowley, Malcolm, ed. *Writers at Work: The Paris Review Interviews*. New York: The Viking Press, 1958.

Ghiselin, Brewster, ed. *The Creative Process*. New York: Mentor Books, 1952.

Hall, Donald, ed. *The Modern Stylists*. New York: The Free Press, 1968.

Kuehl, John. *Write and Rewrite*. New York: Meredith Press, 1967.

Van Gelden, Robert. *Writers and Writing*. New York: Scribner's Sons, 1946.

IX ✐ The Growth
of English

THE ORIGIN OF LANGUAGE

No one knows exactly how languages began. Something in the social, cooperative nature of man impelled him to communicate, and language is the instrument of human cooperation. *Homo sapiens* has never been the largest, the strongest, or the swiftest of animals; in fact, compared even with other primates, he is physically limited. But he has the most nimble brain—a statement that might lead us to conclude that the nature of the human mind formed language, that man's innate capacity for complex thought determined his invention and use of language. The situation, however, is not quite so easy, for the nature of language must also influence the nature of the mind. Imagine a language that has no absolute negative, no *no*, but only *perhaps*. In such a language, the sentence "He is *not* good" would be impossible, and hence the whole thought pattern that the sentence represents would be impossible. "He is *perhaps* good" represents a whole different mental set from "He is *not* good." What we are saying here is that perhaps language shapes mind as much as mind shapes language. But, to avoid a which-came-first-the-egg-or-the-chicken argument, we can plead ignorance about the genesis of language; somehow it came into being, and its nature undoubtedly conditions the kinds of thoughts that men think.

Theories about the genesis of language are picturesquely named. The *ding-dong* theory is the most naive. Its basis is the assumption that somehow words just naturally represent the things they stand for, as if, somehow, the word DOG is intrinsically more canine than, say, GLOD. The ding-dong theory is based on the confusion between word and thing, between symbol and that symbolized.

The *bow-wow* theory assumes that language came about through imitation or *onomatopoeia*. Since the bird makes a sound roughly like *cuckoo,* the bird was named after the sound that he made. The dog says, "Bow-wow," so children call him a "bow-wow." Whether or not this theory has valid basis we can never know. But we can ask how the bow-wow theory explains the genesis of such words as "love," "black," and "see."

The *pooh-pooh* theory advances the hypothesis that vocal sounds came about as an accompaniment to gestures. Thus, the genesis of language is placed firmly in kinetic action—a shake of the fist, a shrug of the shoulders, a smile—accompanied by appropriate sound.

The *yo-he-ho* theory explains language as the result of labor. As men toiled at heavy tasks, they automatically grunted or gasped. Gradually, the vocal sounds became connected with the tasks, and the result was the inception of language.

All of these explanations, it seems to me, reflect man's never-ending urge to find simple solutions to complex problems. If one accepts any of the hypotheses and follows them to their logical conclusions, the results stagger the imagination, primarily because the endless diversity of language does not show bias in any of the areas covered by the four popular theories. If language were particularly exclamatory, we might be prone to accept the pooh-pooh theory; if language were particularly onomatopoetic, we might incline to the bow-wow theory. But, in fact, all of these hypotheses test the credulity of even the most casual observer.

The easiest and most consistent theory is that God created both man and language, and that both have existed *mutatis mutandis* since the Garden of Eden. In an age of faith, such a theory suffices, but no one today takes it seriously.

Though the origin of language is lost in the darkness of prehistory, there is no reason to believe that the development of man's language was any less complex a process than the evolution of man himself. It is safe to assume that ding-dong, bow-wow, pooh-pooh, yo-he-ho, and many other factors played their role in the birth of language.

Although we are uncertain about the ultimate origin of language, we do know that each language did not develop separately, that languages are related to each other, and that there are a number of families. English belongs to the Indo-European family. Before we get into the discussion of that family and of English in particular, however, it is necessary to clarify a few notions about the sounds of language.

In all real senses, speech is primary, and writing is secondary. Writing (as well as printing) is a more or less accurate attempt to record speech sounds, and in some languages, notably English, the system of *orthography* or spelling presents only a rough approximation of speech sounds. We can illustrate this principle with the following series:

> b*ough*
> th*rough*
> th*ough*
> t*ough*

Four different sounds for one spelling! Any language, of course, accommodates any number of sounds, for no two people pronounce all words or most words exactly alike in any precise, scientific meaning of the word "alike." But not all sounds or variations of the same sound in a language are meaningful; in fact, the native is not even aware of the countless variations that he hears. The reason for this is that some variations are meaningful, and some are not. By and large, we hear only the meaningful variations, except, of course, when we hear striking variations from our own dialect. You can test the variations in sound patterns by listening to ten or fifteen people pronounce the *o* in coffee. Chances are, your ear will detect differences, and special equipment would reveal differences in every single pronunciation. But all of this is just common sense: We know that we can recognize individual voices; hence we recognize differences in pronunciation.

The smallest *meaningful* units of sound in language are called *phonemes* (see Chap. III). They are, so to speak, the building blocks of the language. A change in a phoneme of a word either changes the meaning or makes the word into a non-word in the language. The sound that *i* represents is a phoneme, as are the sounds that *p* and *t* represent: p i t. But change the first phoneme, and one gets, perhaps, b i t. Change the middle phoneme, and one gets b a t, b e t, b o t (a non-word in writing, but, depending on pronunciation one of two words in speaking, either *bought* or *boat*), and b u t (in speech, depending on pronunciation, either *but* or *boot*). All of this is extremely difficult to illustrate without a transcription that indicates not conventional orthography, but actual pronunciation—that is, without a phonetic alphabet. There are such alphabets, notably the International Phonetic Alphabet (IPA). However, explaining and learning these phonetic alphabets is a longer task than would be justified by the present discussion. The important thing to remember is that the written language is only a rough approximation of the spoken language. In this book, we will need to resort to approximate, understandable phonetic transcriptions, and the student will need to use his sense of language to follow the discussion of the growth of English, to which we can now turn.

THE FAMILY TREE

As figure 1 indicates, English is a member of a family of languages called the Indo-European. This family includes

    1. Indo-Iranian—Sanskrit, the ancient literary and sacred language; modern Indian tongues; Romany, the language of the Gypsies; modern Iranian and its related dialects.
    2. Armenian.
    3. Tokharian—an ancient language of Chinese Turkestan.
    4. Hellenic—the classical Greek dialects and modern Greek.
    5. Albanian.
    6. Italic—Latin and the so-called modern Romance languages: French, Italian, Spanish, Portuguese, and Rumanian.
    7. Celtic—the native languages of the British Isles.
    8. Germanic—discussed below.
    9. Balto-Slavic—Lithuanian in the Baltic group and Polish, Czechoslovakian, Russian, and Bulgarian in the Slavic group.

The Germanic branch divided into three main stems. The eastern language, Gothic, has no modern offspring and is preserved in Bishop Ulfilas' translation of the New Testament (about 350 A.D.). The northern stem of the Germanic developed into the modern Scandinavian tongues, Icelandic, Norwegian, Danish, and Swedish. It is the Western stem from which English comes. As figure 1 indicates, the High West Germanic developed into modern German; the Low West Germanic developed into a group of sister languages: Plattdeutsch, Dutch, Frisian, and English.

The chart, however, shows the relationship and development of the Indo-European languages in only their broadest outlines. Nothing of the complexity of the changes is given. We will see, for instance, that English was greatly influenced in its development by Scandinavian and French.

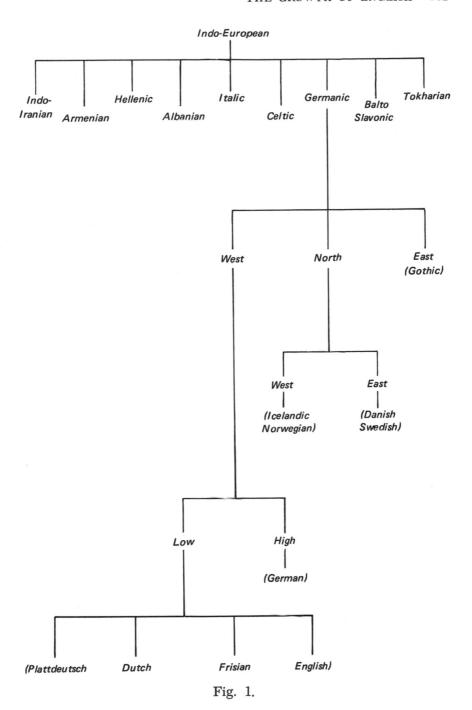

Fig. 1.

THE BEGINNINGS

There is good reason to believe that some 5,000 years ago, the Indo-European peoples were living in a fairly compact group somewhere in Europe or western Asia, we do not know exactly where. By the year 2,000 B.C., the diffusion of this tribe, or tribes, had begun. The peoples wandered from India to Scandinavia and apparently became ascendant wherever they went.

Isolation of a language group is the best way in the world to bring about change in language. As the tribes isolated themselves from the parent Indo-European community, their individual languages began the slow but steady process of development. Even today, with almost universal mass communication, we know that dialects persist within languages and that there is no universal language in the world. The differences among languages are on three levels: in pronunciation or the production of speech sounds, in the lexicon or word stock, and in the structure. Isolation of one group from another brings about changes in all three, and these changes are persistent, as the existence of dialects in modern American English attests.

It is fairly easy to demonstrate that sound changes in the Indo-European languages followed a systematic pattern. This was the simultaneous discovery of Jacob Grimm, a German, and Rasmus Rask, a Dane, in the nineteenth century. The system of changes is called Grimm's Law, and it allows us to reconstruct hypothetical forms of the Indo-European Mother Tongue as well as showing the systematic divergences among languages in the family. The theory of sound shifts is too complex for the present discussion, nor does the general student have use for a detailed knowledge of the matter. But in outline, the theory goes something like this. Even the most casual observer notes a great many cognates in languages, say, English, French, and German:

father	pere	Vater
mother	mere	Mutter
one	un	ein
midnight	minuit	Mitternacht
cook	coq	Koch

Are these similarities coincidental, or do they result from systematic changes? Grimm and Rask described the systematic changes in the Germanic family. In so doing, they demonstrated conclusively the process whereby related languages become distinct and individual.

OLD ENGLISH

But our interest in the history of languages really begins about the year 500 A.D., which marks the inception of English.

In 55 B.C. the Romans conquered Britain, a land inhabited by the uncivilized Britons, a people who spoke Celtic. The Romans protected these people from the incursions of the wild Picts and Scots from the north. For more than 400 years, England remained under the rule and protection of the Roman legions. Around 409 A.D., the Romans withdrew to attend to their affairs at home and left the Britons to fend for themselves. The ensuing chaos left the native inhabitants virtually defenseless, and they were soon conquered by Germanic tribes from the west coast of Europe. The two primary invading tribes were the Angles and the Saxons. We are unsure of the identity of the third tribe, but will follow tradition and call them Jutes. The Angles conquered and settled the Midlands and the northern part of the island to the Scottish border; the Saxons controlled the southern part of England; and the Jutes occupied a small area, roughly what is now Kent.

It is to the languages that the Angles and the Saxons brought with them that we owe modern English, a strange fact when one considers that the "native" language, the Celtic, made little contribution to the development of the language that we speak today. In this situation, one finds perhaps a linguistic-political lesson, namely, that if conquest is complete enough, the conquered culture either withers or dies completely.

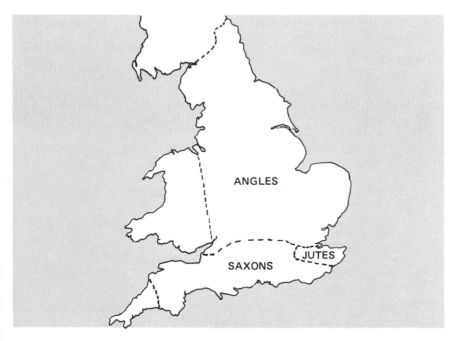

Fig. 2.

The history of fifth- and sixth-century England is virtually a closed book. Obviously, the two ascendant peoples, the Angles and the Saxons, were engaged in consolidating their territories and in fighting off the native Britons, but since there are no records, one can only speculate.

In 597, the conversion of Britain to Christianity began under St. Augustine of Canterbury, and it is really at this point that we can begin to speak about the history of England and the English language. We should not assume that Old English (or Anglo-Saxon, as it is sometimes called) sprang into being overnight; that is not the way of languages. But for convenience, we can date that tongue from about the middle of the fifth century to about 1100.

Here is a transcription of an Old English riddle:

> Moððe word fræt.   Mē þæt þūhte
> wrǣtlicu wyrd,   þā ic þæt wundor gefrægn,
> þæt se wyrm forswealg   wera gied sumes,
> þēof in þȳstro   þrymfæstne cwide
> ond þæs strangan staþol.   Stælgiest ne wæs
> wihte þȳ glēawra,   þē hē þām wordum swealg.

(Old English ð and þ are pronounced like English *th*.)

(A moth ate a word. To me that appeared a strange fate, so that I questioned that wonder, that the worm swallowed up the song of some man, thief in the dark the strongly firm utterance and the secure binding. The stealing spirit was not one whit the brighter, that he swallowed the word.)

The riddle, of course, is about a bookworm that eats up the words of some poet. If you will look closely (and use your imagination), you will see words that are cognate with modern English and German words.

mothe	moth
word	word
me	me
thæt	that
thuhte	thought
wyrd	weird (originally "fate")
wundor	wonder
wyrm	worm
forswealg	(for) swallowed
fræt	Germ. fressen
gefrægn	Germ. fragen

Mothe ward [as in "hospital ward"] frat. May that thoochtuh [with the *ch* pronounced as in German *ich*] ratleecoo würd, thah ich [as in German *ich*] that woondoor yefran, that say würm forswealg [with *a* of *bath*] wear-ah yee-ed soo-mes, thay-oaf in thoo-strow thrümfast-ne cwee-de owned thas strong-an stahthol. Stalyee-est neh was [with the *a* of *bath*] wichte [with the Germ. *ch*] thü glee-ow-ruh, they hay them ward-um swalg [with the *a* of *bath*].

With a little practice, you will be able to give a very rough approximation of what Old English sounded like. Trying to give phonetic transcriptions, of course, once again illustrates the necessity for a reliable phonetic alphabet in language studies.

The differences between Old English and Modern English lie not exclusively in vocabulary and pronunciation, but also in structure. Old English was a language that showed word relationships by their inflectional forms (*i.e.*, it was a *synthetic* language); Modern English is primarily an *analytic* language, showing word relationships by their position in the sentence (*i.e.*, their *syntax*). In Old English, as you remember, all of the following arrangements meant "The man killed the king":

> Se man sloh thone kyning.
> Thone kyning sloh se man.
> Se man thone kyning sloh.
> Thone kyning se man sloh.
> Sloh se man thone kyning.
> Sloh thone kyning se man.

There was no possibility of mix-up, because *se* was the subjective form of the definite article ("the"), and *thone* was the accusative. The same sentences translated word by word into English illustrate the differences between a synthetic and an analytic language:

> The man killed the king.
> The king killed the man.
> The man the king killed.
> The king the man killed.
> Killed the man the king.
> Killed the king the man.

In other words, in Modern English, inflectional forms do not show the relationships of words, but rather syntax does. The following charts indicate something of the complexity of Old English declensions:

A Masculine Noun, *stone*

Singular		*Plural*	
Nominative	stan	stanas	
Genitive	stanes	stana	
Dative	stane	stanum	
Accusative	stan	stanas	

In the process of eliminating inflections, Modern English has preserved only the differentiation between singular and plural, stone/stones.

The Personal Pronouns

		1st Person	2nd Person	Masc.	Fem.	Neut.
Sing.	Nom.	ic	thu	he	heo	hit
	Gen.	min	mim	his	hiere	his
	Dat.	me	the	him	hiere	him
	Acc.	me	the			
Dual	Nom.	wit (we two)	git (ye two)	hine	hie	hit
	Gen.	uncer	incer			
	Dat.	unc	inc			
	Acc.	unc	inc			
Plur.	Nom.	we	ge	hie		
	Gen.	ure	eower	hiera		
	Dat.	us	eow	him		
	Acc.	us	eow	hie		

Modern English has eliminated the dual number. Which forms of singular and plural does it retain? (*Eow* and *eower* were pronounced much like our modern *you* and *your*.)

The Definite Articles

Singular	Masculine	Feminine	Neuter
Nominative	se	seo	thæt
Genitive	thæs	thære	thæs
Dative	thæm	thære	thæm
Accusative	thone	tha	thæt
Instrumental	thy		thy

Plural	
Nominative	tha
Genitive	thara
Dative	thæm
Accusative	tha

Without further examples, we can say that the development of Middle English and then Modern English from Old English largely involved the dropping of inflections and the fixing of syntax, a process that went on over the centuries.

With the conversion of the Angles and the Saxons to Christianity in the late sixth century, borrowings from Latin, the language of the Church, became understandably numerous. Sometimes the Latin words were taken over in a relatively pure form, as, for instance, in modern English the German *Volkswagen* generally retains a close approximation of its native pronunciation and exactly its native spelling. But other Latin words were changed in both spelling and pronunciation. However, considering the dominance of Christianity after 597, the number of Latin borrowings is relatively small. We acquired both *minster* and *monastery* from *monasterium*. *Bishop* was acquired from the Latin *episcopus*, as was *episcopal*. Latin, however, had little influence on the structure of the language.

Sometime around the year 800, the Scandinavians began their incursions into England. These Norse invaders spoke languages closely allied to the West Germanic dialects of the Angles and the Saxons; hence, it is understandable that their language had a more appreciable influence on Old English than did the Latin. Like many invaders, the Scandinavians tended to settle down in the invaded land and to amalgamate with the conquered people. One evidence of the Scandinavians' influence is that they gave more than 1,400 place-names in England, usually the ones ending in *-by*, *-thorpe*, and *-thwaite*. They also contributed such nouns as *egg, fellow, freckle, garden, guess, leg, root, skin,* and *sky*; such verbs as *call, get, give,* and *take*; the adjectives *flat, loose, low, odd,* and *weak*. But a more important contribution—one that attests to the depth of the Scandinavian influence—is the basic structural words that English picked up from the Norsemen. They gave the language its pronouns *they, their,* and *them* and its preposition *with*. In other words, the Scandinavians added to the closed classes of parts of speech—something that the Latin never did. It is important to remember, too, that the confrontation of two languages almost always brings about some kind of modification in the basic nature of one or both. Occupation troops in Germany after World War II got along nicely with German words uttered in English structure and without the niceties of German inflections. If the conquest of Germany by the Americans had taken place in the ages before mass communications, the German language would undoubtedly have altered itself appreciably.

For the modern American, Old English is a "foreign" language, as strange and difficult as German, French, or Russian. But changes were slowly taking place, the changes that contributed to the language that we now speak.

MIDDLE ENGLISH

The most radical changes took place after 1066, when the Normans invaded and conquered England. In order to illustrate the rapid and dramatic nature of the change, one can compare the following passage from the twelfth-century *Peterborough Chronicle* with the Old English riddle that was cited earlier:

This gaere for the King Stephne ofer sae to Normandi and ther wes underfangen, for thi that hi wenden that he sculde ben alsuic alse the eom wes, and for he hadde get his tresor; ac he todeld it and scatered sotlice.

(This year King Stephen travelled over the sea to Normandy and there was accepted, for they thought that he should be just like his uncle was, and because he had gotten his fortune; but he split it up and scattered [it] foolishly.)

The following, from *The Book of the Duchess* (1369) by Chaucer, is, with the exception of one or two words, completely understandable to the modern reader:

> Me thoghte thus: that hyt was May,
> And in the dawenynge I lay
> (Me mette thus) in my bed al naked,
> And loked forth, for I was waked
> With smale foules a gret hep
> That had affrayed me out of slep,
> Thorgh noyse and swetnesse of her song.

In fact, however, if you were to hear these passages read aloud, they would sound almost completely foreign to you. Middle English was moving toward Modern English, but it had not yet arrived.

What happened to the language during the period 1066-1500?

First, the Normans consolidated their conquests. They became the undoubted ruling class of England. These conquerors, then, imported both their customs and their language, and it became the task of the native English to adjust, as they immediately proceeded to do. One estimate is that about 20,000 Normans remained in England after the conquest, and they formed the ruling class in the feudal system which developed. The official and literary language became French, and the native English virtually disappeared as a written language. Of course, the natives still spoke their mother tongue and probably became bilingual to a certain extent. But an example of the ascendancy of Norman French is that the only important Anglo-Saxon written document to be preserved from the period 1066-1200 is the *Peterborough Chronicle* quoted above.

To speak of *the* Middle English language is perhaps misleading, for in the period 1100-1500, several dialects developed: Northern, West Midland, East Midland, Southwestern, and Southeastern. And there were appreciable differences between these dialects. One common example is the voicing of *f* and *s* in the south, so that *for* and *see* would have been pronounced as *vor* and *zee*. One of the interesting detective games in the study of language is trying to determine the dialect of authors or scribes of Middle English manuscripts. Not until the printing press came into use did orthography start to become fixed and virtually universal.

In the handwritten manuscripts, the scribe attempted to approximate the sounds that he heard, and the result was definite regional variations in the kinds of written language used. The situation is much as if the scribe were to write *bird* for the standard American pronunciation, *böd* for the New England pronunciation, and *boyd* for the Brooklyn pronunciation. Middle English dialects, then, had definite characteristics that made each unique.

The sound changes from Old English to Middle English were perfectly regular. For example, O.E. clæne (with the vowel of *bath*) > M.E. *clene* (pronounced *clay-nuh*) > Mdn. E. *clean*; O.E. *hus* (pronounced *hoos*) > M.E. *hous* (pronounced *hoos*) > Mdn. E. *house*. And so on. It is beyond our purpose to chart all of the Middle English sound changes. Suffice it to say that they were perfectly regular and systematic.

The structure of the language also changed from Old English to Middle English. The most important development was the language's loss of inflections. As we have seen, Old English was a synthetic language, highly inflected; Middle English became an analytic language. One notices this fact in reading Chaucer, for his word order is virtually that of Modern English. The supposed reasons for the loss of inflections make interesting speculation. One reason we can eliminate immediately: it has been said that rude, illiterate people, such as the great mass of Middle English speakers, cannot handle the complex niceties of a highly inflected language. But, after all, during the period 500-1100, the masses apparently had no trouble in handling the complexities of Old English inflections. The most likely explanation of the Middle English loss of inflections is the influence of French. After 1066, French met and mingled with English, and the result was undoubtedly a leveling process. Every time two language groups meet, this process occurs, as it did during World War II in the German used by the occupation forces.

The pervasiveness of the influence of Norman French on Middle English is most readily seen in the vocabulary. From 1066 to about 1400, English adopted French words by the droves: authority, council, empire, majesty, parliament, reign, state, tax; baptism, clergy, damnation, faith, immortality, parson, reverence, saint, trinity, vicar; assault, bail, crime, decree, felon, judge, plaintiff, sentence, trespass; army, battle, captain, defense, enemy, guard, lieutenant, navy, sergeant; able, blank, carry, damage, eager, face, gay, horrible. And this is merely a small sampling. The fact that about 30.9 per cent of all English words are derived from French is evidence of the depth of French penetration into the English language.

THE RENAISSANCE

"Renaissance" means "rebirth," and that period from about 1500 to 1650 is called the Renaissance in England. The term itself is misleading, for it implies that out of the dark ignorance and crudity of the Middle Ages a new enlightenment sprang into being. As everyone knows, the English Renaissance did bring a spectacular development in culture and learning: Shakespeare, Bacon, Sidney, Jonson, Lyly, Raleigh, Donne, Marvell, Milton—and on and on. But the Middle Ages were not without culture; they produced, for instance, an extremely rich literature— the cycles of mystery plays, romances like *Sir Gawain and the Green Knight,* and Chaucer's *Canterbury Tales.*

In language, 1500 roughly marks the beginning of Modern English. To read works written before 1450 takes special training; almost anyone can read works written from 1550 on. To be sure, Shakespeare did not use the language of Walter Lippmann, but the differences between the language of 1550 or 1600 and that of 1969 are, comparatively speaking, slight.

By the time of the Renaissance, the old inflectional system had disappeared, which means that syntax generally was fixed once and for all. The two great changes that the language underwent during the Renaissance were in pronunciation and spelling. It was the printing press that fixed spellings, for now texts gained wide distribution with a consequent tendency toward standardization. In Middle English, the word *dead* was likely to appear (according to dialect) in any one of the following forms: *ded, deed, dead, dyad.* In the Renaissance this diversity was lost. The change in pronunciation took place most notably in the system of long vowels, as illustrated by the following table:

Word	Chaucer's Pronunciation	Shakespeare's Pronunciation
place	plah-suh	place
feet	fate	feet
bite	bee-tuh	bite
stone	stahn	stone
fool	foal	fool
mouse	moos	mouse

In the Middle Ages, the purpose of education had been ecclesiastical, the training of priests: the main (if not the sole) purpose of learning was the glory of God. Reading and writing still had about them the aura of the arcane and the mysterious that we see in the etymological alliance of *grammar* and *glamor* (or magic). Often even the aristocracy saw no virtue in literacy and left the task of writing necessary communications to menial scribes. But in the Renaissance, concomitant with the diffusion of printing, learning came to be an admired accomplishment, and schools gradually developed from their exclusively theological character into academies of general learning. It has been estimated that in Shakespeare's time between one-third and one-half of the residents of London could read, including all of the upper, ruling class.

In 1476 or thereabouts, William Caxton established the first printing press in England—a monumental development in the history of Western civilization. Prior to Caxton's time, all texts were hand-copied, primarily by scribe-monks in monasteries. These hand-copied manuscripts were often genuine works of art—the *illuminated* manuscripts now so highly prized by collectors—but obviously so slow a method of reproduction made a general diffusion of learning impossible. The printing press greatly speeded up the process of reproduction and at the same time lowered the cost, so that after 1476, books were generally available, and it was possible, even, for authors to make a living on the sale of copies of their works (though the professional author as we know him did not come into being until the eighteenth century). Since the printing presses were centered in London, they established the language of London as *the* dialect. In hand-copied manuscripts, one is likely to find the Southern dialects, but in printed books of the period, the Midlands dialect prevails.

In a way, it is fair to say that during the Renaissance, English and Latin had equal importance as the languages of the learned. Renaissance man did not view Latin as a dead language; every educated man could handle the classical language proficiently. But there was a decided shift from the Middle Ages, when Latin was *the* language of learning, the tongue used in the universities, in the church, in government, and in literature. The change during the Renaissance was more of a shifting of focus onto English rather than a repudiation of Latin. The following passage from Milton's "Of Education" pretty well sums up what was going on in Renaissance schools, their ideals and their goals:

> The end, then, of learning is to repair the ruins of our first parents by regaining to know God aright, and out of that knowledge to love him, to imitate him, to be like him, as we may the nearest, by possessing our souls of true virtue, which, being united to the heavenly grace of faith, makes up the highest perfection. But because our understanding cannot in this body found itself but on sensible things, nor arrive so clearly to the knowledge of God and things invisible as by orderly conning over the visible and inferior creature, the same method is necessarily to be followed in all discreet teaching.
>
> And seeing every nation affords not experience and tradition enough for all kind of learning, therefore we are chiefly taught the languages of those people who have at any time been most industrious after wisdom; so that language is but the instrument conveying to us things useful to be known.

By "the languages of those people who have at any time been most industrious after wisdom," Milton means, of course, the classical languages, Hebrew, Greek, and primarily Latin.

THE NEO-CLASSICAL VIEW

One lesson that the foregoing pages should have made clear is this: language develops and changes almost by its own volition, according to its own internal laws, and under the influence of its circumstances. Attempting to regulate the growth of language is like trying to regulate the changes of the seasons. One example is the many attempts—by, among others, Theodore Roosevelt and George Bernard Shaw—to regularize English spelling. Another example is the futile "laws" that schoolmarms lay down:

> Do not end a sentence with a preposition.
> Do not start a sentence with a coordinating conjunction.
> Do not split an infinitive.
> Use *shall* and *will* "properly."

These rules blithely ignore the usage of the most effective speakers and writers in the language, and the perceptive student must ask himself whether the schoolmarm (male or female) has actually observed the English language as it appears in speech and writing, not in the handbooks.

The attempt to regulate language, to "preserve" it, came into being about 1660 with the restoration of the English monarchy after the civil wars. Now, any movement to preserve the language as it is reflects an attitude that change is decay, that the growth of the language must be toward corruption, and this is precisely the attitude of the neo-classical period, 1660-1800.

If language is to be regulated, then obviously there must be a regulatory body, a linguistic supreme court or senate that will make the laws, or at least codify them, and then extirpate offending locutions. There were proposals for a British Academy (similar to the French Academy, founded in 1635). In 1667, Richard Sprat's influential *History of the Royal Society* advocated the founding of an academy to purify the language of "fantastical" elements brought to it by religious enthusiasm, and Jonathan Swift was much interested in the possibility of an authoritative group for the regulation of language.

Oddly enough, the desire for regulation of language goes back to a veneration of the classical tongues. In the eighteenth century, it was a widely held view that Latin maintained a primal purity that could serve as the model for all languages; insofar as English corresponded with Latin, it was pure, but any divergence was a sign of falling off from the linguistic Golden Age. The equation is simple: the more the change, the greater the corruption.

The first English dictionaries were in great measure attempts to preserve the purity of language and to guard against corruptive change. Though Samuel Johnson did not compile the first English dictionary, his is the work from which modern dictionary-making stems. Begun in 1747, Dr. Johnson's dictionary is the first milestone in English lexicography, an admirable and sensible work. But Johnson did view himself as a bastion against the barbarian forces of change. In his "Preface" he tells us:

> When I took the first survey of my undertaking, I found our speech copious without order, and energetick without rules: wherever I turned my view, there was perplexity to be disentangled, and confusion to be regulated; choice was to be made out of boundless variety, without any established principle of selection; adulterations were to be detected, without a settled test of purity; and modes of expression to be rejected or received, without the suffrages of any writers of classical reputation or acknowledged authority.

Dr. Johnson set out to establish the authority by which language could be regulated and by which degenerative change could be halted. And in his viewpoint, Johnson was typical of his time.

This period, too, is the beginning of the schism between *descriptive* and *prescriptive* grammar, an important concept in any study of language. A prescriptive grammar is one that makes value judgments and tells what *should be*. A descriptive grammar is one that does not make value judgments and merely delineates what *is*. Almost all modern language study is descriptive rather than prescriptive, but almost all of the grammars used in pedagogy are prescriptive. There is, of course, nothing wrong with value judgments and prescriptions about language; every good teacher is more or less prescriptive, and everyone who deals with language says "such and such is more effective" and "such and such is less effective." The trouble comes when prescriptiveness and descriptiveness are confused, when the old shall-will controversy gets mixed up with what actually goes on in language, when the injunction "Do not end a sentence with a preposition" is viewed as some kind of primal or God-given commandment about language. In fact, grammars are much more successful when they do not prescribe.

By and large, the doctrine of absolute correctness has prevailed into our own day—even though scientific language study is a strong counterforce. But, unfortunately, the scientific study of language has not penetrated very deeply into the curricula of our schools.

CONCLUSION

Every student should have an awareness of the dynamics of language, which grows and changes in almost the same way as an organism. A good way to gain awareness of the dynamics of language is to study its history.

Any pronouncement that English has been developing toward more expressiveness and more versatility should be viewed with a healthy dose of skepticism; in fact, it is better to speak of linguistic change than of linguistic development. For it is axiomatic that all languages express what they must express.

And the English language is still mutant, still moving on in time toward other vocabulary, other typical structures, and probably other pronunciations. This process is neither good nor bad; it just is.

X ℐ A Checklist of Writing Problems

The following is an alphabetical list of problems that students frequently encounter in their writing. In most instances, the entries in the checklist contain cross-references to the other chapters in this book, where fuller discussions of many of the entries appear. The checklist is a handy way to "brush up" on the writing problems that often bother students, but it is not a substitute for the fuller discussions that appear in the other chapters.

ABSOLUTES (see pp. 151-153)

Absolute constructions modify the sentence as a whole:

The crisis passed, he began to recover rapidly.
The semester being concluded, I can now settle down to writing.
The class did not meet, *the professor having been delayed by heavy freeway traffic.*
The floats assembled at 5:00 a.m., *the parade to begin at 10:00.*

Absolutes come about through the combination of two sentences. What is removed from one of the sentences to make it an absolute? The answer is *tense*. Absolute constructions have everything that full clauses do except tense. What is added when tense is removed? The answer is one of the signs of the participle, either present (ing) or past (symbolized by -en). Thus:

The + bell + present + ring

> The class is ready to settle down.

The + bell + ing + ring
(Remember that ing + V must be rewritten as V + ing.)
The + sun + past + have + en + set

> We lit the bonfire.

The + sun + ing + have + en + set

Do not confuse the absolute construction with other participials. Note the difference between the absolute and the present participial (see p. 158 ff.):

Absolute: *The flu having struck,* many students were absent.
Present participial: *Having the flu,* I decided to stay home.

The verbal in the absolute has a subject. The verbal in the participial does not have a *stated* subject (although there is an implied subject).

ACTIVE VOICE

See the entry "Voice" in this checklist. See also p. 158 ff.

ADJECTIVES

Mark Twain said, "As to the Adjective: when in doubt, strike it out." The piling up of adjectives does not necessarily make for vivid style, and too many adjectives cause sogginess. The right word can replace a whole string of adjectives:

She was sad, hopeless, and desperate.
She despaired.

Modern grammar indicates that adjectives and verbs are very much alike and may develop from the same sorts of deep structure constituents. For instance, both verbs and adjectives can be *intransitive*

I *see*
It is *good*

or *transitive*

> I *see a dollar*
> It is *worth a dollar.*

Adjectives occur in three positions: *attributive*

> *White* dogs don't bark
> White dogs don't bark at *little* boys

appositive

> The barn, *huge and lonely,* loomed on the horizon
> Anything *worth a dollar* must be good

and *predicate*

> The work is *difficult*
> His mood seems *sad*
> The weather becomes *cold.*

The section on "embedding" (pp. 119-126) discusses the syntax of adjectives.

ADVERBS

Adverbs modify:

> verbals: He took the plate, *casually* nodding to his neighbor.
> adjectives: She was *completely* beautiful.
> adverbs: Murgatroyd yodels *amazingly* well.
> clauses: He knew *exactly* what he would do.
> phrases: The epidemic extended *nearly* to New Delhi.
> sentences: *Unfortunately,* the plane was five hours late.

The whole class of adverbs can be divided into true adverbs and intensifiers. True adverbs can be defined as movable modifiers; their places in sentences are not fixed:

> *Unfortunately,* the plane was five hours late.
> The plane, *unfortunately,* was five hours late.
> The plane was, *unfortunately,* five hours late.
> The plane was five hours late, *unfortunately.*

Intensifiers are not movable modifiers:

> *very* pretty, *quite* late, *pretty* good, *awfully* happy

Intensifiers, paradoxically, sometimes tend to de-intensify meaning. *He is very intelligent* is much less intense than *He is brilliant. She is very pretty* is less intense than *She is beautiful.* Here again is the old principle of choosing exactly the right word instead of attempting to shape meaning through the addition of modifiers.

AFFECT-EFFECT

These two words are often confused. *Affect* is a verb, not a noun.

> The pollen *affected* my hayfever.
> Wages *affect* the price of steel.
> Noise does not *affect* his concentration.

Effect is a noun, not a verb.

> The *effect* of pollen is a hayfever attack.
> The *effect* of higher wages is rising steel prices.
> The *effect* of noise is hypertension.

But in one meaning, *effect* can be a verb. As a verb, *effect* means "to bring about."

> The medicine *effects* a cure.
> Rising wages *effect* high steel prices.

Affective is the adjective that pertains to the excitation of emotions.

> The music was *affective*.
> The *affective* elements of language sway men's feelings.

Effective is the adjective equivalent of *effect*.

> The medicine is *effective*.
> The most *effective* cure for melancholy is work.

AGREEMENT, PRONOUN AND ADJECTIVE

A pronoun and a pronominal adjective should agree in number with their antecedents.

When the antecedent is compound, the pronoun or adjective should be plural:

> Geoffrey and William said that *they* were going to Chicago.
> Jane and Anthony both grabbed *their* coats and ran.

When the compound antecedent is joined by *not . . . but,* the pronoun or adjective agrees with the antecedent that is affirmative:

> Not Hardy but other novelists wrote *their* works for eternity.
> Not the minor novelists but Dickens alone portrayed *his* age in *his* works.

When the conjunctions are *either . . . or* or *neither . . . nor,* the pronoun or adjective is in the singular:

> Either Ernest or Scott must take *his* place among the immortals.

But the correlative conjunctions cause problems. What should be done in the following case?

> Either Rachel or Frank lost (his/her/their) place.

None of the three alternatives is satisfactory, and the sentence must be completely recast, perhaps as follows:

> Either Rachel lost her place, or else Frank his.

Everybody, anyone, anybody, each, every, etc. take singular pronouns or adjectives in educated usage:

> Everybody took off *his* hat.
> Anyone may be the master of *his* fate.
> Each must do *his* duty.

Once again, however, problems arise. Strict agreement between pronoun and antecedent can bring about awkwardness, if not illogicality:

> The teacher knew every student in the class and told *him* to work hard and succeed.

When this kind of problem arises, it is wise to recast the sentence, perhaps as follows:

> The teacher knew every student in the class and told each one to work hard and succeed.

When the antecedent is a collective noun, meaning governs the number of the pronoun or adjective:

> The family ate *their* evening meal in silence.
> The army defeated *its* foe after three days of battle.
> The group knew that (it/they) (was/were) doomed.

CASE

In English, nouns have only two cases—if we define case on the basis of form. That is, nouns have the common case and the genitive case:

> dog/dog's   girls/girls'   men/men's

But pronouns have three cases:

	1st person singular	2nd person singular	3rd person singular
Nominative	I	you	he, she, it
Genitive	mine	yours	his, hers, its
Objective	me	you	him, her, it
	Plural	Plural	Plural
Nominative	we	you	they
Genitive	ours	yours	theirs
Objective	us	you	them

There are also the adjectival forms:

my hat   *your* purse   *his* money   *her* job   *its* top   *our* home
your yard   *their* garage

Only in the vulgate do the forms become confused:

Them guys robbed the bank of lots of loot.

But sometimes uncertainty about which form to choose leads to "over-correctness." *Us people like music* should be *We people like music.* If one is corrected often enough, he may then "overcorrect" and use *we* when us *is* proper: *Just between we boys . . . Me and Jim went* may lead to the overcorrection of *The committee called on you and I.*

CLAUSES (see chapter 4)

Clauses are sentences within sentences. They have all of the characteristics of sentences, but they function as parts of speech: *nouns, adjectives,* and *adverbs.*

Noun clauses can be

Subjects of Verbs

The crowd

Whoever entered the arena } cheered the champion

Direct Objects of Verbs

I know { my lesson / what is in the book

Indirect Objects of Verbs

Jones gave { the audience / whoever was in the crowd } an encore

Objects of Prepositions

The driver is not sure of { his route / where he should go

Subjective Complements

That is { my desire / what I want

Objective Complements

Everyone called it { silly

{ whatever he wanted to call it

Notice that when noun clauses are introduced by relatives (words like *who, whoever, where, what, that,* etc.), there are no antecedents.

I know *which* side my bread is buttered on.

Compare this kind of construction with those clauses introduced by relatives that have antecedents:

I know the *side which* my bread is buttered on.

When a relative has an antecedent, it introduces an *adjective clause*.

Noun: We see *who is here*.
Adj.: We see the *man who is here*.

As the discussion of embedding indicated, the adjective clause can frequently be pruned so that the construction can result in a mere adjective.

Football stars like girls *who are pretty*.
Football stars like *pretty* girls.
Hand me the book *which is above*.
Hand me the book *above*.
Hand me the *above* book.

Adverb clauses are of a different nature; they are not really embedded in main clauses as are noun and adjective clauses, but result from subjoining one clause to another with a conjunction:

If the ends do not justify the means, what does?
When the ends justify the means, one should act.
Because he is a moral man, he will not prevaricate.
Students succeed *although* professors are incompetent.

COHERENCE

Coherence is the quality in writing that allows the reader to follow the writer's sequence of ideas. When writing is incoherent, the reader cannot easily perceive connections; he flounders about and attempts to supply the links that have either been left out or that are not visible. Of course, coherence depends to a great extent on the logicality of the writer's thought; if two unrelated ideas are yoked, the reader will be puzzled. But coherence also depends on structural, mechanical links that the writer must learn to supply. One of the main ways of achieving coherence is the use of the proper *transitions* in the proper places. (See the discussion of *transitional adverbs* on pp. 59 ff and 136 ff.) Pronoun reference also is important in bringing about coherence (see pp. 134-135). Finally, organization makes for coherence (see pp. 19-21).

COMMA FAULT

The comma fault is joining two or more independent clauses with commas, as though they were coordinate or subordinate.

> With Boileau's translation of 1674 the modern life of Longinus's "On the Sublime" began, until 1674 the Longinian treatise was virtually unknown.
>
> In the fourth lecture Blair answers the question, he immediately takes Longinus to task.

In modern writing, there is a definite tendency to view *then* as a conjunction, so that structures such as the following result:

> We got the job done, then we started the game.

But in educated usage, *then* never serves a conjunctive function. In fact, like other true adverbs, it is a movable modifier:

> | | Then we started the game. |
> | We got the job done. | We then started the game. |
> | | We started the game then. |

Transitional adverbs do not serve a conjunctive function. (See p. 59 ff.) Thus, the following is an error:

> We didn't get the job done, however we started the game.

Remember that transitional adverbs are movable modifiers:

> | | however, we started the game. |
> | We didn't get the job done; | we, however, started the game. |
> | | we started the game, however. |

CONTACT CLAUSES

Sometimes two closely related and fairly short clauses may be joined by a comma, without any conjunction. In fact, this usage is becoming more and more common on all levels of modern English:

> Come to my party, you will enjoy it.
> See *The Graduate*, it's wonderful.

This is not to say, however, that the comma will substitute for sentence punctuation or the semicolon in each and every instance. Contact clauses are used consciously, for stylistic effect, not unconsciously, as a result of negligence.

DANGLING MODIFIERS

Dangling modifiers are sentence elements that seem to modify a word or phrase that they logically should not modify. The result of dangling modifiers is often humor:

> Walking quietly down the bank, the fish was seen in the water.

A dangling participle:

> Sitting on the bench, the pigeons enjoyed the popcorn that I threw to them.
>> (Possible correction: Sitting on the bench, I could see that the pigeons enjoyed the popcorn that I threw to them.)

A dangling gerund:

> After hearing a good concert, the spirits soar.
>> (Possible correction: After hearing a good concert, I feel my spirits soar.)

A dangling infinitive:

> To change a tire, the car should be securely blocked.
>> (Possible correction: To change a tire, one should block the car securely.)

Further examples of sentences

with dangling modifiers	*with dangling modifiers removed*
On entering the torrid zone, the heat almost overcame us.	As we entered the torrid zone, the heat almost overcame us. *Or* On entering the torrid zone, we were almost overcome by the heat.
Living in the city, it has become necessary to learn self-defense.	For anyone living in the city, it has become necessary to learn self-defense.
Being occupied with problems, the doorbell didn't bother him.	Being occupied with problems, he was not bothered by the doorbell. *Or* Murgatroyd being immersed in problems, the doorbell didn't bother him.
Within five miles of his home, sunken in the sand of the beach, he found a pirate treasure.	Within five miles of his home, he found a pirate treasure sunken in the sand of the beach.
The problem can be solved by looking at the agreement of the subject with the verb.	The problem can be solved if one looks at the agreement of the subject with the verb. *Or* To solve the problem, look at the agreement of the subject with the verb.
Tired, wet, and bedraggled, the game was lost by the home team.	Tired, wet, and bedraggled, the home team lost the game.

DISINTERESTED

In the most careful educated usage, *disinterested* is not synonymous with *uninterested*. *Disinterested* means "fair," "impartial," "having no ax to grind." Thus, one would want a *disinterested* judge, but not an *uninterested* judge; a *disinterested* referee, but not an *uninterested* referee.

DOUBLE NEGATIVE

In some languages, the double negative is perfectly acceptable, even necessary. French: Je *ne* sais *pas*. But in English, the double negative is definitely substandard: I do*n't* have *no* money. The avoidance of the double negative in English has nothing to do with meaning or with logic. In language, two negatives do not make a positive. When someone says *I ain't got no money,* we do not presume that he has some money; we know what he means. Avoiding the double negative is merely one aspect of speaking the dialect of the educated.

EDITORIAL WE

In editorials and columns, writers often use the plural pronoun "we" instead of the singular "I." "We firmly believe that the president's statement was . . . ." In its place, the editorial we is a perfectly acceptable convention, but out of its place, it becomes a silly affectation.

FALSE COORDINATION

(For a discussion of coordination, see pp. 136-143.) Coordination is joining like elements with coordinating conjunctions. Sometimes, however, the coordination obviously establishes improper relationships. For instance, in the following sentences, time relationships vital to meaning are suppressed by coordination:

> He was in Vienna last year, and he attended thirty-five operas.
> (While he was in Vienna last year, he attended thirty-five operas.)
> He bought a stereo, and he had enough money.
> (He bought a stereo when he had enough money.)

Cause and effect relationships do not gain expression through coordination:

> He went to college, and he wanted to be an engineer.
> (He went to college because he wanted to be an engineer.)

Note the following:

> Only one of the Jones boys is a success: James is a ditchdigger, *and* John is a bank president.
>> Only one of the Jones boys is a success: James is a ditchdigger, *but* John is a bank president.
>
> He resigned after five years, *and* he didn't like the job.
>> He resigned after five years, for he didn't like the job.

FRAGMENT

As we have seen (pp. 97-98), every sentence is made up of a subject and a verb phrase, even though sometimes transformations make it appear that one element or the other is not present.

> Kernel: John sees the boy.
> See the boy!
> Is the boy seen?
> And so on.

But the invariable rule S———>NP + VP tells us that in its original form, every sentence began as subject and a verb phrase.

We also know that the verb in a sentence is finite. That is, it has tense. (You may recall that the total verb phrase is composed of these elements: tense + (modal) + (have + en) + (be + ing) + V [See pp. 104-115]). Without a finite verb, there can be no sentence. A sentence fragment is a construction that has no finite verb or that is a subordinate construction and hence should be joined with an independent construction.

Examples of constructions with no finite verb:

> The group went to the observatory. *Their purpose being to look at the stars.*
>
> Many people do not understand their destinies. *The will of God intending man to serve His purposes.*
>
> They drove on for fifty miles. *Obviously not being aware that they had missed the turnoff.*

Examples of dependent constructions that are punctuated as sentences:

> There is no alternative to peace. *Because war means annihilation.*
> *Whenever the situation arose.* We coped with the problem of hiring machinists.

Frequently, sentence fragments are both necessary and stylistically justifiable. In answer to questions, one seldom uses complete sentences: "Where are you going?" "To Chicago." "When are you coming back?"

"In May." "Why are you going?" "Because I want to." Fragmentary sentences also emphasize:

> There is only one reason for lying. To protect oneself.

Out of context, it is impossible to say whether a sentence fragment is good or bad, correct or incorrect. In context, the situation becomes clearcut.

GENITIVE

The genitive is often called the "possessive," apparently because it is a case form frequently used to express ownership: Mary's purse, the children's toys. But the concept of ownership begins to fade away in the following examples: the horse's hooves, Einstein's brilliance, Fillmore's problem. For this reason, the term "genitive" seems preferable.

The genitive relationship can be expressed in two ways: with apostrophe -s ('s) or apostrophe and with a prepositional phrase containing "of": Bill's book, Americans' love of freedom, my love of poetry. But the case begins once again to grow hazy: "love of poetry" may not be a genitive at all, for a paraphrase is "love for poetry."

Regardless of the subtleties expressed by what we usually call the genitive case, the main problem is the correct use of the apostrophe. For a discussion of that use, see the chapter on punctuation.

ITS—IT'S

Its is the genitive of it: The house and its yard were well kept; The horse resisted its bridle. It's is the contraction of either it is or it has and can always be read as either. Thus, The car lost it's wheel could be read as The car lost it is wheel, a clearly ungrammatical sentence.

PARALLELISM

Grammatical parallelism means in general that like structures must fill like slots in sentences. To be more specific, for instance, a gerund and an infinitive should not be coordinated: To read and watching movies are my favorite pastimes. Most instances of the violation of parallelism are not so blatant. In the following sentence, a noun and an adjective fill the same coordinated slot, and hence parallelism is violated: The class seems worthwhile [adjective] and a challenge [noun]. Note this instance of unparallel usage: He either goes, or I must stay.

In order to conform to accepted usage, the sentence must be revised to read *Either he goes, or I must stay.*

Often a failure in parallelism results from coordinating items in a series: The president has the power, the means, and should end poverty in America. In this sentence, the coordinated items are

> a noun phrase: the power
> a noun phrase: the means
> a verb phrase: should end poverty in America.

(See also pp. 164-166 and, in this checklist, "Shifted Constructions.")

PASSIVE VOICE

(See "Voice.")

PRONOUN REFERENCE

(See also pp. 134-135). One of the handy devices that the English language gives its users is that of systematic substitutions. *Do* is one of the elements of this device. Instead of saying, *My wife doesn't like Scriabin, but I like Scriabin,* we can say, *My wife doesn't like Scriabin, but I do,* where *do* stands for *do like Scriabin.* The pronouns are obviously an important part of systematic substitution:

> *John* didn't take the course because *John* had a conflict of schedules.
> *John* didn't take the course because *he* had a conflict of schedules.
> The RESTAURANT *served a tremendous variety of foods. That* is what I liked about IT.
> The RESTAURANT *served a tremendous variety of foods, which* is what I liked about IT.

The adjective forms of pronouns also work in systematic substitution:

> The *boy* forgot to take the *boy's* medicine.
> The *boy* forgot to take *his* medicine.

Relative pronouns and relative adjectives also substitute:

> The girl *the girl's* book was on the table entered the room.
> The girl *whose* book was on the table entered the room.

The principle is that pronouns have antecedents from which they gain their meaning. If reference to the antecedent is inexact, the reader must grope. And then he becomes annoyed. Inexact or vague reference is a definite stylistic flaw.

I liked to fish and knew that I would get plenty of *them* before the summer was over.

(*Them* has no antecedent.)

The doctor gave them some pills. *They* were helpful.

(Does *they* refer to "them" or "pills"?)

The president announced that he would request a ten per cent surtax. *This* caused widespread criticism.

(What does *this* refer to? Revision: This announcement caused widespread criticism.)

Further examples of sentences with

reference problems	*eliminated*
I threatened him with expulsion, which terrified him.	My threat to expel him terrified him. *Or* I threatened him with expulsion, an act which terrified him.
During the Christmas vacation, we heard Van Cliburn play Brahms' concerto. This was one of the highpoints of our vacation.	During the Christmas vacation, we heard Van Cliburn play Brahms' concerto. This concert was one of the highpoints of our vacation.
Women are always attracted by uniforms. They look so imposing.	Women are always attracted by uniforms. Military dress looks so imposing.
He went to church dressed in Bermuda shorts, which shocked everyone.	He went to church dressed in Bermuda shorts, and his irreverent attire shocked everyone. *Or* He went to church dressed in Bermuda shorts, and his irreverence shocked everyone.
We bought the car two years ago. Then we went to Europe and Asia, and on our way back we stopped in New York, where we visited our grandparents. While we were gone, it was in storage.	We bought the car two years ago. Then we went to Europe and Asia, and on our way back we stopped in New York, where we visited our grandparents. While we were gone, the car was in storage.
The dentist lectured me about eating too much candy, and I didn't like it.	The dentist lectured me about eating too much candy, and I didn't like what he said.

REPETITION

Though the unnecessary repetition of words, phrases, and ideas is not grammatically incorrect, it is stylistically annoying and makes for awkwardness.

Chinese civilization is interesting, but even more so is Egyptian civilization.

> (Chinese civilization is interesting, but even more so is that of the Egyptians.)

During fall semester, I took an English class, a history class, a psychology class, and a PE class.

> (During fall semester, I took English, history, psychology, and PE.)

Alliteration, the repetition of initial sounds in successive words, can be unpleasant in prose:

> A *b*ig *b*lack *b*ird swooped down from the *c*loudy *c*anopy of sky.
> *G*irls *g*et *g*ood *g*rades.

Repetition, used consciously, can be an effective rhetorical device (see p. 203):

> I came; I saw; I conquered.
> He dreamed of poetry, he ate poetry, he slept poetry; poetry was his entire life.

Tautology is a particularly annoying kind of repetition:

> a rich millionaire   a dead corpse   a beautiful bathing beauty

Redundancy is the unnecessary repetition of ideas:

> . . . early in the morning at 5:00 a.m. . . .
> He frequently went very often to the museum.
> Last summer in July we left for Europe.

SENTENCE FRAGMENT

See "Fragment."

SEQUENCE OF TENSES

In English, we speak of natural sequence, in which the verbs are in the same tense as the notional time that they express, and of attracted sequence, in which one verb influences the tense of the next. Natural sequence:

> Tomorrow the dean *will leave* for New York; he *will remain* there for a week and *will return* via Miami.

Attracted sequence:

> The professor *says* that he *will give* a test tomorrow.
> The professor *said* that he *would give* a test tomorrow.

The tense of "would give" is past, even though the notional time is future.

Unnecessary shifts in tense constitute an annoying stylistic flaw. Often, the inexperienced writer shifts from historical present to past:

> After Jemmy leaves Moll, she *is* disconsolate. She really *loves* Jemmy and *is* distraught at losing him. But Jemmy *did* not go far before he *decided* to return for another farewell.

Shifts within one sentence are particularly conspicuous:

> The team *leaves* International Airport tonight, they *will arrive* in South Bend tomorrow, and they *return* Saturday night.

SHALL-WILL

A great deal of futile to-do has been made over the proper use of *shall* and *will*. The old rule—which by the way never did reflect actual usage—stated that *shall* should be used to show simple futurity in the first person singular and plural; *will* should be used to show simple futurity in the second and third persons singular and plural. To show urgency or resolution, that situation was reversed: *will* would be used for first person and *shall* for second and third:

> I *shall* go tomorrow.
> In spite of every obstacle, we *will* go tomorrow.
> They *will* win the game.
> Regardless of the odds against them, they *shall* win.

No one who is familiar with the language now claims that this distinction is observed on any level of usage. In modern English, *will* is used in every case, except first person interrogative:

> Shall we dance? Shall I take the bus?

SHIFTED CONSTRUCTIONS

Look at the following sentence: The university is near home, it has a good reputation, and you will enjoy going there. The subjects of the three clauses are "university," "it" (synonymous with "university"), and "you," which is a shift from the subject of the first two clauses. A better way of expressing these ideas:

> The university is near home, and it has a good reputation. You will enjoy going there.

Constructions should be grammatically parallel (see "Parallelism"), but also they should be notionally parallel. (The first example sentence illustrates a shift in notional parallelism.)

Another example of a shifted construction:

> The need for social justice is real, for when *you* live in hopeless poverty *you* do not realize the opportunities that *a person* has in a free society if *he* is able to grasp them.

The shift here is from second person to third person. There are many other ways in which parallelism is violated, for instance, by the shift from a phrase to a clause:

> The engineer knew *of the girder's being weak* and *that it needed bracing.*

or by the shift from a noun construction to an adjective construction:

> He has *intelligence* and is *pleasant.* (Revised: He is intelligent and pleasant.)

The idea is to avoid unnecessary shifts in prose. Consistency in the structures of a sentence is a positive virtue.

SPLIT INFINITIVES

A college professor of English—a doctor of philosophy—was on an airplane. Suddenly the stewardess rushed up to him and said, "Doctor, a lady has fainted in the back of the plane. Come quickly." He replied, "There's not much I can do about fainting, but if she had split an infinitive, I could help."

Much senseless furor has raged about the infinitive, split and unsplit—just the sort of controversy that makes the student of language seem like a hopeless pedant involved in the unutterably trivial. As a matter of fact, one should split his infinitives without qualms if the split is less awkward than the unsplit.

The split infinitive in this sentence

> He seemed *to dimly remember* that he had been hit on the head

is preferable to the unsplit infinitive

> He seemed *dimly to remember.* . . .

and the split infinitive in this sentence

> It is necessary *to strictly follow* the instructions to put the car together.

is also preferable to the unsplit infinitive

> It is necessary *strictly to follow* the instructions. . . .

SUBJUNCTIVE

Other parts of this book discuss tense, modals, aspect, and so forth. But verbs also have *mood*:

indicative:

> Norma *sings* in the choir.

imperative:

> *Sing* in the choir!

subjunctive:

> We asked that Norma *sing* in the choir.

Subjunctive mood is usually defined as the form of the verb in a statement of a condition that is contrary to fact:

> If he *were* here, he could solve the problem [but he isn't here].

Note the difference, however:

> If he *was* there, he probably saw the meteor [and we don't know whether or not he was there, but he might have been, and if he was, he saw the meteor].

With all verbs but Be, the subjunctive has a recognizable form only in the third person present singular:

> He *eats* grapefruit.
> I requested that he *eat* grapefruit.
> She *maintains* her youthful appearance.
> Oh, that she *maintain* her youthful appearance!
> It *needs* to be done.
> It *need* not be done.

Be verbs have recognizable subjunctives only in the first and third persons singular:

> I *was* there for the excitement.
> *Were* I only there.
> The king *lives* a full life.
> Long *live* the king.

SYLLABIFICATION

Your dictionary will indicate the division of words into syllables. When words are divided, the split should come only between syllables:

. . . . com-
mensurate.

UPSIDE-DOWN SUBORDINATION (See also pp. 133-134.)

When two ideas are joined by subordination [(Sub)S], the most important—the central idea—should be in the independent clause.

> The landing gear would not come down. The passengers were terrified.
> Upside-down subordination: The landing gear would not come down when the passengers were terrified.
> Improved: When the landing gear would not come down, the passengers were terrified.

But ideas gain importance from context; hence, upside-down subordination in one situation might be perfectly proper in another. Thus, depending on context,

> I was ten years old when Pearl Harbor was attacked.
> When I was ten years old, Pearl Harbor was attacked.

VOICE

All transitive verbs have voice, either *active* or *passive*. The passive voice can be defined as any form of the verb Be plus the past participial form of a transitive verb.

Active	Passive
He *signs* the check.	The check *is signed* (by him).
We *will buy* a new car next year.	A new car *will be bought* (by us) next year.
The group *had seen* the film.	The film *had been seen* (by the group).

Active voice has certain advantages: it is more direct and, as the name implies, it seems to be more active. It is always more economical than passive. Passive is useful at times, however. When one chooses not to express the grammatical subject of a verb, passive works well:

> *Someone* must do the dirty work.
> The dirty work must be done.

For this reason, much scientific writing is in the passive, supposedly because that voice achieves more impersonality and hence more objectivity. Instead of saying *I conducted the test*, the scientist can hide his own identity behind the passive voice: *The test was conducted.*

Passive voice is neither good nor bad—except in context. In some instances, it is unnecessary or out of place; in other instances, it serves a useful function. The point is this: when the writer uses passive rather than active, he should have a reason for doing so.

Index